CORPORATE LAW ̷
OF THE NETHERLANDS

LEGAL AND TAXATION

This book, *Corporate Law and Practice of the Netherlands*,
is the seventh in the **Loeff Legal Series**,
published by Kluwer Law International

Other titles in this series:

Ernst P. Jansen,
Labour Law in the Netherlands
Niels R. van de Vijver,
Securities Regulation in the Netherlands
Willem Verhoeven,
Ships (Arrests; Registration and Mortgages; Enforced Sales in the Netherlands)
Leonard G. Verburg,
The European Works Council in the Netherlands
Peter V. Eijsvoogel,
Telecommunications Regulation in the Netherlands
Steven R. Schuit and Jan-Erik Janssen,
M&A in the Netherlands (Acquisitions, Takeovers and Joint Ventures)
Tom R. Ottervanger, Jacques Steenbergen and Sander van der Voorde,
Competition Law of the European Union, the Netherlands and Belgium

In parallel to the titles of **Loeff Legal Series**, published by Kluwer Law
International, the following titles in **Loeff Legal Series** were published
by Kluwer Juridische Uitgevers:

H. Bert Oosthout,
De Doorstart van een Insolvente Onderneming (Niks of Phoenix),
Niek F.M.M. Zaman,
Juridische Splitsing (Juridisch en Fiscaal)

Kluwer Law International

Sold and distributed
in the USA and Canada by:
Kluwer Law International
675 Massachussetts Avenue
Cambridge, MA 02139, USA
Tel.: +1 617 354 0140
Fax: +1 617 354 8595

Sold and distributed
in all other countries by:
Kluwer Law International
P.O. Box 85889
2508 CN The Hague, The Netherlands
Tel.: +31 70 308 1551
Fax: +31 70 308 1515

Kluwer Juridische Uitgevers

Sold and distributed by:
Libresso
Postbus 23
7400 GA Deventer
Tel.: +31 570 633 155
Fax: +31 570 633 834

CORPORATE LAW AND PRACTICE

OF THE NETHERLANDS

LEGAL AND TAXATION

by

STEVEN R. SCHUIT

LOEFF CLAEYS VERBEKE
AMSTERDAM OFFICE

LOEFF LEGAL SERIES
1998

KLUWER LAW INTERNATIONAL
THE HAGUE • LONDON • BOSTON

Library of Congress Cataloguing-in-Publication Data

Schuit, Steven R.
    Corporate law and practice of the Netherlands: legal and taxation/by Steven R. Schuit.
        p. cm. – (Loeff legal series: v. 6)
    Includes index.
    ISBN 9041105689 (pbk.)
    1. Corporation law – Netherlands. 2. Private companies – Netherlands.
    3. Business enterprises – Law and legislation – Netherlands.
    I. Title. II. Series: Loeff legal series; 6. KKM1050.S38 1998
    346.492'066 – dc21   98-9216

Published by Kluwer Law International
P.O. Box 85889
2508 CN The Hague, The Netherlands
Tel.: +31 70 308 1560
Fax: +31 70 308 1515

Sold and distributed in the USA and Canada by
Kluwer Law International
675 Massachusetts Avenue
Cambridge, MA 02139, USA
Tel.: +1 617 354 0140
Fax: +1 617 354 8595

Sold and distributed in all other countries by
Kluwer Law International
Distribution Centre
P.O. Box 322
3300 AH Dordrecht, The Netherlands
Tel.: +31 78 392 392
Fax: +31 78 546 474

Printed on acid-free paper

ISBN 90-411-0568-9

© 1998, Loeff Claeys Verbeke c/o Kluwer Law International

Kluwer Law International incorporates the publishing programmes of Graham & Trotman Ltd, Kluwer Law and Taxation Publishers and Martinus Nijhoff Publishers.

PREFACE

The corporate and tax laws in Europe are continuously subject to changes from different sources; most importantly from the initiatives of the European Commission. The resulting regulations and directives are important for the protection of creditors and investors, but many significant differences between the national systems continue to exist, often due to historical or cultural differences between the European countries. The corporate law of the Netherlands is a typical expression of the (Rhine) Delta Model or "Polder Model", as frequently discussed by philosophers, politicians and economists. But it is also an expression of a modern, industrialised and outward looking country, where the rule of law prevails. The tax laws of the Netherlands reflect the friendly attitude towards multinationals based in the Netherlands and the investor-friendly attitude of the administration.

This book was written for the benefit of investors, business men, professional advisors and academics. It is the only elaborate treatise focusing specifically on Dutch corporate law in the English language.

Special tribute deserves Jan-Erik Janssen of the Amsterdam office of Loeff Claeys Verbeke, who assisted in the preparation of the manuscript. It was written over time on the basis of experience with business clients that were provided legal assistance in Europe, the US and Asia. He is also the author of the chapter concerning corporate labour participation, (Works Councils). The chapter on taxation was prepared by Eric van der Stoel of the Rotterdam office of Loeff Claeys Verbeke.

This book inevitably contains some generalisations and should not be considered a substitute for legal advice in any particular circumstances.

Steven R. Schuit
Amsterdam, January 1998

ABOUT THE AUTHORS

Steven R. Schuit (1942) of Loeff Claeys Verbeke, Amsterdam office, represents Dutch and foreign clients in Europe, the United States and Asia. He was the resident partner of his firm in New York from 1980 to 1990. He is the general editor of DUTCH BUSINESS LAW (looseleaf), the standard English language treatise about Dutch law, the co-author of M&A IN THE NETHERLANDS, and the editor-in-chief of TIJDSCHRIFT PRIVATISERING, the Dutch legal journal on privatisations.

Jan-Erik Janssen (1969) of Loeff Claeys Verbeke, Amsterdam office, graduated from Nijenrode (the Netherlands School of Business), the Economics Faculty of the Erasmus University of Rotterdam and the Law Faculty of the University of Utrecht. He practices in the mergers and acquisitions area and is the co-author of M&A IN THE NETHERLANDS.

Eric van der Stoel (1959) of Loeff Claeys Verbeke, Rotterdam office, works in the tax department with Dutch corporate income tax and international tax planning as his main areas of practice. Before joining Loeff Claeys Verbeke in 1995, he worked as a tax advisor with one of the major accounting firms. He is a correspondent for TAX NOTES INTERNATIONAL.

Kornelis Dijkman (1967) is specialised in international tax planning. From 1996 until August 1997, he has worked in Milan on the international reorganisation of a large Italian multinational.

Table of Contents

1   GENERAL INTRODUCTION

1.1   General

During the last two decades Dutch law concerning business organisations and corporations has changed dramatically, developing characteristics unknown in any other country.

The emphasis in legislative drafting during this period has been on fostering the interests of both employees and creditors. This higher degree of protection was achieved by reducing the power of shareholders (*see infra* Chapter 7), disclosure to creditors and to the public in general (*see infra* Chapter 11), adopting strict rules concerning capitalisation (*see infra* Chapter 4) and imposing liability on founders and directors in cases of abuse of the corporate form (*see infra* Chapter 8).

Although this development is most noticeable in the context of corporations, it has left its traces in the areas of unincorporated business enterprises and branch offices of foreign corporations[1].

This book describes the laws concerning incorporated and unincorporated business enterprises. Banks, securities and investment operations[2] and insurance companies[3] are covered by special legislation that is not discussed herein. Matters concerning accounting and financial reporting are only superficially described[4].

---

1   Most notably with respect to provisions in the Wet op de ondernemingsraden [WOR] (Works Council Act), 1971 Staatsblad [S.] (Statute Book) 54, *as amended*, and the Handelsregisterwet 1996 [HrW 1996] (Commercial Register Act 1996), 1996 S. 181, *as amended*, that apply to these entities.

2   Reference is made to the following English language publication: N.R. VAN DE VIJVER, SECURITIES REGULATION IN THE NETHERLANDS, Loeff Legal Series, 1997, Kluwer International (The Hague, London, Boston).

3   Reference is made to the following English language publication: J.C.P. EKERING, "Insurance", in: DUTCH BUSINESS LAW; LEGAL, ACCOUNTING AND TAX ASPECTS OF DOING BUSINESS IN THE NETHERLANDS (S.R. Schuit and J. van Helleman, editors) [hereinafter: DUTCH BUSINESS LAW], looseleaf, Kluwer International (The Hague, London, Boston), Chapter 27.

4   Reference is made to the following English language publication: GOPAL RAMANATHAN, "Business Accounting", DUTCH BUSINESS LAW, *supra* at note 3, Chapter 10.

1.2   Corporate Governance

One of the distinct characteristics of Dutch company law is the two-tier management structure comprised of a management board and a supervisory board (*see infra* Chapter 7.1). This structure is mandatory for corporations with equity in excess of NLG 25 million, a Works Council, and fifty or more employees in the Netherlands. Under this mandatory two-tier structure the supervisory board has far-reaching powers, superseding to some extent those of the shareholders and the management board. A Works Council is a representative body of employees that is mandatory for enterprises with thirty-five or more employees in the Netherlands (*see infra* Chapter 12.1). On the basis of its statutory powers, a Works Council may exercise considerable influence on management decisions in such areas as mergers, acquisitions, take-overs and joint ventures, investments, split-ups and divestitures[5]. These and other characteristics emanate from a social and economic environment that long ago accepted the notion that the management board is not subordinate to the shareholders[6], and may even be allowed to take positions that are not in the best interests of shareholders[7]. The management board must protect the "interests of the corporation"[8], which may include the interests of shareholders, employees[9] and, according to certain legal commentators, the corporation's business relations, as well as certain basic societal interests[10].

The reduced power of shareholders is particularly noticeable in relation to the appointment of managing directors. For corporations with a mandatory two-tier structure, the management board is appointed by the supervisory board[11] and the supervisory board fills its own vacancies[12].

---

5   WOR art. 25(1). Reference is made to the following English language publication: L.G. VERBURG, "Employee participation: Works Councils", in: DUTCH BUSINESS LAW, *supra* p. 1 at note 3, Chapter 11.

6   Judgment of January 21, 1955, Hoge Raad [HR] (Supreme Court), 1959 Nederlandse Jurisprudentie [NJ] (Dutch Court Reporter) No. 43.

7   E.J.J. VAN DER HEIJDEN, HANDBOEK VOOR DE NAAMLOZE EN DE BESLOTEN VENNOOTSCHAP [hereinafter HANDBOEK] § 231 (W.C.L. van der Grinten 12th ed. 1992), W.E.J. Tjeenk Willink (Zwolle); C. ASSER, 2, III VERTEGENWOORDIGING EN RECHTSPERSOON: DE NAAMLOZE EN BESLOTEN VENNOOTSCHAP [hereinafter ASSER-MAEIJER 2, III] § 16 (J.M.M. Maeijer, 1st ed. 1994), W.E.J. Tjeenk Willink (Zwolle).

8   The "interests" of the corporation are often defined in terms of its continued existence and growth, and thus its profitability. *See* ASSER-MAEIJER 2, III, *id.*, § 293.

9   Judgment of November 11, 1982, Gerechtshof [Ger.] (Court of Appeal) Amsterdam, 1983 NJ No. 30.

10   HANDBOEK, *supra* at note 7, § 231.

11   Burgerlijk Wetboek [BW] (Civil Code) arts. 2:162/272.

12   BW arts. 2:158(2)/268(2).

Shareholders and the Works Council can make recommendations and veto appointments that would cause the supervisory board to be not "properly constituted". A veto is subject to judicial review[13] (*see infra* Chapter 7.3.c.ii). This structure is in itself a strong defence against corporate raiders. Dutch law contains several other devices that have so far been highly effective in protecting the management board against unfriendly take-overs[14]. The same mechanisms may, however, have an impact in situations where no take-over is contemplated and where shareholders have a legitimate interest in making changes in the composition of the management board and the supervisory board.

Only recently the shareholders, as stakeholders in the corporation, have received more attention both from the angle of the new emphasis in the Netherlands on the concept of shareholders' value and from the angle of accountability of management to shareholders. A report on Corporate Governance in the Netherlands was released on June 25, 1997 by a Committee established by the Amsterdam Stock Exchange. The report contains specific "best practice" recommendations concerning the supervisory board, the management board, the shareholders' meeting, compliance procedures and auditors' review of systems of internal control.

1.3   Harmonisation of European Company Law

Many changes in the law of corporations can be attributed to the European Union (EU) authorities. The EC Treaty[15] provides for the progressive harmonisation of the economic policies of the Member States, in order to promote the proper functioning of the Common Market[16]. This includes the harmonisation of company law. Furthermore, the EC Treaty aims to abolish obstacles to the free movement of goods, persons, services and capital between the Member States[17].

An important principle embodied in the EC Treaty is the right of establishment. Under this principle nationals of Member States have the free-

---

13   BW arts. 2:158(6),(9)/268(6),(9).
14   For an elaborate description in the English language and a legal analysis of friendly public offers and hostile offers in the Netherlands, *see*: S.R. SCHUIT AND J.E. JANSSEN, M&A IN THE NETHERLANDS. ACQUISITIONS, TAKEOVERS AND JOINT VENTURES. LEGAL AND TAXATION [hereinafter: M&A IN THE NETHERLANDS], 1996, Kluwer Law International (The Hague, London, Boston).
15   Treaty establishing the European Economic Community [EC Treaty], art. 2, March 25, 1957, 1957 Tractatenblad [Trb.] (Treaty Book) Nos. 74, 91, *as amended.*
16   EC Treaty arts. 2, 3(h).
17   EC Treaty art. 3(c), Title I, Title III.

dom to establish themselves in the territory of other Member States under the same conditions that apply to the nationals of the host country[18]. This includes the right to pursue activities as self-employed persons, set up branch offices, incorporate companies, and carry on business according to the host country's law[19]. Member States are bound to eliminate the existing restrictions and refrain from introducing new restrictions on the freedom of services or the right of establishment[20].

Companies may prefer to establish in the Member State with the most favourable company law: the so-called "Delaware effect". The divergence of company laws in different Member States is acknowledged by the EC Treaty, which provides for the legal basis for the harmonisation of company law. The Community institutions are responsible for the harmonisation of company law "by coordinating to the necessary extent the safeguards which, for the protection of the interests of members and others, are required by Member States of companies or firms...with a view to making such safeguards equivalent throughout the Community"[21]. Pursuant to Article 220 of the EC Treaty, the Member States shall conclude agreements with respect to, *inter alia*, the retention of legal personality in the event of transfer of the seat of a company to another Member State[22]. Furthermore, certain regulations are based on Articles 100 and 100a of the EC Treaty which call for directives on the harmonisation of statutory and administrative law provisions in the Member States that are of direct influence on the establishment and operation of the Common Market.

Harmonisation is realised by way of directives, treaties, and regulations which approximate the company laws of the Member States and delete important differences between them.

A directive must be implemented into national legislation by all Member States, by way of adoption of national statutes within a prescribed peri-

---

18   EC Treaty art. 52.
19   EC Treaty art. 52 ("... 'companies or firms' means companies or firms constituted under civil or commercial law, including cooperative societies, and other legal persons governed by public or private law, save for those which are non-profit-making" (EC Treaty art. 58)).
20   EC Treaty arts. 52, 53, 59, 62.
21   EC Treaty art. 54(3)(g).
22   EC Treaty art. 220 provides: "Member States shall...enter into negotiations with each other with a view to securing for the benefit of their nationals...the mutual recognition of companies or firms..., the retention of legal personality in the event of transfer of their seat from one country to another, and the possibility of mergers between companies or firms governed by the laws of different countries...".

od[23]. Individuals may rely on the directive to have incompatible national legislation overruled if a Member State fails to implement a directive on time or does so incorrectly[24].

However, in enforcing their rights against the government of a Member State, individuals may only rely on such provisions of the directive which are unconditional and sufficiently precise.

The signing and ratification of so-called Community conventions between the Member States is subject to the normal procedure for treaties under public international law. However, these Community conventions are generally prepared by the Community institutions and are subject to interpretation by the Court of Justice of the European Communities[25]. These conventions can be regarded as law common to all of the Member States[26].

Regulations constitute a truly uniform European company law and represent a new "European" legal regime[27]. Rather than requiring implementation by national legislatures, a regulation has direct effect, *i.e.*, it gives rise to rights which private parties may enforce before national courts[28].

a   The First Directive[29]: Disclosure of Essential Information and the Protection of Bona Fide Third Parties. This directive provides that certain information on the internal governance of companies must be made available to the public through public registers and national gazettes. The information includes the articles of association, names of the board members and the corporate agents, subscribed capital and, in

---

23   Pursuant to EC Treaty, art. 189 "a directive shall be binding, as to the result to be achieved, upon each Member State to which it is addressed, but shall leave to the national authorities the choice of form and methods".

24   The Becker Case, Court of Justice of the European Communities 1982 Report of Cases Before the Court of Justice and Court of First Instance of the European Communities [E.Comm. Ct.J.Rep.] 53.

25   Submission of preliminary questions to the Court of Justice of the European Communities by national judges (EC Treaty art. 177) guarantees the uniform interpretation of Community laws and regulations.

26   In the field of company law no Community convention has yet been concluded. An initiative of the Member States for a convention on cross-border mergers was superseded by the proposal of the Commission for a directive (*see infra* Chapter 1.3.j).

27   Pursuant to the EC Treaty art. 189: "A regulation shall have general application. It shall be binding in its entirety and directly applicable in all Member States".

28   A regulation can be considered as "self-executing". *See Van Gend en Loos*, 1963 E.Comm. Ct.J.Rep. 3.

29   First Council Directive No. 68/151, 11 Official Journal of the European Communities [O.J. Eur. Comm.] (No. L65) 8 (1968), *as amended.*

the case of public companies, the annual financial results. The directive contains detailed provisions on the termination of the existence of a corporation. In addition, this directive limits to a great extent the *ultra vires* defence against *bona fide* third parties (*see infra* Chapter 3.6). This directive has been implemented in Dutch law.

b   The Second Directive[30]: Minimum Disclosure Requirements, the Formation of Public Limited Liability Companies and the Maintenance, Increase and Reduction of Capital. Companies must disclose their corporate form, name, purposes, registered office, share capital, classes of shares and the composition and powers of the various bodies of the company. The directive provides that the minimum issued capital for public companies must exceed 25,000 ECU (European Currency Units). It restricts distributions to shareholders that erode the capital of a company and its statutory reserves. A corporation may therefore only distribute its free reserves. Redemption of capital is restricted and capital may only be reduced in compliance with certain disclosure requirements in order to protect creditors. Moreover, shareholders of a public company have a pre-emptive right in the case of the issue of new shares. Finally, this directive contains an important provision for leveraged acquisitions: a company may not grant loans or security for the acquisition of shares in its own capital (*see infra* Chapter 4.3.g). The Netherlands has implemented this directive.

c   The Third Directive[31]: Mergers of Public Limited Liability Companies within one Member State. This directive deals with statutory mergers within a Member State. The directive provides for the protection of the interests of shareholders, creditors, and employees. In a statutory merger the assets and liabilities of the acquired company are transferred to the acquiring company by operation of law (*see* Chapter 10.3.b). The shareholders of both the acquiring and acquired company receive a proportional interest in the merged company. This right is secured by requiring valuation of the share exchange ratio by an independent expert. This directive has been implemented in the Netherlands. The directive helps to pave the way for cross-border mergers, provided for in the proposed tenth directive (*see infra* Chapter 1.3.j).

---

30   Second Council Directive No. 77/91, 20 O.J. Eur. Comm. (No. L26) 1 (1977), *as amended.*
31   Third Council Directive No. 78/855, 21 O.J. Eur. Comm. (No. L295) 36 (1978).

d   The Fourth Directive[32]: Company Accounts. This directive contains detailed requirements for the preparation of balance sheets, profit and loss statements, and annual reports. The accounts that are required to be maintained in accordance with the directive must give a true and fair view of the assets, liabilities, financial position and results of the company. The directive applies to both private and public companies. Special accounting rules apply to banks and insurance companies[33]. Certain small and medium-sized enterprises specified in national legislation are exempt from the most stringent publication requirements. This directive has been implemented in the Netherlands.

e   Proposal for a Fifth Directive[34]: Company Structure and Management. The proposed Fifth Directive deals with the structure and administration of public companies and the powers and obligations of their corporate bodies. It allows for both a two-tier management structure (management board and supervisory board) and a one-tier management structure (one board composed of executive and non-executive directors). If the directive were enacted in its current form, it would have a significant impact on Dutch corporate law[35]. However, there has been European-wide opposition to this proposal since it was first drafted in 1972.

f   The Sixth Directive[36]: Division of Public Limited Liability Companies. This directive covers divisions of public corporations in which all assets and liabilities are transferred by operation of law to two or more corporations in exchange for shares in the recipient corporations, whereby the dividing corporation ceases to exist. Dutch Parliament

---

32   Fourth Council Directive No. 78/660, 21 O.J. Eur. Comm (No. L222) 11 (1978), *as amended.*

33   For the rules concerning accounts of banks and other financial institutions, *see* 29 O.J. Eur. Comm. (No. L372) 1 (1986). For the rules concerning accounts of insurance companies, *see,* 34 O.J. Eur. Comm. (No. L374) 7 (1991). These directives have been implemented in Dutch law.

34   Proposal for a Fifth Council Directive, 15 O.J. Eur. Comm. (No. C131) 49 (1972); *as amended:* 26 O.J. Eur. Comm. (No. C240) 2 (1983); 34 O.J. Eur. Comm. (No. C7) 4 (1991); 34 O.J. Eur. Comm. (No. C321) 9 (1991).

35   The proposal in its current form limits the issuance of protective preference shares (*see infra* Chapter 5.1.c) to 50% of the issued capital and prohibits, *inter alia,* limitations on voting rights with respect to ordinary shares (*see infra* Chapter 6.3), and qualified majorities for ballots to appoint or remove managing directors or supervisory directors (the latter prohibition would only apply to public limited companies where these rights accrue to the shareholders, *i.e.* not to "large" N.V.s (*see infra* Chapter 7.3.c.ii).

36   Sixth Council Directive No. 82/891, 25 O.J. Eur. Comm. (No. L378) 47 (1982).

recently adopted the statute[37] to implement this directive and to introduce the demerger as well (whereby the demerging corporation does not
cease to exist) as a separate form of a split-up (*see infra* Chapter 10.4).
The statute is applicable to all legal persons. By implementing the directive, the complement of the statutory merger (*see* Chapter 10.3) will be
introduced, offering a relatively straightforward procedure for the restructuring of business enterprises and for structuring joint ventures. The procedure for a division or demerger mirrors to a great extent the procedure
for the statutory merger, including requirements for a split-up proposal, a
fairness opinion and protection of creditors' and employees' interests.

g   The Seventh Directive[38]: Consolidated Accounts. This directive
deals with consolidated annual accounts for groups of companies. The
directive complements the Fourth Directive concerning individual company accounts. Consolidated annual accounts are required where a holding corporation has: (i) the majority of voting rights in its subsidiary; (ii)
the right to appoint or remove a majority of voting rights in its subsidiary; (iii) the right to appoint or remove a majority of the members of the
administrative, management or supervisory board of the subsidiary; or
(iv) the contractual right to exercise a decisive influence over its subsidiary. Where a holding corporation of a group is located outside the Community, Member States have the option not to require consolidation if
the consolidated annual accounts are prepared in conformity with the
requirements laid down in the directive or their national equivalents. The
administrative burden for small and medium-sized enterprises has been
reduced. Since January 1, 1990, all groups of companies established
within the Community must prepare consolidated annual accounts. This
directive has been implemented in the Netherlands.

h   The Eighth Directive[39]: Statutory Auditors. This directive
contains minimum requirements for the educational and professional
qualifications of auditors and requires Member States to ensure their
independence. Dutch law is in conformity with this directive.

---

37   Statute of December 24, 1997, S. 776.
38   Seventh Council Directive No. 83/349, 26 O.J. Eur. Comm. (No. L193) 1 (1983),
     as amended.
39   Eighth Council Directive No. 84/253, 27 O.J. Eur. Comm. (No. L126) 20 (1984).

i   **Draft Proposal for a Ninth Directive[40]: Groups of Companies.** The object of this draft proposal is to create a legal structure for the unified management of a public limited liability company which is controlled by another enterprise, whether owned by an individual or a corporate entity. Such group could be formed by a so-called "control contract" or by a "unilateral declaration of control". The directive would protect creditors of a company that is subordinate to a parent by introducing liability of the parent for the debts of its subsidiaries. At present, no formal proposal has been published by the Commission.

j   **Proposal for a Tenth Directive[41]: Intra-Community Cross-Border Mergers.** This proposal purports to remove difficulties in realising a cross-border merger between Member States and purports to avoid "forum-shopping", *i.e.* cross-border mergers in one Member State in order to avoid certain mandatory laws in another Member State[42]. However, the principle obstacles for a true cross-border merger are in the taxation area, which is not covered by the proposed Tenth Directive.

k   **The Eleventh Directive[43]: Disclosure of Information by Branch Offices.** This directive limits the information to be disclosed by branches of companies. It is intended to harmonise the disclosure requirements for branch offices in the Member States. A branch need only disclose basic information, such as its name, address, and activities, as well as the name of its parent company. The directive permits a branch to submit consolidated annual accounts and annual reports rather than its own accounts, as long as they are prepared in accordance with the Fourth and Seventh Company Law Directives (*see supra* Chapter 1.3.d and g). If the parent company is registered outside the Community, the accounts must nonetheless be prepared in conformity with these directives or their equivalent. Dutch law is in conformity with this directive.

---

40   A preliminary draft for a proposal was circulated informally to the Member States in December 1984.

41   Proposal for a Tenth Council Directive, 28 O.J. Eur. Comm. (No. C23) 11 (1985), *as amended.*

42   The proposal provides, *inter alia*, for minimum requirements with respect to employee participation, provisions with respect to the supervision of mergers and publication requirements.

43   Eleventh Council Directive No. 89/666, 32 O.J. Eur. Comm. (No. L395) 36 (1989). A preliminary draft for a revised proposal was circulated informally to the Member States in 1996.

l   The Twelfth Directive[44]**: Single-Member Limited Liability Company.** This directive ensures the legal recognition of single-member private limited liability companies throughout the Community. The directive applies both to companies whose shares have been held by one shareholder since their incorporation, and to companies whose shares have subsequently come to be held by a single shareholder. The single shareholder involved may be either a natural person or a legal entity. The directive is intended both to protect third parties dealing with such companies and to encourage sole proprietors to incorporate. Matters not regulated by the directive are governed by the company laws of the individual Member States. Dutch law is in conformity with this directive.

m   Proposal for a Thirteenth Directive[45]**: Take-over Bids.** The latest draft of this proposal, dated February 7, 1996, aims to be a "framework directive" instead of a detailed harmonisation. It consists of certain basic principles of a limited number of general requirements which Member States must implement through more detailed rules. The directive would apply to corporations which are wholly or partly listed on an official stock exchange in the Community, but Member States may extend the applicability of this directive. Member States would be obliged to designate a supervisory authority which would be empowered to supervise the take-over rules. The general requirements focus on the protection of minority shareholders, the necessary degree of information and disclosures to shareholders and the role that the management board of the target should play during the offer.

n   Proposals for a Regulation and a Directive Concerning the European Company[46]**.** The Commission has proposed a regulation concerning a statute for a public limited liability European Company ("*Societas Europaea*" or "*SE*") together with a complementary directive on the role of its employees. The proposal intends to offer companies in the

---

44   Twelfth Council Directive No. 89/667, 32 O.J. Eur. Comm. (No. L395) 40 (1989).
45   Proposal for a Thirteenth European Parliament and Council Directive, 32 O.J. Eur. Comm. (No. C64) 8 (1989); amended: 33 O.J. Eur. Comm. (No. C240) 7 (1990); 39 O.J. Eur. Comm. (No. C162) 5 (1996).
46   Proposal for a Council Regulation on the Statute for a European Company, 32 O.J. Eur. Comm. (No. C263) 41 (1989), *as amended*: 34 O.J. Eur. Comm. (No. C176) 1 (1991); and proposal for a Council Directive complementing the Statute for a European Company with regard to the involvement of employees in the European Company, 32 O.J. Eur. Comm. (No. C263) 69 (1989), *as amended*: 34 O.J. Eur. Comm. (No. C138) 8 (1991).

Community the opportunity to form a new corporate entity for cross-border co-operation. Originally, the European Company was to be subject to uniform Community corporate law. However, the last negotiation proposal to a large extent relies on the harmonised, but not uniform, laws of the respective Member States. By way of example, the most recent negotiation proposal for the complementary directive on employees in the European Company allows for four forms of employee participation: (i) on the supervisory board or management board level; (ii) through a separate, special body; (iii) by an agreement between the European Company and an organisation that represents the employees; or (iv) through an agreement between the European Company and its employees. These proposals have encountered severe criticism. However, the recent adoption of the Directive for the European Works Council (*see infra* Chapter 1.3.q) may prove to be the impetus for compromises in this area.

o   The Regulation on the European Economic Interest Grouping[47]. The regulation on the European Economic Interest Grouping (EEIG) (*Europees Economisch Samenwerkingsverband*) took effect on July 1, 1989, and provides for a new separate legal person capable of cross-border co-operation in different Member States. An EEIG may be formed by two or more companies based in the Community, and is analogous to a joint venture in the way it is managed by its members. An EEIG is formed through the execution of a contract or notarial deed that is then registered in the Member State in which it maintains its head office. The EEIG's purpose must be to facilitate and develop its members' economic activities, rather than to pursue its own separate activities. Dutch Parliament has adopted an implementing statute, which contains further rules for EEIGs to be formed in the Netherlands (*see infra* Chapter 2.5.c).

p   The Directive on the Notification of Major Holdings[48]. This directive requires that a significant holding in a company listed on a stock exchange must be reported if certain specified thresholds of the voting rights of the outstanding shares are exceeded. In the event such shareholding falls below these levels, this must also be reported. Subsequently, the company or the competent authority will disclose the information to the public in each Member State where shares of the company are listed. This directive has been implemented in the Netherlands (*see infra* Chapter 1.4).

---

47   Council Regulation No. 2137/85, 28 O.J. Eur. Comm. (No. L199) 1 (1985).
48   Council Directive No. 88/627, 31 O.J. Eur. Comm. (No. L348) 62 (1988).

q   The Directive for the European Works Council[49]. This Directive applies to companies or groups of companies in the Member States (which for the purpose of this directive is defined to exclude the United Kingdom but to include Norway, Iceland and Liechtenstein) with one thousand or more employees of which 150 employees or more are employed in two different Member States. This directive encourages such company or group of companies to negotiate with the employees' representatives as to how its information and consultation obligations should be fulfilled. It allows for both a negotiated European Works Council as well as a negotiated procedure that fulfils these obligations. If negotiations fail, a mandatory European Works Council with the powers listed on the annex to the directive must be formed. These powers are rather limited compared with the powers of a Dutch Works Council, which remain unaffected upon the formation of a European Works Council whether negotiated or mandatory. The directive has been implemented in the Netherlands (*see infra* Chapter 12.3).

1.4   Major Holdings Disclosure Act

The Major Holdings Disclosure Act 1996 (WMZ 1996) places an obligation on an actual or potential of a direct or indirect interest (in terms of shares or voting rights or both) in the capital of an N.V. to disclose its holding if it reaches certain thresholds. These thresholds are set at percentages of 5, 10, 55 and $66^2/3$[50]. The WMZ only applies to N.V.s incorporated under Netherlands law whose shares or depository receipts are officially listed on a securities exchange located and operating in an European Economic Area (EEA) Member State.

Each time one of the thresholds has been reached, the shareholder must forthwith notify the corporation concerned and the Securities Board of the Netherlands (STE)[51]. Upon receipt of any such notice, the STE must publish this message within nine days in a national newspaper in every EEA Member State in which the corporation is listed[52].

The WMZ 1996 covers holdings in terms of voting rights attached to shares and capital interest (*i.e.* shares in respect of which the shareholder

---

49   Council Directive No. 94/95, 37 O.J. Eur. Comm. (No. L254) 64 (1994)
50   The percentages for investment corporations with a variable capital (BW art. 2:76a) are set at 25, 50 and $66^2/3$.
51   Wet melding zeggenschap in ter beurze genoteerde vennootschappen 1996 [WMZ 1996] (Major Holdings Disclosure Act 1996), arts. 2, 3, 1996 S. 629
52   WMZ 1996 art. 7.

does not necessarily have any voting rights). It also covers voting rights which are vested in the pledgee or beneficiary of a life interest (*vruchtge-bruik*) in shares when a right of pledge or life interest is created on the shares. The WMZ contains specific provisions for holdings in corporations by professional intermediaries (*e.g.* securities underwriting and securities lending) and in case of an initial public offering.

2   SELECTION OF BUSINESS ORGANISATIONAL FORM

2.1   General

a   Foreign or Dutch Corporate Law. Any individual, partnership or corporation, whether Dutch or foreign, resident or non-resident, can do business in the Netherlands without being required to adopt a particular legal form. The foreign owner must therefore first determine whether he wants the business in the Netherlands to be conducted through a corporation, a partnership, or a branch (*filiaal*) of the foreign unincorporated business. This raises the question whether the corporation or the partnership should be established under Dutch or foreign law.

b   Representative Office. Many foreign business organisations are represented in the Netherlands by an agent. If that agent is operating from within that foreign organisation, it may keep his representative offices in the form of a Dutch branch of that foreign organisation (*see infra* Chapter 2.2) or adopt a Dutch corporate form, usually a B.V. corporation (*see infra* Chapter 3.2.a). The choice is highly dependent on the nature of the business, the agent's tax position, and the tax status that the foreign organisation is willing to accept in the Netherlands (*see infra* Chapter 2.3).

c   Legal Personality. The law[1] stipulates which private legal forms can claim legal personality, *i.e.*, can be called a "legal person": Associations (*Verenigingen*), Co-operatives (*Coöperaties*), Mutual Insurance Associations (*Onderlinge Waarborgmaatschappijen*), Foundations (*Stichtingen*), Corporations (N.V.s and B.V.s) and EEIGs[2]. General and limited partnerships created under the laws of the Netherlands have no legal personality. A legal person is, in respect of the laws of property, contract, tort and succession, equivalent to a natural person, unless the law stipulates otherwise[3]. A legal person formed under the laws of the Netherlands can have its principal place of business outside the Netherlands. Dutch law recognises the existence of foreign legal entities with legal personality, which are governed by foreign law. In this publication, certain aspects of legal personality have been described in the context of Dutch corporate law only.

---

1   BW art. 2:3.
2   Act of June 28, 1989, art. 3(1), 1989 S. 245.
3   BW art. 2:5.

2.2 Branch Office of a Foreign Corporation

a   General. If a foreign individual or legal entity or its Dutch business has not adopted a Dutch legal form, the Dutch business will be treated as part of the foreign owner's assets and liabilities. These liabilities include all responsibilities and obligations of that business which may arise under Dutch law.

If the Dutch business is wholly owned by a non-resident foreign legal entity, it is considered a branch office (*filiaal* or *nevenvestiging*). A business in the Netherlands can also be jointly owned by two or more corporations or individuals and be established under foreign law. These joint ventures frequently take the form of a general or limited partnership (*see infra* Chapter 2.4). The directors of the foreign legal entity and the persons in charge of the business operations in the Netherlands may be liable for "apparent negligence" in the event of a bankruptcy in the Netherlands (*see* Chapter 8.2.d)[4].

b   Power to Represent the Branch Office. The power to represent a foreign corporation is subject to the law of the country or state of incorporation. The Commercial Register Act 1996 and the implementing Commercial Register Decree 1996, however, requires the branch office of a foreign corporation to register at the Commercial Register (*see infra* Chapter 11). The information registered is binding upon the foreign corporation, even if the registered data is in conflict with the charter or bylaws of the foreign corporation or the laws under which the foreign corporation was formed. Third parties may therefore rely on the registration at the Commercial Register in all respects. The Commercial Register Act 1996 requires the designation of one or more persons who can sign for and bind the corporation. It is prudent to describe in detail the limitations on this authority to sign[5]. The registration is often made by the branch manager. If he states that he has a blank power, he may, as a practical matter, by operation of the Commercial Register Act 1996, have a much wider express authority than even the chief executive officer of the foreign corporation.

A branch office of a foreign corporation may enter into agreements of a wide variety, thereby binding the foreign corporation. Certain agree-

---

4   BW art. 2:138(11); Asser-Maeijer 2, III, *supra* p. 2 at note 7, § 334.
5   For the applicable theory concerning agents and their authority, *see infra* Chapter 7.2.d.iv.

ments will by their nature be governed by Dutch law. To the extent that enforcement is sought in the Netherlands of agreements that purport to be governed by foreign law, Dutch conflict of law rules apply[6].

c   **Name.** A branch office may operate under the name of its head office, its owners, or almost any other name, provided that the name does not confuse the public or infringe the name[7] or trademark rights[8] of third parties (*see infra* Chapter 3.3.c.ii). Regardless of the name used in the Netherlands, third parties can ascertain the name and business of the foreign owner from the files of the Commercial Register (*see infra* Chapter 11).

d   **No Discrimination against Foreigners.** A foreign enterprise (corporation, EEIG, partnership or sole proprietorship) is treated on an equal basis with Dutch enterprises. Dutch law is essentially non-discriminatory towards foreigners, but there are exceptions with regard to the legal form in which the business must be conducted, as well as the formalities to be complied with, most notably in the areas of exchange controls, securities trading, banking and insurance business, oil and gas and small retail trade. Residency or EU nationality requirements apply for the shipping[9], aviation[10] and defence industry. A draft statute is pending before Dutch Parliament that intends to prevent the evasion of Dutch mandatory corporate formalities by using a foreign corporation for a business enterprise that operates exclusively or almost exclusively in the Netherlands[11].

e   **Mandatory Rules.** A business enterprise in the Netherlands, regardless of its legal form, must comply with certain requirements of Dutch law,

---

6   Reference is made to the following English language publication: M. DAS AND J.J. VAN HAERSHOLTHE, "Conflict of Laws" in: DUTCH BUSINESS LAW, *supra* p. 1 at note 3, Chapter 4.

7   Handelsnaamwet [Handelsnaamw.] (Tradename Act) arts. 5, 5a, 5b, 1921 S. 842, *as amended.*

8   Eenvormige Beneluxwet op de merken [BMW] (Uniform Benelux Trademark Law) art. 13, 1962 Trb. 58, *as amended.*

9   Wetboek van Koophandel [WvK] (Commercial Code) art. 311, 1835 S.44, *as amended.*

10   Luchtvaartwet (Act on Aviation) art. 16, 1958 S. 47, *as amended.* The airline industry is organised on the basis of bilateral agreements pursuant to the 1944 Chicago Convention (1947 Trb. 165) and Council Regulation No. 2407/92 on Licensing of air carriers (35 O.J. Eur. Comm. (No. C240) 1 (1992)).

11   Wet op de formeel buitenlandse vennootschappen (Act on Pseudo Foreign Corporations) No. 24139.

including registration at the Commercial Register, establishment of a Works Council if it has fifty or more employees (*see infra* Chapter 12.1), the Merger Code, if it is involved in take-overs or mergers[12], and rules governing registration for various taxes.

2.3 Choice between Branch and Subsidiary

a **Legal Aspects.** Apart from tax aspects, which are generally decisive (*see infra* Chapter 2.3.b), the choice between setting up a branch office of a foreign legal person or a subsidiary established under Dutch law involves a number of considerations. The financial background and reputation of the head office determine the creditworthiness of the branch. A subsidiary will, from a legal point of view, be judged on its own financial standing. A subsidiary possesses the attribute of limited liability, thereby limiting the legal responsibility of the head office. A branch acts directly on behalf of the head office. To mitigate the liability of the head office for the debts of the branch, the head office may consider establishing a subsidiary in its country of residence which acts as a special purpose vehicle for its branch in the Netherlands. In that case, the liability will be limited to the amount of share capital of the special purpose vehicle.

Under Dutch law the management of a subsidiary has its own responsibilities and is entitled to a certain degree of independence from the parent (*see infra* Chapter 7.2.a.i). The management of a branch is completely subject to the control of the head office. Dutch subsidiaries are subject to extensive auditing and publication requirements.

With the exception of registration at the Commercial Register and the disclosure required by the Commercial Register Act (*see infra* Chapter 11.2), no Dutch auditing or publication requirements exist for branches except for those engaged in banking and insurance.

In the absence of contractual restrictions, shares in a subsidiary company can be sold or otherwise disposed of by their owner. A branch is not a legal person separate from the head office, and can therefore be sold only by way of an asset transaction. Obviously, where a special purpose vehicle is used to establish the branch, the shares of this special purpose company can be sold in order to sell the branch.

---

12 Reference is made to the following English language publication: M&A IN THE NETHERLANDS, *supra* p. 3 at note 14.

A Dutch subsidiary gives added weight to the local presence. From a practical point of view it can be important to have the appearance of being Dutch, for instance, in regard to customer relations, marketing and for labour relations.

Branches sometimes suffer from "red tape" requirements imposed by government agencies or contractual parties to prove their authority to enter into agreements or to make certain filings. On the other hand, branches have a fairly unrestricted legal structure. The law of corporations is considerably more complex.

Branches require very little time to establish. The formation of a Dutch corporation, on the other hand, normally takes several weeks (*see infra* Chapter 3.3.b.iv).

Costs for setting up a branch are minimal. (For the costs of corporate formation, *see infra* Chapter 3.3.d).

b **Taxation**[13]**.** Not only do the legal aspects mentioned above play a role in determining the form of the enterprise in the Netherlands, but there are also major tax implications involved in the decision. These are caused by the different tax treatment of the two business forms.

There is no difference in principle between the taxation of a branch or a subsidiary. Both are covered by the Corporate Income Tax Act. Both are also covered by the concept of sound business practice (*see infra* Chapter 13.1.iii.A). There are, however, differences between the treatment given to the two business forms. Although both the branch and the subsidiary are presumed to be independent of the foreign business organisation, certain aspects of the presumed independence of the branch meet resistance from the tax authorities. Consequently, interest and royalties, and often other intercompany charges such as management expenses, are not chargeable to a branch, based on the idea that these charges cannot be made to oneself. However, this is different if the head office itself has to pay interest or royalties. In such a case, the interest or royalties can be charged to the branch. There is a tendency in case law of the Dutch Supreme Court towards a more independent treatment of branches under the direct method of taxation by which the tax treatment comes closer to that of subsidiaries. For a subsidiary, these charges are possible, provided they are made on an arm's length basis. In cases where the direct

---

13   This paragraph was revised by Jan A. Ter Wisch and Eric van der Stoel of Loeff Claeys Verbeke, Rotterdam office.

method of taxation cannot be applied, a ruling may be granted that taxation be based on other methods, such as a percentage of sales.

A subsidiary is a Dutch resident taxpayer and as such is subject to tax on its worldwide income. A branch, being a permanent establishment of a non-resident taxpayer, is taxed only on certain specifically stated Dutch-source income. As a non-resident taxpayer, a branch is not entitled to the benefits a Dutch resident subsidiary enjoys under the Netherlands tax treaties, nor of those under the Decree for the Avoidance of Double Taxation[14], which are available only to resident taxpayers.

The participation exemption[15] (*see infra* Chapter 13.2.c) applies to both a branch and a subsidiary. However, it is more difficult in the case of a branch to establish that the investments involved belong to the branch.

Benefits passed on by a head office to a subsidiary or by a subsidiary to a head office based on their shareholder relationship are treated for tax purposes as informal capital and distributions respectively. Informal capital contributions must be eliminated from the business profits of the subsidiary, whereas distributions must be added to its business profits. They will, however, attract capital contributions tax or dividend withholding tax. In the framework of a branch, any such non-arm's length benefits receive the same tax treatment, but will not attract capital contributions tax or dividend withholding tax, since the former is applicable only to corporations, and branch profits may be repatriated without any withholding tax. Under Dutch tax law no branch profits tax is levied, although some tax treaties concluded by the Netherlands allow a branch profits tax on profits distributed by the branch.

The fiscal unity[16] (*see infra* Chapter 13.2.e) is only available to a subsidiary established under Dutch law and resident in the Netherlands. The Dutch Supreme Court ruled that a corporation which is established under Dutch law but is resident outside the Netherlands, can be part of a fiscal unity. As a result of this case law the Deputy Minister of Finance issued a regulation[17] on the eligibility of corporations established under foreign law for fiscal unity treatment. Under this regulation foreign corporations which are resident in the Netherlands may be included in a fis-

---

14 Besluit voorkoming dubbele belasting (Decree for the Avoidance of Double Taxation), 1989 S. 574, *as amended.*
15 Wet op de vennootschapsbelasting [Vpb] (Corporate Income Tax Act), art. 15(a), 1969 S. 445, *as amended.*
16 Vpb art. 15.
17 August 10, 1994.

cal unity (either as a parent or as a subsidiary) if they are sufficiently comparable to a Dutch limited liability corporation.

For an elaborate discussion on Dutch tax law, *see infra* Chapter 13.

2.4   General Partnership and Limited Partnership

a   Introduction. For the establishment of a business venture under Dutch law, the basic choices are a sole proprietorship (*eenmanszaak*), a private partnership (*maatschap*), a general partnership (*vennootschap onder firma*), a limited partnership (*commanditaire vennootschap*), a European Economic Interest Grouping (*Europees economisch samenwerkingsverband*), or a corporation. A private partnership is most often used for professionals, such as lawyers, accountants, tax consultants and architects, although under Dutch law it can be the business form for all business enterprises. However, if the private partnership conducts business that is not the business of professionals, and conducts this business under a common business name, the rules of a general partnership apply by operation of law. The main characteristics of the general and limited partnership forms available under Dutch law are described below. A sole proprietorship is similar to a general partnership, except that there is only one owner, and consequently no need for a partnership agreement.

b   General Partnership (*Vennootschap onder Firma*)

i   *General.* A general partnership established under Dutch law is based on an agreement between two or more partners, which may be individuals or legal entities.

None of the partners need to be Dutch or resident in the Netherlands. The partnership is not a separate legal person distinct from its owners. A partnership can hold property, sue and be sued, and contract in its own name. Third parties may hold the partners jointly and severally liable for the partnership's debts (*see* iv below). The purpose of the partnership must be co-operation in order to make a profit. By law, the partners must contribute either cash, property, labour, or goodwill. A contribution of business relations or know-how is also acceptable[18].

18   C. ASSER, 5, V BIJZONDERE OVEREENKOMSTEN: MAATSCHAP, VENNOOTSCHAP ONDER FIRMA EN COMMANDITAIRE VENNOOTSCHAP [hereinafter ASSER-MAEIJER 5, V] § 37 (J.M.M. Maeijer, 6th ed. 1995), W.E.J. Tjeenk Willink (Zwolle).

ii *Commercial Register.* General partnerships must be registered at the Commercial Register[19]. The registration requires the disclosure of, *inter alia*, the names of the partners, their nationality and signatures, and a description of the partnership's business[20].

iii *Partnership Agreement.* A written partnership agreement is recommended, although not mandatory. It should cover the partnership's name, the partnership's purposes or objects, the authority of the partners to bind the partnership (the scope of authority is determined by the partners), the manner in which profits and losses are to be distributed among the partners, the capital contribution of each partner, the consequences of the resignation and expulsion of a partner, and the dissolution of the partnership.

The partnership will not necessarily be dissolved if one of the partners resigns. The remaining partners may continue the business and keep the assets if this is provided in the partnership agreement. The agreement should be drafted with a view to its tax consequences (*see* vi below).

iv *Liability of the Partners.* Details of the partnership's purposes and the authority of the individual partners to represent the partnership should be disclosed at the Commercial Register[21]. In the absence of a proper registration, third parties may hold all partners jointly and severally liable for any action performed by any partner on behalf of the partnership, whether or not this action falls within the partnership's purposes[22]. A proper entry in the Commercial Register ensures that the unlimited personal liability of each of the partners can only be invoked to the extent the liability is incurred by a partner acting within the scope of his authority as disclosed[23].

v   *Annual Accounts.* The annual accounts of the partnership need not be disclosed to the public or filed at any register or agency. However, a partnership engaged in banking or insurance must comply with the applicable disclosure rules.

---

19 WvK art. 23.
20 HrW 1996 art. 8, Handelsregisterbesluit 1996 [HrB 1996] (Commercial Register Decree 1996) arts. 9(1), 12, 1997 s. 147.
21 HrW 1996, art. 8(1), HrB 1996, arts. 9(1), 12.
22 WvK art. 29.
23 WvK art. 17,18; HrW 1996 art. 18.

vi *Tax Treatment of Profits and Losses.* For tax purposes, the partnership's income flows through to the individual partners. It is treated as income of the partners in the manner set out in the partnership agreement and is reported on their individual income tax returns. Non-residents are subject to Dutch income tax only on certain sources of income, such as business income derived through a permanent establishment (*see infra* Chapter 13.2.g.ii). The profit share of a non-resident partner qualifies as Dutch taxable income.

vii *Distribution of Profits and Losses.* Profits can be distributed according to the partnership agreement. If the profits are retained, they must be included in the income statement submitted by each partner for tax assessment. Dutch law does not permit the establishment of a partnership in which a partner is liable for all losses or specific losses, without having a share in the profits[24].

viii *Capacity to Sue.* Although it is not a separate legal person distinct from its owners, the partnership can sue or be sued[25].

ix *Position of Creditors.* In the event of an attachment of partnership assets or bankruptcy of the partnership, the claims of the business creditors of the partnership have priority over those of the creditors of the individual partners, with respect to the assets of the partnership[26].

x *Partnership Shares.* The partnership agreement may provide for the transfer of partnership shares. Shares in the partnership may even be in the name of a bearer of a share certificate. The use of this legal device may, however, have far-reaching negative tax implications.

c **Limited Partnership (*Commanditaire Vennootschap*)**

i *General.* A limited partnership is similar to a general partnership, but has one or more limited partners, referred to in Dutch as "silent" partners (*stille vennoten*), whose liability is limited to the amount of their capital contributions[27].

---

24 ASSER-MAEIJER, 5, V, *supra* p. 21 at note 70, § 70.
25 Wetboek van Burgerlijke Rechtsvordering [Rv.] (Code on Civil Procedure) art. 4(4), 1828 S. 14, *as amended*; BW art. 7A:1682.
26 Judgment of November 26, 1897, HR, W7074.
27 WvK art. 20(3).

ii   *The Managing Partners.* A limited partnership has one or more managing partners whose liability is that of a general partner, *i.e.*, unlimited. To avoid the adverse effects of unlimited liability, the managing partner may be a limited liability corporation, the shares of which may be held by the limited partners (this arrangement is similar to the well-known German *GmbH und Co. K.G.*).

iii   *Management by Limited Partners.* If a limited partner is involved in management (directly or by proxy) or if his name is disclosed, his liability will be *unlimited* (even if third parties know of his status as a limited partner)[28].

iv   *No Shares.* A limited partnership by shares is no longer permitted[29].

v   *Tax Treatment of Profits and Losses.* For tax purposes, a limited partner is treated as a general partner (*see supra* Chapter 2.4.b.vi).

2.5   Other Legal Forms of Doing Business

a   The Association (*Vereniging*) and its Qualified Forms

i   *General.* An association in its general form is prohibited from having as its purpose the making of profits for distributions to its members[30]. For this reason, an association in its general form is not a desirable form for doing business. There are, however, sub-categories of the legal form of an association that may be used for specific business purposes and that can distribute profits to their members[31]: the co-operative and the mutual insurance association (*see* below). For a conversion of any association to an N.V. or B.V., *see infra* Chapter 10.5. An association in its general form cannot own real property, and its managing directors are jointly and severally liable for the actions of the association if the articles of association (hereinafter the articles) are not drawn up in notarial form, and do not comply with certain mandatory rules[32]. An association with articles drawn up before a civil-law notary must register with the Chamber of Commerce (*see infra* Chapter 11)[33].

---

28   WvK art. 21.
29   Statute of May 28, 1975, 1975 S. 277.
30   BW art. 2:26(3).
31   BW art. 2:53a.
32   BW art. 2:30.
33   BW art. 2:29(1).

ii   *The Co-operative (Coöperatie)*[34]. A co-operative is a popular organisa-
     tional form for agricultural businesses. Several co-operatives in the
     Netherlands own considerable business operations. One of the largest
     banks, Rabobank, largely geared to the agricultural business, is a co-
     operative.

iii *The Mutual Insurance Association (Onderlinge Waarborgmaatschappij)*[35].
     The legal form of a mutual insurance association (hereinafter a mutu-
     al) is used only in the insurance industry, in which case the policy
     holders are the members of the association.

iv   *Limitation of Liability.* The co-operative and the mutual are basically
     subject to the same rules. The initials W.A., B.A. or U.A. are usually
     part of the name, and indicate the extent of the members' liabil-
     ity. U.A. stands for *uitgesloten aansprakelijkheid, i.e.,* an absolute limi-
     tation of the liability of the members and former members for the
     actions by the co-operative or the mutual[36]. B.A. stands for *beperkte
     aansprakelijkheid, i.e.,* the restricted liability of the members, as deter-
     mined in the articles and disclosed at the Commercial Register. W.A.
     stands for *wettelijke aansprakelijkheid, i.e.,* the personal liability of the
     members, each for an equal part.

v   *Commercial Register.* Both the co-operative and the mutual must file
     registrations at the Commercial Register similar to the registrations
     required for corporations (*see infra* Chapter 11).

vi   *Executive Powers.* The co-operative and the mutual must each have a
     management board, and may have a supervisory board[37]. If the co-
     operative or the mutual qualifies as "large" for more than three con-
     secutive years, it must have a supervisory board[38]. The test for this
     qualification is similar to the test for a corporation to qualify as a
     "large" corporation (*see infra* Chapter 7.1.b.ii). Many decisions of the
     management board of a "large" co-operative or mutual require prior
     approval by the supervisory board[39]. The duties of board members
     and the rules concerning the personal liability of managing directors
     of corporations (*see infra* Chapter 8) apply similarly to managing

---

34   BW art. 2:53(1).
35   BW art. 2:53(2).
36   BW art. 2:56(1).
37   BW art. 2:57.
38   BW arts. 2:63f, 2:63c.
39   BW art. 2:63j.

directors of co-operatives and mutuals, as do the rules concerning the powers of the managing directors of a corporation (*see infra* Chapter 7.2)[40].

vii *Annual Accounts.* Strict rules concerning auditing, the prescribed format, adoption and publication of annual accounts and the annual report, apply to co-operatives and mutuals[41]. Associations in their general form that conduct a business enterprise having a net turnover of at least NLG 6 million must comply with these rules as well[42].

b   The Foundation (*Stichting*). A *stichting*[43] has certain similarities to a foundation in the United States. Unlike its US counterpart, however, a *stichting* is not necessarily limited to charitable purposes. To the extent that the legal concept of a trust is recognised under Dutch law, a *stichting* functions in much the same way as a common law trust. It has no members, and cannot make distributions to its managing directors or its founders. Any distributions to third parties must have a charitable or non-commercial purpose[44]. The purposes of a *stichting* can include commercial activities. For a conversion of a *stichting* to an N.V. or B.V., *see infra* Chapter 10.5. There are several *stichtingen* with large business enterprises. The legal form of a *stichting* is often used for the issuance of depository receipts by a corporation (*see infra* Chapter 5.5) and for the exercise of control by the management board over the shareholders by use of priority shares and preference shares (*see infra* Chapter 5.1.c). A *stichting* can be formed only by a notarial deed[45]. It is a separate entity, distinct from its founders or managing directors. It can own property, contract in its own name, and sue or be sued. The *stichting* must register with the Chamber of Commerce (*see infra* Chapter 11)[46]. Foundations that conduct a business enterprise having a net turnover of at least NLG 6 million must comply with the rules for the format, adoption and publication of annual accounts and the annual report[47].

---

40   BW arts. 2:53a, 2:44, 2:45.
41   BW art. 2:58.
42   BW arts. 2:49, 2:360(3). The minimum turnover threshold may be altered by Royal Decree to conform to EC legislation (BW art. 2:398(4)).
43   BW art. 2:285(1).
44   BW art. 2:285(3).
45   BW art. 2:286(1).
46   BW art. 2:289.
47   *See* BW arts. 2:300, 2:360(3).

c **European Economic Interest Grouping.** The EC Regulation[48] concerning the creation of the European Economic Interest Grouping (EEIG, *see supra* Chapter 1.3.o) has been implemented into Dutch law by a separate statute[49]. However, many material aspects remain governed by this Regulation directly, and it should be noted that the interpretation of this Regulation and its implementation in Dutch law are subject to the jurisdiction of the Court of Justice of the European Communities. Nevertheless, each Member State has been given certain choices in its implementation of the Regulation, and consequently each country has its own EEIG. In the Netherlands, the EEIG (*Europees Economisch Samenwerkingsverband*, or *EESV*) has legal personality, but in many other respects shows great similarity to the general partnership (*see supra* Chapter 2.4.b). The most notable differences are that:

a   the EEIG must serve the interests of its members (entrepreneurs or professionals, corporations or individuals) and not have corporate purposes of its own;

b   its members must be domiciled or resident in one of the Member States;

c   an EEIG must have at least two members from two or more different Member States;

d   while the activities of the EEIG must be of support to its members, the EEIG itself should not be an independent profit centre. However, the making of profit by the EEIG in itself is not prohibited;

e   the EEIG cannot hold shares in the capital of its members;

f   it cannot have more than 500 employees;

g   membership is personal. The transfer by a member of its participation in the EEIG requires the approval of all other members;

h   the provisions concerning the liability of board members in case of bankruptcy (*see infra* Chapter 8.2.d) and the investigation into the affairs of the legal person (*enquête, see infra* Chapter 9.2.b) also apply to the EEIG;

i   the EEIG must have its annual accounts audited by an independent auditor.

An EEIG is not considered an independent taxpayer. Like a general partnership, it serves for tax purposes as a transparent vehicle in which profits and losses are attributed to its members.

---

48   Council Regulation No. 2137/85, 28 O.J. Eur. Comm. (No. L199) 1 (1985).
49   Statute of June 28, 1989, 1989 S. 245.

3   TYPES OF CORPORATIONS; FORMATION; CORPORATE PURPOSE

3.1   Introduction

a   General. Any corporation incorporated under foreign law can validly carry on business in the Netherlands. Foreign corporations continue to be governed by the corporate laws of the jurisdiction of their incorporation and this law will be recognised by Dutch courts, unless it conflicts with Dutch public order, even if the main centre of activities of the corporation (*siège réel*) is in the Netherlands rather than in the country or state of incorporation. An attempt by a foreign corporation to transfer the corporate seat to the Netherlands will not be recognised in the Netherlands and a Dutch court may declare the corporation void or non-existent. For a transfer of the seat of a Dutch corporation, *see infra* Chapter 10.7.

Most Dutch law concerning corporations is statutory law, contained in Book 2 of the Civil Code. Dutch law recognises two different types of corporations: the N.V. (*Naamloze Vennootschap*) and the B.V. (*Besloten Vennootschap*). Both the N.V. and B.V. are separate legal entities, distinct from their shareholders, with a capital divided into shares[1]. The N.V. and the B.V. can be used for the same business purposes, can own and transfer property, lend money, buy and sell securities, engage employees, contract and borrow in their own name, participate in other ventures and sue or be sued. Due to limitations on the transferability of its shares, the B.V. is a privately held or close corporation, while the free transferability of N.V. shares makes the latter a public corporation (*see infra* Chapter 3.2).

b   The Concept of the Group (*Concernrecht*). Dutch law recognises that corporations often do not operate on a stand-alone basis. A significant number of business organisations consist of a holding company, several sub-holding companies and a considerable number of subsidiary companies. Larger groups may also have, within the group, a management company and a finance company. There is no standard pattern for any group structure. Any group has its own history, tax parameters, organisational requirements, production and service locations, sales outlets, financing arrangements, captive insurance plans, etc.

---

1   BW arts. 2:64(1)/175(1).

The diversity of these group arrangements created a need for legislative reform and clarification, especially with respect to such matters as annual accounts and disclosure requirements, the rules concerning "large" corporations (*see infra* Chapter 7), and the requirements of the Works Councils Act.

Dutch law defines a "subsidiary" (*dochtermaatschappij*) as a legal person in which a parent company (i) can exercise more than one-half of all eligible voting rights at a general meeting of shareholders, or (ii) can appoint or remove more than one-half of the management or supervisory boards (assuming all votes are cast)[2]. The parent company's rights may be derived from a shareholders' agreement (*see infra* Chapter 6.4) and may be held either by the corporation alone or jointly with any of its other subsidiaries. A general or limited partnership in which one or more corporations or any of their subsidiaries is fully liable to creditors is deemed to be a "subsidiary" of such corporations. A corporation may also be a subsidiary of more than one shareholder. This situation may occur, *inter alia*, if one of its shareholders, pursuant to the articles or a shareholders' agreement, is entitled to appoint or remove the majority of the managing directors and another shareholder is entitled to appoint or remove the majority of the supervisory directors[3].

Dutch law defines a "group" (*groep*) as an economic structure in which legal persons, partnerships, or both are united in one organisation (*i.e.* centralised management)[4]. If a party has majority control over a company that qualifies as "centralised management", that other company will be a group company of the first party[5]. Equity interests are not conclusive evidence for the qualification of a company as a group company. A minority participation or a participation of 50% may suffice, provided ancillary provisions granting decision-making powers exist. Consequently, a company may be a group company in more than one group.

A "participation" (*deelneming*) exists when a legal person or partnership, for its own account, either directly or through one or more subsidiaries, has an equity interest in another company, with the objective of having a long-term association with that other company for the furtherance of its own business purposes. Contributing one-fifth or more of the issued capital creates a rebuttable assumption of a "participation"[6]. A company par-

---

2   BW art. 2:24a.
3   Asser-Maeijer 2, III, *supra* p. 2 at note 7, § 610.
4   BW art. 2:24b.
5   Asser-Maeijer 2, III, *supra* p. 2 at note 7, § 608.
6   BW art. 2:24c.

ticipates in a partnership if it or its subsidiary as a partner (i) is fully liable towards its creditors, or (ii) has as its objective a long-term association with that partnership for the furtherance of its own business purposes.

For the statutory definition of a "dependent company" (*afhankelijke maatschappij*), *see infra* Chapter 7.1.b.ii.

Dutch law has to some extent adopted a consistent theory concerning groups of affiliated companies. The reality of the group as a business concept has had an effect on the development of theories concerning the responsibility of a parent for the actions of its subsidiary and *vis-à-vis* the creditors of the subsidiary (*see infra* Chapter 3.5), the availability of subsidiary assets as collateral for loans made to the parent or to sister corporations (*see infra* Chapter 4.7), and the extent and nature of the instructions that a parent may give to the management board of a subsidiary (*see infra* Chapter 7.2.a.i).

c   Investment Company with Variable Capital (*Beleggingsmaatschappij met veranderlijk kapitaal*). Investment companies, both open-end and closed-end, that meet the requirements stated below are exempt from certain strict rules concerning the capital of the corporation. These exemptions relate to the power of the management board to decide on the issuance of new shares and the pre-emptive rights of shareholders (*see infra* Chapter 4.4.b), the repurchase of shares (*see infra* Chapter 4.6.b and Chapter 4.3.f), and the redemption of shares (*see infra* Chapter 4.6.c). Investment companies qualify for these exemptions only if they meet the following requirements[7]:

a   the investment company must be an N.V.;

b   the investment company must have the exclusive purpose to invest its assets with spread risk, with the objective to share the benefits with its shareholders;

c   the articles must empower the management board to issue, acquire and dispose of shares in the capital of the investment company;

d   the shares, other than priority shares (*see infra* Chapter 5.1.c), will be quoted on a stock exchange;

e   the articles must state that the N.V. is an investment company with variable capital; and

f   the issued capital of the investment company in excess of the shares acquired and held by it must equal at least 10% of the authorised capital (*see infra* Chapter 4.1.a) stated in the articles[8].

---

7   BW art. 2:76a(1).
8   BW art. 2:98(8).

d   Corporate Formalities. Dutch corporate law is complex and generally strict, while maintaining flexibility in certain areas. Great emphasis
is placed on the articles (*see infra* Chapter 3.3.c), capitalisation and subscription (*see infra* Chapter 4), the annual accounts, disclosure requirements at the Commercial Register (*see infra* Chapter 11), and the
representation of labour in management decisions (*see infra* Chapter 12).
The management board must keep a record of all shareholders' resolutions
available for inspection by shareholders and the holders of depository
receipts[9] (*see infra* Chapter 5.5). Subject to any special requirements stated
in the articles, resolutions of the management board or the supervisory
board can be adopted in any manner, without any formalities being
required. Shareholders' resolutions require special attention (*see infra*
Chapter 6.2).

e   No Bylaws. A corporation is formed by the execution of a deed of
incorporation, which contains the articles. Bylaws of the type commonly
drawn up in the United States are unknown in the Netherlands. The articles are considerably less detailed than most bylaws, but have a similar
practical function. However, the articles can only be amended by a
shareholders' resolution (*see infra* Chapter 10.2) and must be filed at the
Commercial Register for public inspection (*see infra* Chapter 11). Internal
rules governing the distribution of powers and the decision making process of the management board and the supervisory board may be adopted
in the form of a regulation or manual (*see infra* Chapter 7.2.a.i).

3.2   Public and Private Corporations

a   Differences between an N.V. and a B.V.. N.V. shares can be in
bearer form and may then be freely negotiable[10]. However, the transfer of
registered N.V. shares may (but need not) be restricted in any way; the
shareholders are free to set forth transfer restrictions in the articles[11]. B.V.
shares must be registered shares[12] and, as a general rule, cannot be freely
transferred. Consequently, B.V. shares cannot be listed on the Amsterdam
stock exchange. The articles of a B.V. must contain one of the transfer
restrictions imposed by law (*see infra* Chapter 5.4.c.ii)[13]. Share certifi-

---

9   BW arts. 2:120(4)/230(4).
10   BW art. 2:82(1).
11   BW art. 2:87(1).
12   BW art. 2:194(1).
13   BW art. 2:195(2).

cates can only be issued to N.V. shareholders; B.V. shareholders cannot obtain certificates evidencing title to their shares. Furthermore, a B.V. may, within specific statutory restrictions, give loans for the acquisition of its shares[14], whereas an N.V., with the exception of loans for employees' shares, may not (*see infra* Chapter 4.3.g)[15]; the amount of treasury shares permitted is limited to 50% for the B.V.[16] as opposed to 10% for the N.V. (*see infra* Chapter 4.3.f)[17], and the respective mandatory minimum capital requirements differ[18] (currently NLG 40,000 for a B.V.[19] and NLG 100,000 for an N.V.)[20]. There are other differences, but these are usually of minor significance for business matters. Both the B.V. and the N.V. can be a statutory "large" corporation (*see infra* Chapter 7.1.b). Many substantial corporations in the Netherlands have adopted the B.V. form (in contrast to the situation in certain other Member States, such as the United Kingdom, where the close corporation form is available only to the small or medium-sized corporation). The specific audit and disclosure requirements are almost identical for N.V.s and B.V.s., irrespective of whether they are "large" corporations.

b   Modification of Corporate Form. An N.V. may convert to a B.V.[21] and a B.V. may convert to an N.V.[22]. This conversion of form does not affect the corporation's existence or identity (which would have disastrous tax consequences)[23]. A decision of the shareholders to convert the corporate form is executed in the same way as other amendments to the articles (*see infra* Chapter 10.2)[24]. For the conversion of an association, a co-operative, a mutual insurance association and a *stichting* to an N.V. or B.V. and *vice versa, see infra* Chapter 10.5.

---

14   BW art. 2:207c(2).
15   BW art. 2:98c(1).
16   BW art. 2:207(2)(b).
17   BW art. 2:98(2)9b).
18   Different rules apply to investment companies with variable capital (*see supra* Chapter 3.1.c).
19   BW art. 2:178(2).
20   BW art. 2:67(2).
21   BW arts. 2:18, 2:183(1).
22   BW arts. 2:18, 2:72(1).
23   BW art. 2:18(8).
24   BW art. 2:18(2).

3.3   Formation

a   General. The formation of a Dutch corporation is subject to a number of formalities and time-consuming. Administrative review by the Ministry of Justice (*see infra* Chapter 3.3.b.iv) often takes several weeks. The corporation can only be formed upon receipt of the official clearance by the Ministry, known as a certificate of no objection (*verklaring van geen bezwaar*). The corporation can then be formed either by an individual acting in his own capacity or on the strength of a power of attorney[25]. One or more parties, known as the founders, must appear before a Dutch civil-law notary, or be represented pursuant to a power of attorney and confirm their desire to form the corporation with articles as read to them, in full or in summary form.

The initial management board is appointed in the deed of incorporation[26]. Each of its members is jointly and severally liable for the obligations of the corporation until the moment that the corporation has been properly registered and the minimum capitalisation requirements have been met[27].

b   Incorporation

i   *The Deed of Incorporation.* A corporation comes into existence upon the execution before a Dutch civil-law notary of the deed of incorporation (*akte van oprichting*), which contains the articles (*statuten*)[28]. The articles are subject to and must be consistent with the law[29]. The deed of incorporation cannot be executed prior to the receipt of a certificate of no objection from the Ministry of Justice (*see* iv below). Bylaws of the US type are unknown. An organisational meeting is required, but only for the purpose of designating an auditor (*see infra* Chapter 6.1.b)[30].

ii   *Procedure.* The draft deed of incorporation is prepared by a Dutch civil-law notary or an attorney specialised in corporate matters. The civil-law notary or attorney submits the final draft to the Ministry of

---

25   BW arts. 2:4(1), 2:64(2)/175(2).
26   BW arts. 2:132/242.
27   BW arts. 2:69(2)/180(2).
28   BW arts. 2:66(1)/177(1).
29   BW arts. 2:68(2)/179(2).
30   BW art. 2:393(2).

Justice, and arranges for payment of the filing fees[31]. The notarial deed must be in the Dutch language[32]. The civil-law notary is required by law to retain the original of the deed. Certified copies may be issued to the founders and the management board[33].

iii   *The Founders.* The deed of incorporation must be signed by the civil-law notary and by the founders or their duly authorised representatives. Both corporations and individuals may be founders. Each founder must subscribe to part of the capital[34]. The aggregate contribution to the issued capital is required by law to be at least one-fifth of the authorised capital (*see infra* Chapter 4.1.b)[35]. Issued capital is the sum of the nominal value of all shares issued, commonly referred to in US corporate law as "stated capital". Dutch law does not recognise the concept of an incorporator whose sole function is to establish the corporation without any participation.

All of the shares may be held by a single individual or corporation[36]. For the disclosure and recordation requirements of a company with a single shareholder, *see infra* Chapter 5.2.c. The founders may be of any nationality and may be domiciled anywhere.

A founder can be represented only by a written power of attorney[37], which must conform to the requirements of the law applicable to the founder. A power of attorney by telex or telefax is acceptable to most civil-law notaries. Once incorporated, the corporation does not automatically cease to exist should the power turn out to be invalid. The courts may, however, dissolve such a corporation (*see infra* Chapter 10.6.b.ii)[38].

iv   *The Certificate of No Objection.* The certificate of no objection has two functions. First, it is an instrument by which the Ministry of Justice exercises administrative control over the contents of the deed of incorporation, and, once incorporation has taken place, over amend-

---

31   BW arts. 2:68(1)/179(1).
32   BW arts. 2:65/176.
33   Wet op het Notarisambt (Act on the Notarial Profession) art. 42, 1842 S. 20, *as amended.*
34   BW arts. 2:64(2)/175(2).
35   BW arts. 2:67(4)/178(4). Different rules apply to investment companies with variable capital (*see supra* Chapter 3.1.c).
36   BW arts. 2:64(2)/175(2).
37   BW arts. 2:65/176.
38   BW arts. 2:4(2), 2:21(1)(a).

ments to the articles. The certificate of no objection does not, however, immunise the articles from subsequent objections concerning their legality. The certificate's second function is even more important. Before issuing the certificate, the Ministry investigates, on the basis of criminal, bankruptcy and other records, whether there is reason to fear abuse of the corporate form.

The certificate can be refused only on the following grounds: if there is a danger, in light of the intentions or prior records of those who will determine or take part in the determination of the corporate policy, that the corporation will be used for unlawful activities or that creditors will be prejudiced by its activities; if the deed of incorporation is contrary to public order or law; if the founders have not subscribed to at least one-fifth of the corporation's authorised share capital (*see infra* Chapter 4.4.a); or that the filing fee due to the Ministry of Justice has not been paid[39]. Refusal to issue a certificate of no objection can be appealed to the Court of Appeal from Decisions of the SER, Product and Trade Boards (*College van Beroep voor het bedrijfsleven*)[40].

The notary or attorney must also submit to the Ministry, together with the draft of the deed of incorporation, details regarding the identity of the founders, the names of the first members of the management board and, where applicable, the supervisory board; for foreign corporate shareholders, recent annual accounts; for foreign individuals, a letter from a bank stating that the individual is known to the bank and normally meets his obligations[41]; and, if the corporation is to engage in banking or the insurance business, certain certificates from The Netherlands Bank or the Insurance Chamber. This procedure is often time-consuming and only the most urgent cases can, at the discretion of the Ministry, be expedited. Any subsequent changes to the articles require a new notarial deed and a new certificate of no objection from the Ministry (*see infra* Chapter 10.2).

v   *Personal Liability of Managing Directors.* The management board, or the civil-law notary on its behalf, must register the corporation's data and deposit a certified copy of the deed of incorporation at the Commercial Register of the Chamber of Commerce (*see infra* Chapter

---

39   BW arts. 2:68(2)/179(2).
40   BW arts. 2:174a/284a.
41   Ministerie van Justitie, Departementale Richtlijnen 1986 (Ministerial Directives) [hereinafter RICHTLIJNEN] § 2, 1985 Staatscourant [Stcr.] (Government Gazette) 227.

11)[42]. The management board must also ensure that, at the date of incorporation, at least 25% of the nominal value per issued share is paid up, and that the total nominal value paid up equals at least NLG 100,000 (for an N.V.), or NLG 40,000 (for a B.V.) (*see infra* Chapter 4.3.b). Until both of these mandatory requirements are complied with, the managing directors are jointly and severally liable for the obligations of the corporation, in addition to the corporation's liability for such obligations[43] (*see also infra* Chapter 8.3.b.ii).

vi *Defective Incorporation.* A corporation that was formed without complying with all formalities stated under v above, was otherwise not formed in conformity with the law or has articles that violate the requirements of the law is subject to an action by the public prosecutor or other interested party to have it dissolved by the court[44]. The court will allow for an action by the founders to redress the defects[45].

However, when business is conducted in the name of a corporation whose deed of incorporation was not signed by a Dutch civil-law notary, or if the certificate of no objection was not obtained from the Ministry of Justice, the corporation never came into existence[46]. In the meantime, the estate is liable for all of its obligations, jointly and severally with its present managing directors or those who were acting as such, absent of which the persons who created these obligations in the name of the corporation are liable[47]. This *de facto* corporation should be clearly distinguished from the corporation "to be formed" (*see infra* Chapter 3.4.b).

Dutch law does not recognise the concept of corporations by estoppel as it exists in the United States.

c **Articles of Association**

i *General Introduction.* The rules governing a corporation's conduct are set forth in the law and in the articles. Dutch corporate law does not recognise or require bylaws, separate and distinct from the articles.

---

42   BW arts. 2:69(1)/180(1).
43   BW arts. 2:69(2)/180(2).
44   BW art. 2:21(1).
45   BW art. 2:21(2).
46   BW art. 2:4(1).
47   BW arts. 2:4(3),(4).

The articles must not be in conflict with mandatory provisions of law[48]. The law requires that the following subjects be dealt with in the articles[49]:

a   the name of the corporation (*see* ii below);

b   the official seat (*see* iii below);

c   the purposes or objects of the corporation (*see* iv below);

d   the authorised share capital specified by type of shares (the issued share capital must be stated in the deed of incorporation (*see supra* Chapter 3.3.b.i)); and

e   a provision for the event that a member of the management board fails in or is prevented from performing his duties.

In order to give management, shareholders and others a more complete and balanced picture of the corporation's structure, practice has demonstrated the value of stating in the articles various additional legal provisions that apply mandatorily to the corporation.

ii   *The Name.* The name must contain an indication of the corporate form, either the abbreviation "N.V."[50] or "B.V."[51]. It cannot contain any such indication in a foreign language[52].

Any name is acceptable as long as it is not too general or too vague (city names are, for example, prohibited), does not imply that the corporation has powers or purposes that it does not have, is not confusing or deceptive to the public, and does not violate the trade name or trademark rights of others[53]. A name search is usually conducted with the assistance of the Commercial Register and, sometimes, the Benelux Trademark Office. Their opinion is generally sufficient for this purpose, but does not give full protection against claims for trade name or trademark infringement. Names referring to a certain business activity may only be used if the corporation is actually engaged in that business[54]; the words "bank"[55] or "insurance company" can be used only if the corporation meets the statutory requirements applicable to banks or insurance companies. An investment company

---

48   BW art. 2:21(1)(b).
49   BW arts. 2:66(1)/177(1), 2:67(1)/178(1), 2:134(4)/244(4).
50   BW art. 2:66(2).
51   BW art. 2:177(2).
52   RICHTLIJNEN, *supra* p. 36 at note 142, § 5.
53   Handelsnaamw. arts. 5, 5a, 5b; BMW art. 13; Richtlijnen § 5.
54   RICHTLIJNEN, *supra* p. 36 at note 142, § 5.
55   Wet Toezicht Kredietwezen 1992 [WTK] (Act on the Supervision of the Credit System) art. 83(1), 1992 S. 722, *as amended.*

with variable capital (*see supra* Chapter 3.1.c) must refer to this status whenever its name is used[56].

The full name (including the N.V. or B.V. abbreviation), the official seat and the registration number must be on the corporation's stationery and on all other papers (except telexes, telegrams and advertising announcements) emanating from the corporation (*see infra* Chapter 11.1.c)[57].

If the business is carried out under a trade name which is different from the corporate name, the trade name must also be filed with the Commercial Register[58].

iii   *The Seat.* The official seat is normally the principal office of the corporation. It can be in any municipality in the Netherlands[59]. The official seat must be stated in the articles. Frequently, it will be the municipality in which the corporation's principal office is situated, but this need not be so.

Under the Commercial Register Act 1996, providing for one national registration only, a corporation must register with either the Commercial Register at its official seat or the district in the Netherlands in which it has its principal place of business[60].

Dutch law does not recognise the concept of a registered office or registered agent. A corporation can be sued by serving process on a member of its management board or on its head office[61]. For a transfer of seat, *see infra* Chapter 10.7.

iv   *The Corporate Purposes or Objects.* The purposes or objects may consist of a short general description of the corporation's major activities. The purposes clause can be changed only by an amendment to the articles. It can be very general, normally specifying the principal business or activity of the corporation, coupled with such language as "and to engage in any other similar business." Investment companies with variable capital (*see supra* Chapter 3.1.c), must include in the purposes

---

56   BW art. 2:76a(2).
57   BW arts. 2:75(1)/186(1); HrW 1996, art. 25(1).
58   HrW 1996 art. 8(1); HrB 1996 art. 9(1).
59   BW arts. 2:66(3)/177(3).
60   BW arts. 66(1),(3); HrW 1996 art. 6(1).
61   Rv art. 4(3).

clause a reference to defined activities[62]. The corporate purposes provision can limit the power of the corporation. Unless the articles state otherwise, a corporation has the power to engage in any lawful business, to own property, to buy or sell securities, to lend money, to enter into contracts, to sue, to borrow money, to issue notes or bonds, to grant mortgages of its property as security, to fix the compensation of employees and managing directors, to participate in ventures as a partner or a manager, to own shares in another corporation, and to act as a founder of another Dutch or foreign corporation. While it may be argued that in theory the powers of a corporation cannot extend beyond promoting its own individual interest[63], it is nevertheless useful for subsidiaries to include in their purposes clauses a statement that the interests of the corporation include the interests of the parent and other corporations of the group and that its assets can serve as collateral on behalf of other corporations of the group. As part of the articles, the purposes provision is available for public inspection. If the corporation acts in a way that exceeds the scope of its express or inherent powers the doctrine of *ultra vires* (*see infra* Chapter 3.6) may operate to nullify the transaction, if it can be shown that the other party knew, or should have known, that the transaction was beyond the scope of the corporation's purposes[64]. These other parties to the transaction cannot, however, invoke this doctrine, even if they can prove that the corporation knew that the act exceeded its purposes. Therefore, they are bound by the transaction whether or not it is within the scope of the corporation's purposes (*see infra* Chapter 3.6). Managing directors who act beyond the corporation's purposes may be personally liable for damages incurred by the corporation[65].

v   *Infinite term.* The articles may not contain any limitations on the duration of a corporation's existence[66].

d   Costs of Formation. The costs of corporate formation include a filing fee of NLG 200, due to the Ministry of Justice upon submission of all documents; a fee not exceeding NLG 200 to the Chamber of Commerce for a name search on possible trade name infringement; and a fee of several hundred guilders to a trade mark agency for a name search on possible trademark infringements.

---

62   BW art. 2:76a(1)(d).
63   For a different view, *see supra* Chapter 3.1.b.
64   BW art. 2:7. This provision does not impose a duty to make inquiries.
65   BW art. 2:9.
66   BW art. 2:17.

The national fee schedule for the notarial fee charged for incorporation is linked to the amount of the corporation's authorised capital. The fee schedule allows the fee to be adjusted to reflect the work involved. The fees for consultants such as attorneys, tax specialists, and auditors reflect the work involved.

The annual levy of the Commercial Register (*see infra* Chapter 11.4) is calculated on the basis of a schedule that takes into account such variables as equity and loans made to the corporation[67].

The capital contribution tax is 1% of the higher of the value either of the net capital contribution or of the paid-up portion of the nominal value of the issued shares. The capital tax must be paid within one month after incorporation[68]. In the event of a merger, take-over or internal reorganisation, subsequent capital tax reductions and exemptions can be obtained (*see infra* Chapter 13.4).

3.4 Pre-Incorporation Transactions

a   General. The initial steps in forming a corporation are undertaken by a corporation or an individual who arranges the necessary funding for the new corporation, recruits the management, and outlines the corporate structure. This individual is not always the founder. Certain individuals may wish to enter into business transactions for the account of the new corporation prior to its inception, assign existing business to the new corporation, or encumber the new corporation with certain commitments made prior to the date of incorporation.

b   The Corporation "To Be Formed". Dutch law recognises the existence of the corporation prior to its formation. Consequently, the corporation to be formed can enter into contracts[69]. There are, however, significant limitations.

All transactions must be ratified[70], expressly or implicitly, by the corporation after its incorporation, *i.e.*, by the management board, in order to

---

67   A draft statute (No. 25029) is pending before Dutch Parliament to introduce an annual levy based on the legal form and size (in terms of turnover and employees) of the corporation.

68   Wet op belastingen van rechtsverkeer [BRV] (Tax Act on Legal Transactions) arts. 35, 36, 38, 39, 1970 S. 611, *as amended.*

69   BW arts. 2:93(1)/203(1).

70   BW arts. 2:93(1)/203(1).

be binding on the corporation. Ratification of a contract that is detrimental to the corporation can constitute an act of mismanagement (*see infra* Chapter 8.2). Until ratification occurs, the founders or other persons acting on behalf of the corporation "to be formed" are personally bound and liable unless otherwise stipulated[71]. Upon ratification, the corporation is bound, with retroactive effect. If the corporation cannot honour the contract, and the founders, such other parties or their representative knew or could reasonably be expected to have known of the corporation's future inability to perform, they will be personally liable. Bankruptcy within one year after the date of incorporation creates a rebuttable statutory presumption of this knowledge (*see infra* Chapter 8.2.d)[72]. If the contract is not ratified, it is not enforceable against the corporation. If a transaction with a corporation to be formed entails the transfer of title to property prior to incorporation, the title may legally be deemed to accrue to the founders or other parties acting on behalf of such corporation. Upon ratification the title will transfer to the newly formed corporation by operation of law, without any taxes being incurred. These rules do not apply to the following actions by the founders provided the actions will be incorporated in the deed of incorporation: (a) the issue of shares; (b) the acceptance of contributions to these shares; (c) the appointment of managing and supervisory directors; and (d) potentially onerous transactions as listed in Chapter 3.4.c below[73]. For potential liabilities with respect to these actions, *see infra* Chapter 3.4.d below.

To avoid confusion about the actual existence of the corporation or the intention to contract on behalf of the corporation to be formed, it is customary to indicate that the corporation is in the course of formation by adding the abbreviation "i.o." (*in oprichting*) after the name of the corporation.

c   **Potentially Onerous Agreements.** In order to be relieved from personal liability, to the extent possible, the founders or other parties acting on behalf of the corporation "to be formed" may wish to ensure that the corporation will honour certain obligations from its inception, without any need for ratification by the management board. A mere agreement to this effect with the other founders or parties acting on behalf of the corporation "to be formed" will not suffice. This result can only be achieved by setting forth the obligations in the deed of incorporation or by reference to the obligations in an attachment to the deed of incorporation. This is, however, limited under Dutch law to the following types of transactions[74]:

71   BW arts. 2:93(2)/203(2).
72   BW arts. 2:93(3)/203(3).
73   BW arts.
74   BW arts. 2:94(1)/204(1).

a subscriptions for shares that impose special obligations on the corporation;
b acquisitions of shares on conditions other than those available to the general public (applies to N.V.s only);
c transactions that confer a benefit on a founder or third party incorporator; and
d capital contributions other than in cash.

After incorporation, these types of transactions may be entered into only with the prior approval of the shareholders, except if and to the extent that the management board is so authorised in the articles[75]. The notes to the annual accounts for the year in which any such transaction is entered into must disclose this transaction[76].

d **Liability of the Founders.** A founder may incur liability[77] if he does not exercise sufficient care in placing the initial shares, accepting contributions to the shares, or appointing the initial management board (and supervisory board, if there is one), or by entering into any of the types of transactions set forth in Chapter 3.4.c above. This cause of action is similar to a mismanagement claim (*see infra* Chapter 8.2.b and d).

e **Organisational Expenses.** The corporation is responsible for the payment of all reasonable expenses related to its formation. The total amount of these expenses, or an estimate thereof, must be disclosed at the Commercial Register[78].

3.5 Disregarding the Corporate Entity

The theory of piercing the corporate veil, whereby the separate existence of a corporation is ignored, finds limited application in the Netherlands. The theory in its purest form makes the shareholders fully responsible for the actions of the corporation under certain defined circumstances. This theory is approximated in Dutch law in cases involving abuse of a subsidiary by a parent corporation. The parent corporation may be liable for damages to creditors of the subsidiary. This is, in fact, brought as a tort claim against the parent for abuse of its power as the controlling share-

---

75 BW arts. 2:94(2)/204(2).
76 BW art. 2:378(3).
77 BW arts. 2:93(4)/203(4), 2:9, 2:138.
78 BW arts. 2:69(1)/180(1).

holder of the subsidiary[79]. Moreover, a parent which had actual involvement in the management of the affairs of the subsidiary, may be held liable if it allowed the subsidiary to incur debts knowing that the creditors of the subsidiary would remain unsatisfied[80]. However, successor liability has consistently been denied by the Supreme Court[81].

A mismanagement claim, on the other hand, is not against the parent, but is instituted against the board of the mismanaged corporation. The board may be responsible to the corporation for damages (*see infra* Chapter 8.2). Furthermore, a corporation that serves as a director of another corporation may be liable for mismanagement and, by analogy, the individual directors of the "director-corporation" may also be personally liable (*see infra* Chapter 8.1.d). If a bankruptcy is caused by "apparent negligence" in the three-year period prior to the date of bankruptcy, members of the management and supervisory board may be held personally liable for the deficit, as well as others (such as shareholders) who *de facto* managed the affairs of the corporation (*see infra* Chapter 8.2.d).

3.6 *Ultra Vires*

This doctrine focuses on the purposes or objects clause in the articles (*see supra* Chapter 3.3.c.iv). The purposes of a corporation can merely give guidance to the interpretation of the interest that a corporation may have in a certain transaction[82]. If a corporation acts in gross violation of its own interests, it may be acting *ultra vires*. Courts will interfere only when the challenged action could not possibly be in the "interests of the corporation". The interests of a subsidiary prevail over the interests of its parent (*see also infra* Chapter 8.2.b.i). Consequently, a subsidiary may act *ultra vires* by providing collateral for a third party loan to its parent corporation, thereby incurring a serious risk to its own future financial security (*see also infra* Chapter 4.7). A corporation may only void a transaction that could not conceivably be within the scope of its purposes, when the other party knew the corporate purposes and should have known that

---

79   Judgment of September 25, 1981, HR, 1982 NJ No. 443; Judgment of November 2, 1984, HR, 1985 NJ No. 446; Judgment of May 9, HR, 1986 NJ No. 792; Judgment of February 19, 1988, HR, 1988 NJ No. 487; Judgment of October 6, 1989, HR, 1990 NJ No. 286; Judgment of November 8, 1991, HR 1992 NJ No. 174; Judgment of November 18, 1994, HR 1995 NJ No. 170.
80   Judgment of February 19, 1988, HR, 1988 NJ No. 487.
81   Judgment of November 3, 1995, HR, 1996 NJ No. 215.
82   Judgment of February 7, 1992, HR, 1992 NJ No. 438; Judgment of October 16, 1992, HR, 1993 NJ No. 98.

this transaction was *ultra vires*. The other party is not required to make inquiries[83]. The mere availability at the Commercial Register of the articles containing the purposes provision does not create a presumption of the requisite knowledge. The other party cannot invoke the nullity, but can require the corporation to decide within a reasonable period of time whether or not it intends to proceed with the transaction[84].

---

83 BW art. 2:7.
84 BW art. 3:55(2).

4 CORPORATE FINANCE; FUNDING

4.1 Equity and Debt

a **General.** Although for corporate finance and accounting purposes a conceptual delineation is made between equity and debt, progressively this distinction has blurred in practice. Certain financing and tax schemes have spurred the development of various "hybrid" financing instruments that possess attributes that mystify a classification as either equity or debt on the basis of the conventional criteria (fixed return vs. sharing of business risks etc.)[1]. Examples thereof that have gained recent popularity include profit participation rights (*winstrechten*) issued in the form of profit participation certificates (*winstbewijzen*) (*see infra* Chapter 5.1.b) and subordinated loans. Although the holder of a profit participation certificate does not have any voting rights, he is entitled to share in the corporation's profits and, depending on the articles, may have certain specified additional rights (*see infra* Chapter 5.1.b). This instrument bears some resemblance to a non-voting share, non-existent in the Netherlands. In the example of subordinated loans, the rights of a subordinated creditor with respect to interest payments and for the liquidation proceeds rank below the rights of other creditors, which may provide the corporation with debt that can be considered "near-equity".

b **Equity.** The issued capital is the aggregate nominal value of the issued or placed shares (*i.e.* issued and not redeemed). Nominal value (also called par value) is essential to the capital concept. Issued capital is part of equity. Equity refers to shareholders' funds. It includes the amount actually contributed to capital, amounts due as further contributions by the shareholders, additional paid in capital (capital surplus), reserves and retained earnings[2]. Bearer shares must be fully paid in upon issuance[3]. Contributions to registered shares, *i.e.*, shares issued to a named shareholder can, under certain circumstances, be made in instalments that can be called upon by the corporation. The unpaid portion acts as a cushion to support the equity. The total nominal value of the issued shares (*i.e.*,

---

1   For convertible debt securities and cumulative preferred profit sharing shares, *see infra* Chapter 5.1.e and Chapter 5.1.c.
2   BW art. 2:373(1).
3   BW art. 2:82(3).

the issued capital) has great significance in Dutch corporation law, but bears *no* direct relationship to shareholders' equity, the value of the shares, the value of the assets, or the cash position of the corporation. The issued capital must at all times be at least one-fifth of the authorised capital stated in the articles[4]. For the various types and classes of shares, *see infra* Chapter 5.1.

There are no rules on debt-equity ratios for corporations other than banks and insurance companies.

4.2   Preservation of Equity

There is a wide variety of diverse statutory provisions aimed at defending the corporation, to the extent possible, against a deterioration of its equity. Although Dutch Parliament cannot legislate against losses incurred in the ordinary course of business (as opposed to those resulting from mismanagement) it has done the following:

a   set rules for the preservation of issued capital (*see infra* Chapter 4.3) and for any reduction of issued capital, (*see infra* Chapter 4.6);

b   set rules concerning the payments on shares for the amounts that may exceed the nominal value (*i.e.*, capital surplus contributions, *see infra* Chapter 4.4.a);

c   restricted the use of corporate assets for the benefit of persons other than the corporation (*see infra* Chapter 4.3.e and g). This includes empowering the corporation to void a transaction that violates the corporate purposes (*see supra* Chapter 3.6);

d   set strict rules for the presentation of annual accounts, for audits, and for the accounting profession;

e   required the disclosure of annual accounts (*see infra* Chapter 11.2) and of certain proposed reductions in the issued capital of the corporation (*see infra* Chapter 4.6);

f   set strict rules for the accounting of the financial results of subsidiaries, group companies, and affiliates; and

g   subjected members of the management board and supervisory board to liability for mismanagement and other malfeasance in cases of noncompliance with certain statutory requirements (*see infra* Chapter 8.2 and 8.3).

---

4   BW arts. 2:67(4)/178(4).

4.3 Preservation of Issued Capital

a   Objective. The rules concerning capital to a large extent reflect the implementation of the Second and Fourth EC Company Law Directives (*see supra* Chapter 1.3.b and d). These rules focus on the concept of the nominal value per share and of the issued and paid-in share capital. Their prime objective is to prevent the dilution of the issued capital, which might leave creditors and shareholders with a mere shell.

Although a potential creditor of a corporation might check the Commercial Register for the amount of the issued and paid-in capital (*see infra* Chapter 11.2) and may rely on the published annual accounts of the corporation, in a large number of cases the amount of the issued capital will be only a small fraction of eventual claims. Nevertheless, the rules concerning the preservation of capital must be observed strictly. If the rules have not been strictly observed, the transaction may be void and the managing directors may be personally liable.

b   Minimum Capital. In order to ensure that the capital will not fall below an absolute minimum level that will remain available to the corporation to the extent not deteriorated by losses, the law requires a *minimum capital* of NLG 100,000 for an N.V.[5] and NLG 40,000 for a B.V.[6]. The statutory amount of the minimum capital may be increased. For N.V.s, increases are pegged to mandatory increases prescribed by EC legislation[7]. For B.V.s, the minimum capital can be increased pursuant to a Royal Decree that refers to a price index[8]. In order to be listed at the Amsterdam Stock Exchange (AEX-Effectenbeurs nv), the equity of an N.V. must be at least NLG 10,000,000[9]. There are specific rules applicable to the minimum capital of banks and insurance companies.

The minimum capital may be an amount that is very small in relation to the nature of the business of the corporation and the risks it may incur in its ordinary course of business. In the case of inadequate capitalisation, the creditors may want to "pierce the corporate veil" (*see supra* Chapter 3.5).

---

5   BW art. 2:67(2).
6   BW art. 2:178(2).
7   Second Company Law Directive, *supra* p. 6 at note 30, art. 6(3).
8   BW art. 2:178(2); Act of December 12, 1985, 1985 S. 656, art. IX.
9   A company seeking a listing on the *Nieuwe Markt Amsterdam* (NMAX) (which was recently introduced and can best be compared to the Alternative Investment Market in England) must have equity of at least ECU 1,000,000.

The paid-in capital is that part of the issued capital for which contributions have actually been made. It must amount to at least 25% of the issued capital, but in any event not less than NLG 100,000 in the case of an N.V., or NLG 40,000 in the case of a B.V.[10] If at any time after formation, the aggregate of the amount contributed to the issued capital, any amounts called up and the balance sheet reserves formed pursuant to the law (called statutory reserves) or the articles is below the minimum capital prescribed by law, a B.V. is required to maintain an additional statutory reserve in the amount of the shortfall[11], but only to the extent this reserve can be formed, for example, out of profits. An N.V., however, must at all times have a minimum paid in capital (*i.e.*, contributions must have been made) equal to or in excess of NLG 100,000. If it fails to comply, it must either be dissolved (*see infra* Chapter 10.6.b) or convert itself into a B.V. (*see infra* Chapter 10.5).

A shareholder is liable for the unpaid balance on his shares, but not in excess of their nominal value[12]. He is also liable for the amount of the subscription price in excess of nominal value. Dutch law allows for assessable shares (*aandelen met stortingsplicht boven de nominale waarde*) only if the articles provide for it at formation or thereafter by an amendment unanimously adopted by all shareholders concerned[13]. Assessable shares are uncommon but possible. It can be particularly useful in joint ventures where parties want to avoid the formalities that an increase of the issued capital beyond the authorised capital may entail. Even after selling shares that are not fully paid up, the initial shareholder remains liable for the unpaid balance until he is released from such obligation by the management board and, where applicable, the supervisory board[14]. The release becomes effective one full year after the transfer. The corporation's share register is not open to the public, except with regard to shares that are not fully paid up[15].

c   Shareholders and Creditors. The issued share capital is considered a guarantee for the corporation's liabilities. Upon dissolution of the corporation, the claims of shareholders are subordinate to claims of debenture holders and other creditors. Shareholders have a claim upon liquidation that is, in fact, subordinate to all other debts of the corpora-

---

10   BW arts. 2:67(3)/178(3), 2:80(1)/191(1).
11   BW art. 2:178(3).
12   BW arts. 2:81/192.
13   RICHTLIJNEN, *supra* p. 36 at note 142, §§ 19, 30.
14   BW arts. 2:90(1)/192(1) require a certified deed of transfer.
15   BW arts. 2:85(4)/194(4).

tion[16]. A shareholder may not, without the corporation's consent, set off the corporation's claims against the amount due for payment on his shares[17]. The trustee in bankruptcy may contest any such consent granted prior to bankruptcy.

d   Nominal Value. Shares must have a nominal value[18]. The nominal value is a fixed amount per type of share. It is an arbitrary figure stated in the articles. The articles may provide for shares with different nominal values[19]. Shares without a nominal value are not permitted[20]. The share capital and the nominal value of each share must be expressed in Dutch guilders[21]. Shares may, of course, be issued at a price above their nominal value. The consideration in excess of the nominal value is called capital surplus or share premium.

e   Contributions to Capital. The required contribution to the issued capital must be made at the time of issuance of the shares (*see infra* Chapter 4.4). There are two forms of capital contributions; contributions in cash[22] and contributions in kind (non-cash contributions)[23]. Cash contributions can be made either in Dutch currency or a foreign currency. At the time of formation, the civil-law notary must obtain a statement from a Dutch bank (or another bank within the European Economic Area that is under governmental supervision)[24] that upon formation the money is indeed available to the corporation, or that the bank has received the required amount of cash in an account in the name of the corporation "to be formed" (*see supra* Chapter 3.4.b). This statement must be issued not more than five months prior to the date of incorporation. The deed of incorporation may state that the corporation accepts this contribution, even though the amount of cash available at the date of formation may differ from the amount originally paid into the bank account[25]. If the cash payment was made in a foreign currency, the statement must state its equivalent in Dutch guilders[26]. The statement by the bank is deposited with the

---

16   BW art. 2:23b(1).
17   BW arts. 2:80(4)/191(3); Judgment of December 23, 1937, HR, 1938 NJ No. 538. For an N.V. this includes any capital surplus amounts (BW art. 2:191(3)).
18   BW arts. 2:67(1)/178(1), 2:79(1)/190.
19   BW arts. 2:67(1)/178(1).
20   BW arts. 2:67/178.
21   HANDBOEK, *supra* p. 2 at note 7, § 161.
22   BW arts. 2:80a(1)/191a(1).
23   BW arts. 2:80b(1)/191b(1).
24   BW arts. 2:93a(3)/203a(3).
25   BW arts. 2:93a(1)/203a(1).
26   BW arts. 2:93a(2)/203a(2).

Commercial Register (*see infra* Chapter 11.1.a) for public inspection. After formation, a statement from a bank is required only when foreign currency is contributed[27].

The corporation may allow a shareholder to contribute only partially to the nominal value of his shares and agree that the remainder, up to a maximum of 75%, must be contributed when called for by the corporation[28]. The issuance of shares at a discount to their nominal value is allowed only in cases of issuance by an N.V. to a professional underwriter, and the discount may not 6% of nominal value. The underwriter is not entitled to contribute in instalments, and he must pay in cash[29]. These shares are thereafter regarded as issued at nominal value.

In general, non-cash contributions are viewed with suspicion, both at the time of formation[30] of the corporation and thereafter[31]. Several provisions counter the issue of "watered shares", *i.e.* nominal value shares issued for a non-cash contribution that has a value below the aggregate nominal value of the issued shares. In addition, as a complement to these rules, Dutch law contains certain statutory provisions that subject certain transactions, which differ in their *form* from contributions to shares, but judged on their *substance* are equivalent, to similar control rules. The German "buzz word" for these statutory provisions, "*Nachgründung*", has become the Dutch term as well.

Contributions of property and other non-cash items to shares are restricted to assets that can be objectively appraised. Promises to perform work or services cannot serve as capital contributions[32]. The contributed assets must be described and an auditor's statement must show that their value exceeds the aggregate nominal value of the issued shares[33]. The auditor's statement and, in case of an N.V., the description of the assets, must be deposited with the Commercial Register for public inspection[34]. Exemptions apply to group companies (*see supra* Chapter 3.1.b)

---

27 BW arts. 2:93a(6)/203a(6).
28 BW arts. 2:80(1)/191(1).
29 BW art. 2:80(2).
30 BW arts. 2:94a/204a.
31 BW arts. 2:94b/204b.
32 BW arts. 2:80b(1)/191b(1).
33 BW arts. 2:94a(2)/204a(2), 2:94b(2)/204b(2).
34 BW arts. 2:94a(1),(2)/204a(1),(2), 2:94b(2)/204b(2). A violation of these provisions is a criminal offence, *see* Wet op de Economische Delicten [WED] (Act on Economic Offences) art. 1(4), 1990 S. 258, *as amended.*

for which another group company has assumed liability pursuant to a statutory procedure. If a non-cash contribution of property is proposed at the time of formation, it must be stated in the deed of incorporation or in an attachment thereto (*see supra* Chapter 3.4.c). Thereafter, approval by a majority vote of the shareholders is required for non-cash contributions. The articles may delegate this power to the management board[35].

During the two-year period following its first registration at the Commercial Register, a corporation is prohibited from entering into any transaction involving assets that were personally owned by any founder (for N.V.s) at any time during the one-year period preceding the formation date or were owned during that time by any person who is a shareholder (for B.V.s)[36]. The acquisition of assets as well as any preparatory action serving to acquire assets in the future, such as an option agreement, falls under the scope of these *Nachgründung* rules[37]. The prohibition does not apply to acquisitions: (i) made at a public auction or stock exchange; (ii) completed within the normal course of business of the corporation; (iii) for which an accountant's statement has already been issued; or (iv) resulting from a statutory merger (*see* Chapter 10.3)[38]. The risk of non-compliance with the *Nachgründung* rules is that a transaction may be voided by the corporation[39] during the three-year period following such transaction. The directors may be liable for breach of their fiduciary duties (*see infra* Chapter 8.1.a) towards the corporation when they neglect to seek the nullity of such transaction. The prohibition can be set aside by a resolution of the shareholders' meeting, subject to a description and auditor's statement described above for non-cash contributions to shares.

---

35   BW arts. 2:94(2)/204(2).
36   BW arts. 2:94c(1)/204c(1).
37   Numerous schemes have been developed in practice to set aside the *Nachgründung* rules (*see* C.E.M. VAN STEENDEREN, "Nachgründung", in: VENNOOTSCHAPSRECHT IN EG-PERSPECTIEF, p. 19 (A.G. Lubbers & W. Westbroek, 1st ed. 1993), Kluwer (Deventer)). Schemes with merit include: (a) formation of the corporation by a foundation which issues depository receipts for shares to its founders. The shares are fully paid up in cash and the property intended to be acquired is then purchased by the corporation from the holders of the depository receipts and not from its shareholders; (b) formation by the corporation of another corporation that acquires the property from the shareholders of its parent; or (c) sale of property to the corporation followed by an issuance of shares; the corporation's obligation to pay the purchase price will be set off against its claim for the cash contribution to the shares.
38   BW arts. 2:94c(6)/204c(6).
39   Or the trustee, in the case of bankruptcy of the corporation.

f   Treasury Shares (*Ingekochte Aandelen*). Dutch law allows a corporation to acquire its own shares[40]. There are, however, significant limitations:

a   a corporation cannot subscribe for shares that it will issue at formation or at any time thereafter[41];

b   the nominal value of the shares held in treasury must be fully paid[42];

c   an N.V. may not, directly or indirectly through its subsidiaries, acquire or hold in ownership or hold as a pledgee more than 10% of its own stock[43]. For a B.V., this amount is 50%[44];

d   a corporation may not repurchase shares in an amount that would bring its net worth below the aggregate of the amount contributed to the issued capital, any amounts called up, and statutory reserves and reserves required by the articles[45];

e   the articles of an N.V. must allow for a repurchase, by action of the management board, subject to authorisation by the shareholders prior to the actual repurchase[46]. A general authorisation cannot exceed an eighteen-month period[47]. The articles of a B.V. must permit a repurchase and may confer this right of authorisation to holders of a specific class or type of shares or to the supervisory board, in which case the authorisation may be general and unlimited in time[48];

f   a repurchase is prohibited during the last six months of the corporation's financial year if the annual accounts for the preceding financial year were not adopted and approved, where applicable, during the first six months[49];

g   parties who purchase shares in their own name for the account of the corporation are, in the case of a B.V., deemed to have purchased for their own account[50] or, in the case of an N.V., under a statutory obligation to transfer the acquired shares to the corporation[51].

---

40   For this purpose the term "shares" encompasses depository receipts issued therefor (BW arts. 2:98(9)/207(5)). Different rules apply to investment companies with variable capital (*see supra* Chapter 3.1.c and BW art. 2:98(8)).

41   BW arts. 2:95(1)/205.

42   BW arts. 2:98(1)/207(1).

43   BW art. 2:98(2).

44   BW art. 2:207(2).

45   BW arts. 2:98(2)/207(2).

46   For an N.V. this authorisation is not required for an acquisition for the purpose of transferring such shares to employees of such N.V. or a group company (*see supra* Chapter 3.1.b), provided the articles so permit and the shares are listed on an exchange (BW art. 2:98(5)).

47   BW art. 2:98(4).

48   BW art. 2:207(2)(d).

49   BW arts. 2:98(3)/207(3).

50   BW art. 2:207b.

51   BW art. 2:98b.

h circularly owned shares are restricted. A subsidiary of an N.V. or B.V. may not subscribe for shares issued by the parent. It may, however, purchase shares of a parent and repurchase its own shares held by its parent company only to the extent this parent corporation may do so[52]; and
i voting rights cannot be exercised on treasury shares[53].

Repurchased shares remain part of issued capital until redeemed (*ingetrokken*) (*see infra* Chapter 4.6.c). Redemption has the effect of reducing issued capital by the amount of the total nominal value of the repurchased and redeemed shares. Treasury shares may not be shown in the annual accounts as assets[54]. Equity must be reduced by the price of the repurchased shares. The value attributed to an investment in a subsidiary is reduced by the price at which the subsidiary purchases shares of the parent company.

g   Financial Assistance Rules. Dutch law generally prohibits corporations from giving financial assistance to third parties (whether shareholders or others) if this assistance is "for the purpose of" the subscription or acquisition by third parties of its shares or depository receipts issued therefor. These financial assistance rules were incorporated into Dutch law to implement the Second EC Company Law Directive (*see supra* Chapter 1.3.b). These rules purport to preserve corporate equity and to protect creditors.

Implementation of this directive in the Netherlands created statutory provisions which differ in their treatment of N.V.s[55] and B.V.s[56] (an N.V. may, however, convert to a B.V., *see infra* Chapter 10.5). For both N.V.s and B.V.s the financial assistance rules prohibit the corporation from providing collateral, guaranteeing payment of the acquisition price or otherwise guaranteeing or binding itself with or for third parties "for the purpose of the subscription or acquisition by third parties of its shares or depository receipts issued therefor"[57]. In addition, N.V.s are prohibited from granting loans for this purpose[58]. The respective prohibitions also extend to subsidiaries (*see supra* Chapter 3.1.b). A B.V. may only provide loans for this purpose up to an amount that does not exceed

---

52   BW arts. 2:98d(1)/207d(1).
53   BW arts. 2:118(7)/228(6).
54   BW art. 3:373(3).
55   BW art. 2:98c.
56   BW art. 2:207c.
57   BW arts. 2:98c(1)/207c(1).
58   BW art. 2:98c(1).

the distributable reserves (*see infra* Chapter 4.8.a.ii) and provided that the articles so permit[59]. Finally, the financial assistance prohibitions do not apply to N.V. shares acquired by or for the account of employees of the corporation or its group companies (*see supra* Chapter 3.1.b)[60].

Due to the sweeping language of the law, the financial assistance prohibitions effectively discourage various forms of leveraged acquisitions that are common in the United States[61]. Several alternative means of financing a leveraged acquisition have developed in practice. However, in the absence of case law which provides a conclusive interpretation of the financial assistance prohibitions, great care should be exercised.

4.4   New Issuance of Shares

a   General. A new issuance of shares increases the issued capital, which must at all times remain within the limits of the authorised capital[62]. The authorised capital can only be increased by an amendment to the articles (*see infra* Chapter 10.2). The ministerial certificate of no objection will be refused if, at the time of execution of the notarial deed required for an amendment to the articles, subscription has not been made for at least one-fifth of the newly authorised capital[63]. If the subscription price is above the nominal value of the shares, the premium can be paid in cash or in any other form as negotiated with the corporation. In the case of an N.V., if the subscription price of the shares is above their nominal value, the share premium must be paid at the time of issuance[64]; for a B.V. the time of payment of the share premium is negotiable. The distribution of power within the corporation for the issuance

---

59   BW art. 2:207c(2). It is sufficient that the articles do not prohibit such transaction (ASSER-MAEIJER) 2, III, *supra* p. 2 at note 7, § 163). The B.V. must maintain a non-distributable reserve in the amount of such loans (BW art. 2:207c(3)).

60   BW art. 2:98c(2). Similarly, with respect to N.V.s, these provisions do not apply to banks and similar institutions registered under the Act on the Supervision of the Credit System (WTK), to the extent such transactions are concluded in the normal course of their businesses (BW art. 2:98c(3).

61   As the financial assistance rules apply to share acquisitions only, in the Netherlands a leveraged buy-out (LBO) in the form of an asset acquisition is often easier to finance than an LBO in the form of a share acquisition. For a more elaborate analysis of the financial assistance rules, *see* M&A IN THE NETHERLANDS, *supra* p. 3 at note 14, Chapter 3.

62   BW arts. 2:79(2)/190.

63   BW arts. 2:68(2)/179(2), 2:67(4)/178(4).

64   BW art. 2:80(1).

of new shares, and the pre-emptive rights that existing shareholders may have to these newly issued shares, are discussed below. The power to issue shares is normally accompanied by the power to determine the consideration therefor. If the consideration is below fair market value, the value of the shares of the existing shareholders will be diluted. This may lead to an action in court based on the grounds that the determination of the consideration violated principles of good faith (*see infra* Chapter 8.1.a).

The power to issue new shares and to determine the consideration therefor may also be of significance in hostile take-over situations. The key element of this device is the ability of either the management board or holders of a specific type of shares (*e.g.*, priority shareholders, *see infra* Chapter 5.1.c) to place preference shares overnight to fend off a raider.

The issued shares are placed by the management board. In the case of a public offer, the management board must observe the applicable stock exchange regulations. The formalities for the issuance of shares are similar to the formalities for the transfer of shares (*see infra* Chapter 5.4). As noted before, a corporation cannot subscribe to its own shares, and is severely restricted in purchasing shares initially issued to others (*see supra* Chapter 4.3.f).

b   N.V. Corporation. The shareholders of an N.V. have the power to decide on the issuance of new shares and to determine the consideration for these shares. The shareholders may delegate this power to the management board or the supervisory board for a certain period not exceeding five years[65]. During this period, the delegation cannot be revoked, unless otherwise stated in the delegation resolution, but it can be renewed from time to time. If there are different types of shares, the power of the shareholders to issue shares of a specific type and to delegate this power to the board is subject to the prior approval of the holders of that type of shares[66]. Within eight days after the issuance of new shares the corporation must file information concerning the type and number of shares with the Commercial Register[67].

Shareholders of an N.V. have a statutory pre-emptive right to purchase newly issued shares of the type owned, proportional to their existing

---

65   BW art. 2:96(1). Different rules apply to investment companies with variable capital (*see supra* Chapter 3.1.c).
66   BW art. 2:96(2).
67   BW art. 2:96(3). A violation of this provision is a criminal offence, *see* WED art. 1(4).

shares in the capital of the corporation[68]. The shareholders can, in various ways, exclude or restrict this pre-emptive right. They can also delegate to the management board or the supervisory board (whichever was originally delegated the power to issue new shares) the right to exclude or restrict the shareholders' pre-emptive rights. This delegation is limited to a period of five years, cannot be revoked, unless otherwise stated in the delegation resolution, and may be renewed from time to time[69]. A shareholders' resolution to restrict or exclude pre-emptive rights or to delegate this power requires a qualified majority of two-thirds of the votes cast if less than half of the issued shares is represented at the meeting[70]. Within eight days after the resolution about the restriction or exclusion of pre-emptive rights was taken, the corporation must file the complete text thereof with the Commercial Register[71].

Pre-emptive rights are not available for new shares with a consideration other than cash, unless the articles provide otherwise, or with respect to shares issued to employees of the corporation or its group companies (*see supra* Chapter 3.1.b). Except as otherwise provided in the articles, holders of preference shares have no pre-emptive rights, and holders of ordinary shares have no pre-emptive rights with respect to preference shares[72].

c   **B.V. Corporation.** The issued capital of a B.V. may be increased by a resolution of the shareholders. The shareholders can delegate this power to the management board or supervisory board. This delegation can be revoked at any time[73]. Furthermore, the articles may confer the power to issue new shares to the supervisory board or the management board.

Unless the articles state otherwise, each existing B.V. shareholder has a pre-emptive right to purchase newly issued shares of the type owned, proportional to his existing shares in the capital of the corporation, except for shares issued to employees of the corporation and its group companies[74]. The shareholders can, each time for one single issuance of shares, restrict or exclude the pre-emptive rights of existing shareholders, unless the articles provide otherwise[75].

---

68 BW art. 2:96a(1). Different rules apply to investment companies with variable capital (*see supra* Chapter 3.1.c).
69 BW art. 2:96a(6).
70 BW art. 2:96a(7).
71 BW art. 2:96a(7). A violation of this provision is a criminal offence, *see* WED art. 1(4).
72 BW art. 2:96a(2),(3).
73 BW art. 2:206(1).
74 BW art. 2:206a(1).
75 BW art. 2:206a(1).

Except as otherwise provided in the articles, holders of preference shares have no pre-emptive rights and holders of ordinary shares have no pre-emptive rights with respect to preference shares[76].

4.5   Stock Options

A corporation can give options on either treasury shares or shares that will be newly issued. Unless restricted in the articles, treasury shares can be sold by the corporation on terms that the management board deems appropriate, without any restraints. Options for newly issued shares, however, are subject to the same rules as an original issue (*see supra* Chapter 4.4)[77], including the rules for pre-emptive rights[78].

4.6   Reduction of Issued Capital

a   General. Three different methods are available for the reduction of issued capital:
i   repurchase of shares (*inkoop*);
ii   redemption of shares (*intrekking*); and
iii reduction of nominal value (*afstempelen*).
Each method has its merits and limitations.

All three methods are subject to strict rules concerning publication and public notification for the benefit of creditors. The public notification must be made by a filing with the Commercial Register and the publication of a notice of this filing in a nationally distributed daily newspaper. Creditors may oppose the contemplated action within a two-month period after the date of the publication. Additional waiting periods and posting of security are required in some cases[79]. Disputes are subject to the exclusive jurisdiction of the competent District Court. Irrespective of whether any creditors object, the reduction of issued capital may never bring the issued capital below the statutory minimum capital threshold. If the proposed reduction would bring the issued minimum capital below 20% of the authorised capital (*see supra* Chapter 4.3), an amendment of the articles is required.

---

76   BW art. 2:206a(2).
77   BW art. 2:96(5)/206(2).
78   BW arts. 2:96a(8)/206a(6).
79   BW arts. 2:100/209.

b   Repurchase (*Inkoop*)[80]. A corporation may repurchase shares provided those shares have been paid up in full. The repurchase may not bring shareholders' equity below a certain level. Shareholders' equity equals the aggregate issued capital, increased by reserves and accrued profits. The rule is that the acquisition price for the repurchased shares shall not bring the amount of shareholders' equity below the issued and called-up part of the corporation's share capital together with any statutory reserves and reserves required by the articles[81]. In other words, the price for the repurchased shares must be paid out of distributable reserves. Violation of this rule may result in personal liability of the managing directors[82]. A repurchase of shares requires cash from the corporation and results in a reduction of the issued capital only upon a subsequent redemption (*see infra* Chapter 4.6.c). Since the corporation, together with its subsidiaries, can own only a certain percentage of its own shares (10% for an N.V.; 50% for a B.V), a cancellation creates room for further repurchases. For this purpose, shares pledged to an N.V. or its subsidiaries are counted as shares held by the corporation[83].

c   Redemption (*Intrekking*). A redemption of shares is only possible with shares held in treasury or with the approval of all holders of the shares of that class. A shareholder whose shares have been redeemed will receive the nominal value of those shares to the extent paid. However, if prior to the issue of the shares, redemption of a specific type of shares was permitted under the articles, the redemption will include all shares of that type (*e.g.*, preference shares), unless such redemption relates to balloted shares (*uitgelote aandelen*), as provided for in the articles prior to their issuance[84]. The redemption of a certain type of shares (usually preference shares, *see infra* Chapter 5.1.c) is often part of an anti-takeover device.

d   Reduction of Nominal Value (*Afstempeling*). A reduction of nominal value is often effectuated when a new capital issuance is being considered and earlier losses have reduced the value of the shares below their nominal value[85]. A nominal value reduction is therefore usually part of a recapitalisation effort. Reduction of nominal value is possible

---

80   Different rules apply to investment companies with variable capital (*see supra* Chapter 3.1.c).
81   BW arts. 2:98(2)(a)/207(2)(a).
82   BW arts. 2:98a(1),(2)/207a(1).
83   BW art. 2:98(2)(b).
84   BW arts. 2:99(2)/208(2).
85   BW arts. 2:99(3)/208(3).

with or without partial payment of the nominal value to the shareholders and exemption of their obligation of contribution to shares[86]. Since the law prohibits an issuance below nominal value (*see supra* Chapter 4.3.e), a reduction of nominal value allows for a fresh influx of capital. This method is also applied in order to make distributions to the shareholders from contributions to the issued capital, but never more than is allowed under the rules concerning minimum capital and issued capital (*see supra* Chapter 4.3.b). An amendment to the articles is required for a reduction of the nominal value of shares[87].

4.7 Debt Financing of the Group; Central Cash Management

Due to several major bankruptcy cases in the Netherlands, considerable attention has been given to the financing practice of corporations affiliated in a group (*see supra* Chapter 3.1.b) whereby the parent corporation or a financing subsidiary creates a debt with collateral from other subsidiaries, including corporations that either do not share in the benefits, or do not do so in a proportional amount. The *ultra vires* doctrine (*see supra* Chapter 3.6) provides the framework for determining whether the subsidiary may validly make collateral available to its parent and, through the parent, to its sister companies. It can be argued that upstream guarantees are valid even when the financing does not serve the interests of the subsidiary. The best test of the validity of this financial assistance by the subsidiary is whether the pledge on the assets jeopardises the corporation's existence[88].

Even more complex are questions concerning central cash management systems, often employed in groups. Is the cash need of an ailing subsidiary a proper justification for the resulting cash shortage of an affiliated corporation that may finally starve to death even though it contributed largely to the central cash management system? No consensus exists in the Dutch legal community about this business phenomenon. Cross-collateralisation between corporations of the same group is deemed legally acceptable, provided the cross-financing and cross-collateralisation are properly disclosed with the Commercial Register and it is reasonably unlikely that these arrangements will threaten the continued existence of the corporations that made the cash payments[89]. No court decision is available with regard to the legality of central cash management systems.

---

86   BW arts. 2:99(3),(4)/208(3),(4).
87   BW arts. 2:99(1)/208(1).
88   Judgment of December 19, 1995, Ger. Arnhem, 1996 NJ No. 307.
89   Asser-Maeijer 2, III, *supra* p. 2 at note 7, § 615.

4.8 Distributions

a Dividends

i *Profit Allocation; Dividend Allocation.* The shareholders' meeting has the power to adopt the annual accounts. If the corporation has the status of a "large" corporation (*see infra* Chapter 7.1.b.ii) the annual accounts must be adopted by the mandatory supervisory board, subject to the approval of the shareholders' meeting[90]. The right to adopt the annual accounts does not, however, imply the right to allocate profits. The shareholders' meeting has the power to create reserves and allocate profits and consequently to determine the amount of dividends to be distributed[91]. However, the articles may grant the power to create reserves out of profit to the management board, the supervisory board, or a specific type or class of shares (*e.g.*, priority shares, *see infra* Chapter 5.1.c). Unless the articles state otherwise, the claim for payment of dividends is created by a resolution of the shareholders, which requires the prior adoption of the annual accounts[92]; for "large" corporations the adopted annual accounts must first be approved by the shareholders' meeting before dividends can be paid.

All shareholders share in the profit in proportion to the nominal value of their shares in the capital of the corporation, unless otherwise provided in the articles[93]. Treasury shares attract dividends, unless the articles state otherwise[94]. Cumulative preference shares (*see infra* Chapter 5.1.c) with payments in arrears rank first with respect to payments of the arrearages. Thereafter, payments on all other preference shares must be made in the amount of the stated preferences, followed by payments on the ordinary shares. Dividends may be paid either in cash or in kind. Corporations listed on the Amsterdam Stock Exchange (AEX) may distribute cash or shares but not property. A shareholder's claim for payment expires after five years, unless a longer period is granted under the articles[95].

---

90 BW arts. 2:101(3)/210(3). A violation of these provisions is a criminal offence, *see* WED art. 1(4).
91 BW arts. 2:105(1)/216(1).
92 BW arts. 2:105(3)/216(3).
93 BW arts. 2:92(1)/201(1), 2:105(6)/216(6).
94 BW art. 2:105(5)/216(5).
95 BW arts. 2:105(7)/216(7).

ii *Legality.* Dividends can be paid only to the extent that the corporation's equity (*see supra* Chapter 4.1.b) exceeds the actual contributed amount and the called up part (*see supra* Chapter 4.3.e), of the issued capital plus the statutory reserves and reserves required by the articles[96] (the equity preservation test). Consequently, so-called "nimble dividends", *i.e.*, dividends paid out of current profits despite the existence of an accumulated loss that could not be eliminated by current profits, are not permitted.

There are no solvency or cash flow requirements that the corporation must meet before dividends can be paid. A corporation may, if the articles so permit, distribute an interim dividend, declared and paid before the annual accounts are adopted (or, for a "large" corporation, approved), provided that at that time the equity preservation test can be met[97]. For N.V. corporations, the equity preservation test must be met as of a date not earlier than the first day of the third month prior to the month in which the payment of an interim dividend is announced[98]. In addition, the management board of an N.V. must prepare a statement of assets and liabilities as of the date of the test, to be signed by each managing director and filed with the Commercial Register[99].

To the extent that, upon their subsequent adoption or approval, the annual accounts indicate a failure to meet the equity preservation test, any regular or interim dividends previously paid in that financial year must be repaid to the corporation[100]. For N.V. corporations the right to rescind dividend payments is limited to dividend recipients who knew or should have known that the distribution of the dividend was illegal[101].

iii *Stock Dividends; Bonus Dividends.* Dividends can take the form of a distribution of shares of the corporation. Stock dividends normally mean that shareholders receive newly issued shares out of current profits. The aggregate market value of the newly issued shares is the amount of the dividend. The issued capital account is increased by the

---

96 BW arts. 2:105(2)/216(2).
97 BW arts. 2:105(4)/216(4).
98 BW art. 2:105(4).
99 BW art. 2:105(4). A violation of this provision is a criminal offence, *see* WED art. 1(4).
100 BW art. 6:203(2).
101 BW art. 2:105(8).

amount of the aggregate nominal value of the issued shares. Bonus dividends are similar to stock dividends, except that the dividend is paid out of a reserve, usually the capital surplus account.

iv   *Dividend Withholding Tax.* Profit distributions made by Dutch resident companies whose capital is divided in shares are subject to dividend withholding tax at a rate of 25%[102]. The tax must be withheld by the distributing company[103]. If the dividend is received by a Dutch resident taxpayer, the dividend withholding tax can be credited against the individual or corporate income tax due[104]. However, the dividend withholding tax can under certain circumstances be reduced, for example, due to the application of tax treaties or domestic provisions implementing the EC Parent-Subsidiary Directive (*see infra* Chapter 13.3).

b   **Redemption.** A redemption can be achieved by two different means; either through a repurchase and subsequent cancellation of shares, or through a direct redemption (*see supra* Chapter 4.6.c).

---

102   Wet op de dividendbelasting [DIV] (Dividend Withholding Tax Act) art. 7, 1965 S. 621, *as amended.*
103   DIV art. 7.
104   Algemene Wet inzake Rijksbelastingen [AWR] (General Act on Taxation) art. 15, 1959 S. 301, *as amended*; Wet op de vennootschapsbelasting [Vpb] (Corporate Income Tax Act) art. 25, 1969 S. 445, *as amended.*

5   SHARES; SHARE TRANSFER

5.1   Types and Classes of Shares

a   N.V. and B.V.. Although their articles may create different types of shares, B.V.s can only issue uncertificated shares; bearer shares cannot be issued[1]. N.V.s may issue both certificated bearer shares, certificated shares registered in the name of the holder and uncertificated registered shares[2]. The legal position of the holder of a certificated registered share and an uncertificated registered share is very similar. The only difference lies in the evidence *vis-à-vis* the issuing corporation[3]. No difference exists with regard to possible title defects (such as the absence of clean title of the previous owner) or formalities for the transfer of these shares.

b   Non-Voting Shares. Unless the articles provide otherwise, all shareholders have equal rights in proportion to the nominal value of their shares[4]. Provisions in the articles concerning payment on shares, voting rights, profit-sharing, and participation in liquidation proceeds may limit, but not completely eliminate, these inherent rights. Non-voting shares do not exist in the Netherlands. It is permissible to create a trust office, which in effect separates the voting power from the beneficial interest in the shares (*see infra* Chapter 5.5). It is also possible to include in the articles a provision that permits a profit distribution to persons other than shareholders. A "profit participation right" (*winstrecht*) so created may be issued in negotiable form as a profit participation certificate (*winstbewijs*) and may even be listed on the Amsterdam Stock Exchange (AEX), subject to the applicable listing requirements. Profit participation rights are of a contractual nature. The creation of profit participation rights must be permitted in the articles[5]. The beneficiary of a profit participation right (*i.e.* the holder of a profit participation receipt) has a right to share in the corporation's profits, as outlined in the contractual terms of this right, but can never be granted any rights to cast votes in a shareholders' meeting. In addition to the profit sharing other rights may be granted to these benefi-

---

1   BW art. 2:175(1).
2   BW art. 2:82(1).
3   Rv art. 184(2)
4   BW arts. 2:118/228, 2:92(1)/201(1).
5   BW arts. 2:105(1)/216(1).

ciaries, to the extent these additional rights are not by law the exclusive pre-rogatives of the shareholders[6]. To the extent these rights are created in the articles, they cannot be affected or abrogated by an amendment to the articles without the consent of every such beneficiary, unless stated otherwise in the articles prior to the creation of these rights[7]. In general, the corporation has a duty of good faith towards these beneficiaries (*see infra* Chapter 9.2.c)[8]. Profit participation receipts are often given to the founders of the corporation and are then called founders receipts (*oprichtersbewijzen*). Profit participation rights are unusual. For the granting of founders receipts at incorporation, *see supra* Chapter 3.4.c. The assignment of profit partici-pation rights to third parties can have significant tax effects.

c   **Types of Shares.** *Ordinary or common shares* are shares for which no special provisions are made. When dividends are paid in the form of shares (*see supra* Chapter 4.8.a.iii.), these shares are usually ordinary shares.

Preference shares have a preference over ordinary shares in the payment of dividends up to and limited to a percentage of their nominal value as stat-ed in the articles; the articles may provide that the preference also relates to liquidation proceeds. Holders of preference shares may have the same voting rights as holders of ordinary shares. Preference shares may be used to raise equity at times that profits do not allow sufficient return to the holders of ordinary shares. Preference shares may also offer the managing directors a means of maintaining their control over the corporation. The issuance of these shares dilutes the voting rights of the holders of ordinary shares. The issuance of preference shares may be delegated to the manage-ment board for a five-year period in the case of an N.V. and for an unlim-ited period in the case of a B.V. (*see supra* Chapter 4.4.b and c).

Cumulative preference shares are preference shares with an additional right to carry forward all preference dividends not paid in previous years (because of lack of profits or otherwise), to be paid in full before any pay-ment to the holders of ordinary shares.

Cumulative profit-sharing preference shares (*i.e., participating preference shares*) are cumulative preference shares which, after satisfaction of their preference, confer on the holder a claim to dividends out of the balance of the profits on an equal or proportional basis with the holders of ordinary shares.

6   ASSER-MAEIJER 2, III, *supra* p. 2 at note 7, § 198.
7   BW arts. 2:122/232.
8   Judgment of January 27, 1956, HR, 1956 NJ No. 48.

Priority shares give their holders certain powers stated in the articles. Priority shares may be used to acquire control over certain actions of the shareholders' meeting or the management board (called "oligarchic" control) by shareholders who are usually founders, managing directors or supervisory directors of the corporation. With respect to a public corporation, legal title to these shares is for practical reasons often held by a *stichting* (*see supra* Chapter 2.5.b). Priority shares also represent a widely used instrument for minority shareholders to retain control over the corporation. Their powers[9] may include:

a the right to make binding nominations to shareholders regarding the appointment, suspension and dismissal of board members. This nomination right cannot be created when the corporation is a "large" corporation (*see infra* Chapter 7.2.c.ii). The shareholders cannot appoint persons other than those proposed. However, binding nominations may be rejected by the shareholders by a two-thirds vote representing more than half of the issued share capital[10];

b the right to veto the issuance of new shares;

c the right to create reserves out of annual profits; and

d the right to veto proposed amendments to the articles.

Warrants are securities issued by an N.V. corporation creating an option to acquire shares at a specific price during a specific period of time.

Claims are securities, issued by an N.V. corporation, that allow the holder to acquire shares from the corporation upon the issuance of new shares, for a consideration that is usually below market value.

Scrips are securities, issued by an N.V. corporation, that are convertible into shares but which do not carry any shareholders' rights until conversion.

d   Classes of Shares. It is possible to create different classes of shares for different groups of shareholders within the same type of shares. In practice, this is limited to registered ordinary shares. Classes are created by a special provision in the articles, principally to allow pre-emptive rights on shares of the same class, to require the approval of shareholders of a specific class of shares prior to the sale of any shares of that class (*see infra* Chapter 5.4.c), or to provide for differences in profit distribution or profit retention for each class of shares.

---

9   RICHTLIJNEN, *supra* p. 36 at note 142, § 17.
10   BW arts. 2:133(2)/243(2), 2:134(2)/244(2).

e   Convertible Debt Securities. Convertible debentures (including bonds) are debt securities that, under conditions set out in the terms of the loan, provide for the option to convert the debt into shares. Whether this conversion is to be called for at the option of the corporation or the holder of the debenture, the rules concerning the issuance of new shares must be complied with prior to the issuance of the convertible debentures (*see supra* Chapter 4.4.a). Voting rights are not available to the holders of such securities prior to conversion.

5.2   Certificates; Registration

a   Share Certificates. Share certificates should not be confused with the Dutch word "*certificaten*", which refers to depository receipts (*see infra* Chapter 5.5).

Share certificates can only be issued to N.V. shareholders. The issuance of share certificates to B.V. shareholders is specifically prohibited[11]. Bearer shares are negotiable instruments[12]; registered shares are not. Consequently, a transfer of registered shares may be subject to certain defects in the title of previous owners, including the seller[13]. Except in cases of fraud, a bearer share certificate evidences title to the shares[14]. N.V. shareholders with registered shares and B.V. shareholders can prove their title to shares only (a) if they are founders, or successors in the rights of one or more founders, by reference to the deed of incorporation, together with documents constituting complete chain of title (*e.g.*, all transfer deeds, *see infra* Chapter 5.4.b), or (b) if they own shares issued after incorporation, by showing the appropriate corporate resolution and documents constituting a complete chain of title. A deed of transfer for shares often contains a waiver of the right to rescind (or nullify) the transfer. Although such a waiver may give some comfort to a buyer, it does not shield the owner of the shares against nullity actions. Furthermore, a certificate may be required from the management board that it has no knowledge of any share transfer other than as shown, and that the shares are still outstanding. In short, N.V. shareholders with registered shares and B.V. shareholders may encounter difficulty in establishing title to shares. However, since all registered shares, other than registered shares issued by listed compa-

---

11   BW arts. 2:175(1), 2:202.
12   BW art. 3:86.
13   BW art. 3:88.
14   BW art. 3:119.

nies, are required to be transferred by a deed of a Dutch civil-law notary, who must do a title search, the exposure with regard to title defects is limited (*see infra* Chapter 5.4).

The share certificate for an N.V. share can be in the name of the shareholder (called a registered share certificate) or can be made out to bearer. A bearer certificate cannot be issued until the full amount of the nominal value of the shares it represents has been paid in[15]. Share certificates must be signed by one or more managing directors or supervisory directors. Facsimile signatures are valid. Holders of the certificate are presumed to know the contents of the articles. Consequently, the share certificate does not usually specify any rights or limitations other than the type of shares, the number of shares, the nominal value, and the class (if any).

The form, colour and other particulars of share certificates are prescribed by royal decree[16]. If N.V. shares are listed on the Amsterdam Stock Exchange (AEX), compliance with the applicable stock exchange regulations is required.

For the notification of certain percentages of voting rights or capital interests in an N.V. listed on an official stock exchange in the European Economic Area, *see infra* Chapter 5.4.a.

b   Shareholders' Register. If the shares are registered, which is always the case for B.V. shares, the management board must keep a register stating[17]:

a   the names and addresses of the shareholders;

b   the amount contributed to the nominal value of each share;

c   any transfers of shares not fully paid up at the date of transfer, as well as any releases that may have been given to selling shareholders from their obligation to make further payments on these shares;

d   the date of transfer of shares not fully paid up at the date of transfer; and

e   any manifest pledge or life interest (*see infra* Chapter 5.3.a and c) affecting the shares, together with the name and addresses of the pledgees or the beneficiaries of the life interest.

---

15   BW art. 2:82(3).
16   Koninklijk Besluit [KB] (Royal Decree) of January 8, 1947, S. H7.
17   BW arts. 2:85(1)/194(1). A violation of these provisions is a criminal offence, *see* WED art. 1(4).

Shareholders[18] have the right to inspect the register. The shareholders' register is not open for public inspection, except for shares for which the nominal value has not been fully paid[19].

Every shareholder and pledgee or beneficiary of a life interest in shares of the corporation has the right to obtain an affidavit of his registration, free of charge[20]. As discussed above, this affidavit is not conclusive legal evidence that the registered person is the rightful owner, pledgee, or beneficiary, or that the shares are properly paid up. The affidavit is not negotiable.

The register must remain at the corporation's main offices in the Netherlands (except for N.V.s that under foreign law or stock exchange regulations must maintain part of their shareholders' register in that foreign country)[21]. The articles may provide that shareholders are entitled to a certified copy, and that a copy of the register shall be kept in the custody of a Dutch civil-law notary or attorney.

c   Disclosure; Single Shareholder. A corporation with a single shareholder is subject to certain public disclosure rules. Single-member corporations are N.V.s or B.V.s with one shareholder who directly holds all of the issued shares. The single shareholder may be another corporation (including the parent) or a natural person. Treasury shares of the single-member corporation or shares held by its subsidiaries are ignored for the determination of the number of shareholders[22].

Once a shareholder qualifies as a single shareholder of an N.V. or loses this qualification, he must notify the corporation within 8 days[23]. Shareholders of a B.V. corporation are known to the corporation, and consequently no special notification by the single shareholder is required. The corporation must within one week[24] notify the Commercial Register about the name and domicile of the single shareholder.

---

18   Pledgees and beneficiaries of a life interest that have the "information rights" similar to holders of depository receipts issued with the support of the corporation (*see infra* Chapter 6.6) have this right as well, except (for N.V.s only) with respect to that part of the shareholders' register that is allowed to be kept outside the Netherlands (BW arts. 2:85(4)/194(4), 2:88(4)/197(4), 2:89/198).
19   BW arts. 2:85(4)/194(4).
20   BW arts. 2:85(3)/194(3).
21   BW arts. 2:85(4)/194(4).
22   BW arts. 2:91a(4), 2:137(1)/247(1).
23   BW art. 2:91a(1),(2). A violation of these provisions is a criminal offence, *see* WED art. 1(4).
24   HrW 1996, arts. 5(1), 9(2); HrB 1996 art. 14(g). A violation of these provisions is a criminal offence, *see* WED art. 1(4).

5.3   Security Interests and Other Encumbrances[25]

a   Pledge (*Pandrecht*). The existence of the underlying debt determines the existence of the pledge[26]. The pledge automatically ceases to exist once the debt is satisfied.

The pledge on bearer shares (N.V.s only) can be created by: (i) an agreement between pledgor and pledgee and compliance with the formalities to remove the share certificates from the pledgor's possession (possessory pledge or *vuistpandrecht*)[27] or (ii) by the execution of an instrument before a Dutch civil-law notary, or by an instrument signed by the pledgor, officially registered with the local tax registration bureau (*Inspectie Registratie en Successie*)[28], in which case it is not necessary to remove the share certificates from the pledgor's possession (non-possessory pledge or *bezitloos pandrecht*)[29]. The pledgor is required to make the representation in the instrument that he has the power to pledge the shares and, as the case may be, that certain limited rights are vested in the shares. Any misrepresentation in this respect may give rise to a claim against the pledgor, but it will not protect the pledgee against any defect in the pledge created in his favour.

For a pledge on registered shares the same formalities must be complied with as for the transfer of such shares (*see infra* Chapter 5.4.a and b)[30]. The management board must register pledges disclosed to it in the shareholders' register (*see supra* Chapter 5.2.b). The articles of both N.V.s and B.V.s may exclude or limit the right to pledge registered shares[31].

Bearer shares deposited in the Negicef clearing house system (providing for transfers by administrative entries) can be pledged subject to the provisions of the Securities Depository Act[32].

---

25   This paragraph was revised by Christian M. Stokkermans of Loeff Claeys Verbeke, Amsterdam office
26   BW art. 3:7.
27   BW art. 3:236(1).
28   Registratiewet (Act on Registration) 1970 S.610.
29   BW art. 3:237(1),(2).
30   BW arts. 3:236(2), 2:86/196, 2:86c. Registered shares in a company, shares or depositary receipts of shares which are listed on an official stock exchange, can also be pledged by execution of an instrument before a Dutch civil-law notary or by an instrument registered with the local tax registration bureau without acknowledgement by or notification to the company (BW art. 2:86c(4)).
31   BW arts. 2:89(1)/198(1).
32   Wet giraal effectenverkeer [WGE] (Securities Depository Act) arts. 20, 21, 42, 1977 S. 333, *as amended.*

The pledgor and the pledgee may agree that the voting rights pertaining to the pledged shares will remain with the pledgor, or will be assigned to the pledgee. However, if a transfer of the shares concerned to the pledgee would be subject to any transfer restriction included in the articles, the assignment of the voting rights to such pledgee shall be subject to the approval of the shareholders' meeting or such other corporate body that under the articles is competent to approve any transfer of shares under the transfer restriction provisions. Authorised to grant or deny such approval shall be the shareholders' meeting, unless under the company's articles another corporate body is competent to grant the approval for any transfer of shares[33].

b   Foreclosure (*Executie*). The pledgee can foreclose the shares without a title of enforcement or court order being required[34]. Any restrictions on the transfer of shares (*see infra* Chapter 5.4.c) will apply[35]. The shares must be sold at a public auction. Until the secured debt has become due and payable, the pledgor and the pledgee may not agree to foreclosure of the collateral by private sale[36]. The pledgor may also seek a court order for a private sale.

In order to start the foreclosure proceedings, the non-possessory pledgee of bearer shares must first obtain possession of the share certificates. If the instrument was not made in notarial form, a court order is required in order to obtain the necessary power to instruct a court bailiff to seize the share certificates[37].

c   Life Interest (*Vruchtgebruik*). This is a personal beneficial interest which an owner of assets grants to another person. It is also known as life estate or *usufruct*. A life interest in shares may include voting rights[38] and the right to receive distributions, but will normally not include the right to sell or encumber the shares[39]. The articles of an N.V. or a B.V. cannot preclude a shareholder to create a right of life interest in any of his shares[40].

---

33   BW arts. 2:89/198
34   BW art. 3:248.
35   BW arts. 2:89(5),(6)/198(5).
36   BW art. 3:251(1),(2).
37   Rv art. 496(1),(2).
38   BW art. 2:88/197.
39   BW arts. 3:201, 3:212, 3:216.
40   BW arts. 2:88(1)/197(1).

5.4 Transfer of Shares

a **N.V. Shares.** Bearer shares are transferred by surrendering the share certificates, unless the shares have been deposited with the Necigef central clearing house organisation which provides for transfers by book entries as regulated by law.

Registered shares are transferred by a deed of transfer executed before a Dutch civil-law notary[41]. The notarial deed contains certain specified details about the parties, the corporation and the shares being transferred[42]. The articles may require the share certificate to be surrendered to the corporation, in which case transfers may be completed by an endorsement and a replacement of the old certificate by a new certificate in the name of the new owner[43]. Shares that are listed on a recognised stock exchange in the European Economic Area, or likely to be admitted to such an official stock exchange in the near future, can be transferred without the involvement of a Dutch civil-law notary[44].

Unless the N.V. is a party to the transfer, shareholder rights can only be exercised by the new shareholder after the corporation has acknowledged the transfer of the registered shares (*erkenning*), or the notarial deed has been served upon the corporation by a Dutch court bailiff (*betekening*)[45]. The acknowledgement can be placed in the deed of transfer or by means of a dated statement on a notarial transcript or on a certified copy of the deed[46]. In the absence of a request from any of the parties to the transaction to acknowledge the transfer, the corporation itself can acknowledge the transfer by means of entry of the new shareholder in the register of shareholders[47].

If certificates of registered N.V. shares have been issued, the acknowledgement of transfer is placed on the existing certificate, or a new share certificate is issued upon presentation to the corporation of the existing

---

41   BW art. 2:86(1).
42   BW art. 2:86(2).
43   BW art. 2:86c(3).
44   Unless the latter category of shares is listed and deposited with the Necigef central clearing house organisation, such shares are transferred by a deed of transfer. Unless the corporation is a party to the transfer, this deed must either be acknowledged in writing by the corporation, or be served upon it by a Dutch court bailiff (BW art. 2:86c).
45   BW art. 2:86a(1).
46   BW art. 2:86b.
47   BW art. 86a(2).

certificate. If the amount of the nominal value has not been fully paid, the deed of transfer should be notarised or filed with the tax authorities, in order to ascertain the date of transfer.

Actual or potential holders of a direct or indirect interest (in terms of shares or voting rights or both) in the capital of an N.V. whose shares or depository receipts are listed on an official exchange in a European Economic Area State must notify[48] the corporation and the Securities Board of the Netherlands (STE)[49] when any of the following thresholds are reached or passed: 5%, 10%, 25%, 50% and 66⅔% (*see supra* Chapter 1.4).

b   B.V. Shares. B.V. shares, which are by definition registered shares, are transferred by a deed of transfer executed before a Dutch civil-law notary (*see supra* Chapter 5.4.a)[50]. The procedure for the transfer of registered shares in a B.V. is similar to that for the transfer of registered N.V. shares. Unless the B.V. is a party to the transfer, shareholder rights can only be exercised by the new shareholder after the corporation has acknowledged the transfer (*erkenning*), or the notarial deed has been served upon the corporation by a Dutch court bailiff (*betekening*) (*see supra* Chapter 5.4.a)[51]. The acknowledgement can (i) be placed in the deed of transfer or by means of a dated statement on a notarial transcript or on a certified copy of the deed, or (ii) be made by registering the transfer in the shareholders' register[52]. The corporation itself can also acknowledge the transfer at its own initiative once it has actual knowledge of the transfer[53]. If the shares are not fully paid up, the deed of transfer must be notarised or filed with the tax authorities, in order to ascertain the date of transfer.

c   Share Transfer Restrictions

i   *N.V. Shares.* Any restrictions on the transfer of N.V. shares must be set forth in the articles[54]. Restrictions can only apply to registered shares. Bearer shares are always freely transferable. Permissible restrictions may include a limitation that registered shareholders be individuals or

---

48   WMZ 1996 arts. 2(1), 3(1).
49   Stichting Toezicht Effectenverkeer [STE] (Securities Board of the Netherlands).
50   BW art. 2:196(1).
51   BW art. 2:196a(1).
52   BW arts. 2:196a(1), 2:196b.
53   BW art. 2:196a(2).
54   BW art. 2:87(1).

entities having certain qualifying characteristics, such as residency in the Netherlands, a specified family affiliation, or the absence of share-holdings in a directly competitive industry. Restrictions shall not, however, render transfer impossible or extremely onerous[55]. The Ministry of Justice may refuse to issue a certificate of no objection (*see supra* Chapter 3.3.b.iv), if it believes that a restriction is unfair. Among restrictions considered to be unfair are those in which the price to be received by the transferor is inequitable (*e.g.*, below fair market value, as determined by an independent expert, at the request of the seller)[56] and those in which the qualifying characteristics of those to whom shares may be transferred are too limited. In practice, restriction clauses for N.V. shares are often similar to corresponding B.V. provisions.

ii *B.V. Shares.* The transfer of B.V. shares *must* be restricted and speci-fied in the articles according to mandatory legal provisions, which allow only limited flexibility[57]. The transfer must be subject either to approval by the corporation's management or supervisory board (*see infra* iii below) or such other corporate body (*e.g.*, the shareholders' meeting) as set forth in the articles, or to rights of first refusal of the other shareholders (*see infra* iv below). Combinations of both alterna-tives are also permitted.

The restrictions apply to all transfers, regardless of the underlying reason (sale, gift, inheritance, foreclosure, etc.). However, unless the articles provide otherwise, these restrictions do not apply to a transfer to a shareholder's spouse, certain relatives, another shareholder, or the corporation itself[58].

The articles may limit the transfer of shares to persons who meet spe-cific criteria (*see* i above). Any share transfer restrictions in the articles must be such that a shareholder, upon his request, receives a price equal to the value of his shares as determined by one or more inde-pendent experts[59]. The articles may provide for standards for expert

---

55 BW art. 2:87(1).
56 RICHTLIJNEN, *supra* p. 36 at note 142, § 31.
57 BW art. 2:195(2).
58 BW art. 2:195(1).
59 BW art. 2:195(5). The experts must also be independent from the corporation. The external accountant of the corporation may be appointed as an expert (Richtlijnen § 26). The internal auditor may be appointed only when the parties consent thereto (ASSER-MAEIJER 2, III, *supra* p. 2 at note 7, § 219).

valuation of the shares, provided they do not lead to an apparently unreasonable valuation. The offer price of any third party may not be made the exclusive valuation standard of the expert[60].

Clauses restricting the transfer of shares may be circumvented when shares are held by a corporate shareholder. For example, corporation A has a transfer restriction provision. Shareholders of corporation A are corporation B and Mr. C. The sole shareholder of corporation B is Mr. B. In order to make the transfer restriction effective, an agreement between Mr. B and Mr. C is required. Otherwise, Mr. B may freely sell his shares in corporation B, which in practical terms abrogates Mr. C's rights under the transfer restriction. For this purpose, the articles may limit the ownership of the corporation's shares to individuals.

iii *Approval Procedure.* The articles can make the transfer of shares subject to the approval of the management board, the supervisory board, the shareholders' meeting, or the holders of a certain type or class of shares, such as priority shares[61]. If the approval is not granted, the seller must be given the name of one or more acceptable prospective buyers who are prepared to purchase the shares at an appropriate price. For tax reasons, the corporation may be named as a prospective buyer only if the seller agrees[62]. Approval is deemed to be given if no prospective buyer is named.

If the parties fail to agree, the price at which the proposed buyer will purchase the shares must be determined by independent experts. A shareholder may, upon determination of the price by the experts, withdraw his request for an approval to sell.

iv *Right of First Refusal.* The articles may specify which shareholders have this right and in respect of which types of shares[63]. It is possible to provide in the articles that the right of first refusal may only be exercised by shareholders of particular types or classes and in a specific order of priority. It is also possible to make the proposed sale subject to both approval (*see* iii above) and rights of first refusal.

A shareholder proposing to sell may withdraw his offer within one month after notification of the identity of the proposed purchaser

---

60   RICHTLIJNEN, *supra* p. 36 at note 142, § 26.
61   BW art. 2:195(3).
62   BW art. 2:195(6).
63   BW art. 2:195(4).

and the price offered. If it appears that not all shares offered for sale will be purchased for cash, at the request of the prospective transferor at a price determined by independent experts[64], the selling shareholder may, within three months thereafter, freely transfer the shares to whomever he chooses[65].

d   Compulsory Transfers

i   *Loss of Qualifications.* A shareholder may be required to sell and transfer his shares in certain situations set forth in the articles, which may include the holding of shares in competitors, engagement in competitive activities, death (in case of individuals), bankruptcy or liquidation (in case of a corporate shareholder).

ii   *Force-Outs.* A shareholder owning 95% or more of a corporation's issued capital may initiate legal proceedings to require all of the other shareholders to transfer their shares to him[66]. A force-out action is subject to the jurisdiction of the Enterprise Chamber (a division of the Amsterdam Court of Appeal, *see infra* Chapter 9.1), with a right of appeal to the Supreme Court on questions of law only[67]. The price for the shares to be transferred is determined by the Enterprise Chamber, which may order expert valuation. The Enterprise Chamber will refuse the mandatory transfer of a minority interest of 5% or less only[68] (i) if the sellers would suffer considerable financial damage that would not be compensated by the sales price, or (ii) in case the articles attribute special powers to the minority shares and the minority shareholders can effectively use this power in the corporation (*i.e.* priority shares; *see supra* Chapter 5.1.c)[69], or (iii) if the majority shareholder has renounced his right to initiate these legal proceedings (which may be particularly relevant in joint ventures.

---

64   BW art. 2:195(5).
65   BW art. 2:195(4).
66   BW arts. 2:92a(1)/201a(1).
67   BW arts. 2:92a(2)/201a(2).
68   BW arts. 2:92a(4)/201a(4).
69   Asser-Maeijer 2, III, *supra* p. 2 at note 7.

5.5 Depository Receipts for Shares (*Certificaten*)

a   General. Depository receipts[70] are instruments issued by a trust office (*administratiekantoor*), representing certain shares of a corporation held by the trust office. The receipts refer to the sort and type of shares, but are not identical to the underlying shares. The rights conferred on receipt holders are determined by the provisions according to which the receipts are issued. These provisions are called the "trust conditions" (*administratievoorwaarden*). The receipt holder has no rights *vis-à-vis* the corporation but only *vis-à-vis* the trust office (with a number of exceptions, *see infra* Chapter 5.5.e). The trust office is usually a foundation (*stichting, see supra* Chapter 2.5.b) formed by the corporation. The financial position of the receipt holder is secured by a statutory pledge on the shares[71]. In most cases, the trust conditions stipulate that distributions by the corporation to the trust office as shareholder flow to the receipt holder, and grant the trust office the exclusive voting rights on the shares held by it. Depository receipts are often used as an anti-takeover device.

b   Types of Depository Receipts. A distinction can be made between registered depository receipts and bearer depository receipts (BDRs). For a B.V., no bearer depository receipts may be issued[72]. Another distinction can be made between: convertible receipts (*royeerbare certificaten*), which can be converted into the underlying shares upon request and payment of a nominal fee; partially convertible receipts (*gedeeltelijk royeerbare certificaten*) which can be converted only upon satisfaction of certain trust conditions; and non-convertible receipts (*niet royeerbare certificaten*) which are convertible only upon the liquidation of the trust office.

c   Stock Exchange Rules. The listing rules of the Amsterdam Stock Exchange (AEX) contain special rules for depository receipts and trust offices, and require the trust office to be independent from the corporation in which it holds shares[73]. This is of particular importance when the trust office has been formed and its board appointed at the corporation's initiative in order to avoid interference by a shareholder or a take-over bid.

---

70   Depository receipts reflect certain rights to which shareholders in a corporation are entitled. These rights should not be confused with profit participation rights (*see supra* Chapter 5.1.b), which are created by a provision in the articles, for persons other than shareholders.
71   BW art. 3:259.
72   BW art. 2:202.
73   Fondsenreglement, AEX Listing Rules, Exhibit X, art. 13, (1997).

d   The Practical Use of Depository Receipts. Depository receipts are used to facilitate trade on the Amsterdam Stock Exchange in foreign shares, particularly if these shares are registered or if the nominal value of such shares is unusual or impractical for Dutch investors (*e.g.*, expressed in a foreign currency), as well as to protect a corporation against corporate raiders.

e   Rights of Receipt Holders. Holders of depository receipts do not have the right to vote the underlying shares. However, they do have the right to share in the corporation's profits. In addition, if the depository receipts are issued with the corporation's concurrence, their holders also have the right to attend and participate in shareholders' meetings[74] and to obtain any reports, statements and other documents to which shareholders are entitled. For these "information rights", *see infra* Chapter 6.6.

f   Meetings of Receipt Holders. The trust conditions may provide for meetings of receipt holders. Most trust offices hold meetings only upon the request of a specified percentage of receipt holders. The receipt holders may have voting rights at such meetings. Only in exceptional cases do the trust conditions require the trust office to cast its vote at the shareholders' meeting in accordance with instructions given by the receipt holders.

g   Transfer of Depository Receipts. The transfer of bearer depository receipts is effected by surrendering the certificate therefor to the transferee[75] (unless they are deposited with the Necigef central clearing house organisation which provides for transfers by book entries as regulated by law). Registered depository receipts (for which no certificate needs to be issued) are transferred by assignment[76].

---

74   BW arts. 2:117(2)/227(2).
75   BW arts. 3:93, 3:90(1).
76   BW art. 3:94.

6 SHAREHOLDERS

6.1 Basic Powers

a Appointment of Managing Directors and Supervisory Directors.
In the Netherlands, the shareholders do not have the supreme authority within the corporation, and the management board is not hierarchically subordinate to them[1]. The shareholders have, in fact, a very limited role in the management and operations of the corporation[2]. The shareholders *cannot* operate as the executive of the corporation (which is the exclusive power of the management board), give detailed instructions to the management board, or, particularly in the case of "large" corporations (*see infra* Chapter 7.3.a.ii), overrule decisions of the supervisory board made pursuant to the powers vested in that board by the law or the articles.

If the corporation is not a "large" corporation the shareholders' primary power is the power to appoint[3], suspend and remove[4] managing directors and supervisory directors. In the case of an optional supervisory board, *i.e.*, one provided for in the articles[5] but not required by law, the shareholders' meeting may not assign this power to the supervisory board[6]. If, however, the corporation is a "large" corporation and not fully or partially exempt (*see infra* Chapter 7.1.b.iv), the managing directors are appointed, suspended and removed by the mandatory supervisory board[7].

With respect to the appointment of managing and supervisory directors, the shareholders may be required to accept nominations made by the management or supervisory board, by a particular type or class of shareholders, usually the holders of priority shares (*see supra* Chapter 5.1.c), or by any other person or institution, stated in the articles. These nominations can always be overruled by a qualified majority of two-thirds of the votes cast, representing more than half of the issued shares[8]. The articles cannot subject the appointment of directors to the approval of any third parties.

1   Judgment of January 21, 1955, HR, 1959 NJ No. 43.
2   BW arts. 2:107(1)/217(1), 2:129/239.
3   BW arts. 2:132/242, 2:142(1)/252(1).
4   BW arts. 2:134/244, 2:144(1)/254(1).
5   BW arts. 2:140(1)/250(1).
6   BW arts. 2:132/242, 2:142(1)/252(1).
7   BW art. 2:162/272, 2:134(1)/244(1).
8   BW arts. 2:133(2)/243(2), 2:142(2)/252(2).

b   Annual Accounts; Annual Report; Dividends. The shareholders'
meeting has the power to adopt the annual accounts[9]. If the corporation is
"large" and not fully or partially exempt (*see infra* Chapter 7.1.b.iv), the
right to *adopt* the annual accounts is vested in the supervisory board,
while the final *approval* of the adopted annual accounts is vested in the
shareholders' meeting[10].

The management board must prepare the annual accounts and submit
them to the shareholders' meeting within five months following the end
of the financial year, save for a one-time extension of up to six months[11].
The annual accounts are accompanied by the auditor's opinion[12] and the
annual report of the management board[13]. The annual report of the management board (which does not include the annual accounts)[14] is final
and cannot be amended by the shareholders' meeting or the supervisory
board. The annual accounts prepared by the management board may
include a proposed allocation of profits. If the right to adopt the annual
accounts is vested in the shareholders' meeting, the final allocation of
profits is made by the shareholders, subject, however, to any provisions in
the articles for the formation of and allocation to certain reserves and to
any powers that the articles may vest in that respect in the management
board, the supervisory board or the priority shareholders (*see supra* Chapter 5.1.d). The allocation of profits includes the determination of
amounts available for dividend (for the distribution of dividends, *see supra*
Chapter 4.8.a). It is therefore not the management board which determines whether dividends will be paid and in what amounts.

If the law or the articles require that the books and accounts be audited,
the shareholders have the power to appoint the auditors[15]. The auditor's
internal report, known as the management report[16], is only submitted to

9   BW arts. 2:101(3)/210(3). Non-compliance with these provisions is a criminal
     offence, *see* WED art. 1(4).
10   BW arts. 2:101(3)/210(3), 2:163/273.
11   BW arts. 2:101(1)/210(1).
12   BW art. 2:393(6).
13   BW arts. 2:101(1)/210(1).
14   BW art. 2:391. The annual report is not the glossy, printed report containing the
     annual accounts familiar to US lawyers and accountants. It is a report by the mana-
     gement board that explains the annual accounts, and indicates the board's views on
     the development of the enterprise. It must be in Dutch. The use of another language
     is permitted only if so resolved by the shareholders before the beginning of the finan-
     cial year, and if during that year no shareholder objects (BW art. 2:362(7)).
15   BW art. 2:393(2).
16   BW art. 2:393(4).

the management board and, where applicable, the supervisory board. This report must include the auditor's findings in respect of the reliability and continuity of the automated data processing[17]. Its findings may become part of the auditor's opinion[18], which is among the documents that the management board must submit to the shareholders. Any interested person has standing to enforce the statutory obligation to have the accounts audited[19].

As a general rule, all corporations are subject to the requirement to file their annual accounts and other information with the Commercial Register (*see infra* Chapter 11.1).

c   Approval of Major Corporate Changes. The shareholders have the right to approve major changes in the corporate structure, including amendments to the articles, statutory mergers, statutory split-ups, dissolution, and the sale of all or substantially all of the corporate assets (*see infra* Chapter 10).

d   Good Faith Requirements. The law requires a shareholder to behave reasonably and equitably in all situations towards all parties connected with the corporation, including other shareholders, the management board, the supervisory board, the Works Council and the corporation itself[20]. This does not imply that shareholders must uphold the corporation's interests, or that they have any obligation towards other shareholders[21]. These good faith requirements may, however, form the grounds for an action to have a resolution of a corporate body voided by court order (*see infra* Chapter 9.2.c)[22].

6.2   Shareholders' Actions

a   Shareholders' Meeting. Shareholders' meetings must be held in the Netherlands. The meeting must be held at the official seat or at a place designated in the articles[23].

---

17   BW art. 2:393(4).
18   BW art. 2:393(5).
19   BW art. 2:393(7).
20   BW art. 2:8.
21   Judgment of June 30, 1944, HR, 1944 NJ No. 465.
22   BW art. 2:15(1)(b).
23   BW arts. 2:116/226.

An annual general meeting must be held at least once a year[24]. All other meetings are referred to as "special" or "extraordinary" meetings.

The annual meeting must be held within six months of the end of the corporation's financial year, unless the articles specify a shorter period[25]. Notice for meetings must be given by the management board or the supervisory board at least fifteen days prior to the date of the meeting[26]. The articles of private corporations and subsidiary corporations often permit a notice to be given by shareholders representing 20% or more of the issued share capital. If the board refuses to convene a meeting, one or more shareholders holding at least 10% of the issued share capital may convene a meeting by obtaining an order of the president of the competent District Court[27]. N.V.s that have issued bearer shares can give notice only by an announcement in designated nationally circulated newspapers. In all other cases, the notice must be sent by mail. Failure to give proper notice may render the meeting voidable[28], unless notice is waived by a unanimous vote representing all of the issued share capital[29].

The agenda of the meeting is determined by the party giving notice. Resolutions on subjects not properly set forth in the notice are valid only if carried by a unanimous vote of a meeting at which all shareholders are present or represented[30]. B.V.s must state the purpose of the meeting in the notice[31]. N.V.s may refer to an agenda of the meeting that is available for inspection by shareholders at the offices of the corporation[32]. Any proposal to amend the articles must, however, be mentioned in the notice[33]. In the event that annual accounts[34] or amendments to the articles[35] are to be discussed, proposals must be made available at the offices of the corporation for inspection by the shareholders prior to the meeting. The chairman of the supervisory board or the president of the management board normally serves as chairman of the shareholders' meeting. The chairman may appoint a secretary to keep minutes and pre-

---

24   BW arts. 2:108(1)/218(1).
25   BW arts. 2:108(2)/218(2).
26   BW arts. 2:115/225.
27   BW arts. 2:110/220.
28   BW art. 2:15(1)(a).
29   BW arts. 2:115/225.
30   BW arts. 2:114(2)/224(2).
31   BW art. 2:224(1).
32   BW art. 2:114(3).
33   BW arts. 2:123(1)/233(1).
34   BW arts. 2:102(1)/212.
35   BW arts. 2:123(3)/233(3).

pare the attendance list. The minutes of meetings at which certain important actions are undertaken or discussed must be prepared by a civil-law notary[36]. The management board must keep a record of all shareholders' resolutions available for inspection by the shareholders and the holders of depository receipts (*see supra* Chapter 5.5 and *infra* Chapter 6.6). They are entitled to receive a copy or excerpt from this record[37].

The law does not require a quorum for the transaction of corporate business. The articles often contain quorum provisions requiring a certain percentage of shareholders to be present, or represented by proxy, when particular subjects (*e.g.*, amendments to the articles or the dissolution of the corporation) are to be voted on at the shareholders' meeting.

b   Actions without a Meeting ("Unanimous Consent Resolutions"). Corporations with few shareholders (or just one) may have a provision in the articles enabling the shareholders to adopt resolutions without a meeting[38]. These resolutions are valid only if the votes are cast in writing (or by telex, telefax, or telegram) and the resolution is passed by a unanimous vote of all shareholders. The managing directors and the members of the supervisory board have an advisory vote in the meeting of shareholders (*see infra* Chapter 6.3). This advisory vote cannot be ignored, even when circumstances would normally indicate the shareholders' concurrence with the resolution. The advisory vote can be solicited by a conference call or by a draft resolution circulated and consented to prior to its adoption[39]. Unanimous consent resolutions may be adopted outside the Netherlands. The management board must keep a record of all unanimous consent resolutions.

6.3   Voting

The right to vote is concomitant with the ownership of shares. Voting rights can never be separated from the shares. While N.V.s may have bearer shares (*e.g.*, all shares listed on the Amsterdam Stock Exchange (AEX) are bearer shares), the articles of an N.V. often require that the share certificates be deposited prior to the meeting at the corporate head office or another designated place (often the offices of a commercial bank). The

---

36   BW arts. 2:124(2)/234(2), 2:330(4).
37   BW arts. 120(4)/230(4).
38   BW arts. 2:128/238.
39   Judgment of March 10, 1995, HR, 1995 NJ No. 595.

notice of the meeting must state this requirement. An N.V. shareholder cannot be required to make the deposit more than seven days prior to the meeting[40]. The articles of a B.V. may require a shareholder to give notice of his intended presence at the meeting; however three days notice is sufficient[41].

Each shareholder has at least one vote[42]. Non-voting shares are not permitted. The voting rights are, in principle, proportionate to the nominal value of the shares[43]. According to detailed provisions of the law, the articles may grant reduced voting rights per shareholder according to certain non-discriminatory thresholds[44] (*e.g.*, six votes for 10%, seven votes for 20%, etc.), thereby reducing the voting power of large shareholders. The articles may also otherwise depart from the proportionality between equity interests and voting interests, provided a single shareholder shall not have more than a certain number of votes specified by law (six in case the authorised capital is divided in 100 or more shares; otherwise the maximum is three)[45].

The managing directors and the supervisory directors have an advisory vote in the meeting of shareholders. A shareholder may be represented by proxy. The proxy instrument must be in writing. The articles may prohibit certain persons from being proxy-holders, but attorneys, civil-law notaries and register accountants (*registeraccountants*) may always represent a shareholder as a proxy-holder[46].

As a general rule, proxies may be revoked at any time before the vote has been taken. Personal attendance of the shareholder at the meeting revokes any proxy given for that meeting[47]. The death or guardianship of the shareholder causes revocation of the proxy by operation of law. The proxy also terminates upon the transfer of the title to the shares. Subject to the foregoing limitations, an irrevocable proxy may be given, provided it is coupled with an equity interest[48].

---

40   BW art. 2:117(3).
41   BW art. 2:227(3).
42   BW arts. 2:118(1)/228(1).
43   BW arts. 2:118(2)/228(2).
44   BW arts. 2:118(4)/228(4).
45   BW arts. 2:118(5)/228(5).
46   RICHTLIJNEN, *supra* p. 36 at note 142, § 11.
47   ASSER-MAEIJER 2, III, *supra* p. 2 at note 7, § 289.
48   Judgment of November 13, 1959, HR, 1960 NJ No. 472.

Pledgees[49] and beneficiaries of a life interest[50] (*see supra* Chapter 5.3) may have voting rights. These voting rights are inherent in and concomitant with their equity interest, and cannot be revoked by the personal attendance of the legal owner of the shares, by the transfer of title to the shares, or by the death or mental incompetence of the shareholder.

The shareholders have access to the shareholders' register (*see supra* Chapter 5.2.b). Proxy solicitations and proxy battles are unusual in the Netherlands. There are, therefore, no special rules governing this phenomenon.

The holders of certain types or classes of shares, usually priority shares (*see supra* Chapter 5.1.c), may have the right to veto certain shareholders' decisions, especially those providing for amendments to the articles or the dissolution of the corporation (*see infra* Chapter 10.6.b).

6.4   Shareholders' Agreements

Shareholders may enter into agreements concerning most of the rights incidental to the ownership of their shares. Shareholders' agreements are, as a general rule, valid and enforceable, but they bind only the parties thereto. The rights and obligations set forth in the agreement are not incidental to the shares and do not bind future shareholders. The effectiveness of shareholders' agreements may be enhanced by penalty clauses, the use of irrevocable proxies and covenants to bind a successor or assignee under a penalty provision (*kettingbeding*).

Most joint venture agreements that call for the formation of one or more corporations to conduct the joint venture business contain provisions concerning the financing of the joint venture, a right of first refusal in the event a participant wishes to sell its equity stake, and the use that the parties may make of their voting rights. These agreements cannot, however, set aside the powers that the management board and the supervisory board derive from the law and the articles.

It is generally held by legal commentators that a shareholder cannot sell or otherwise dispose of his voting rights separately from his legal or beneficial ownership rights in the shares, albeit that a voting agreement with other shareholders is allowed. However, a shareholder cannot agree to

---

49   BW arts. 2:89(3)/198(3).
50   BW arts. 2:88(3)/197(3).

vote according to instructions from the management board or the supervisory board, and a voting agreement, like any other agreement, cannot violate the law, the articles, or principles of good morals (*goede zeden*)[51].

Several types of voting agreements have been specifically approved by the Dutch Supreme Court. A voting agreement is valid if it purports to avoid a deadlock in a shareholders' meeting and allows a third party to resolve the deadlock[52]. The third party must act in good faith. The same practical result can be achieved by a provision in the articles that in case of a tied vote among shareholders, a third party will resolve the matter[53]. A voting agreement may provide for a voting pool that requires certain shareholders to vote as a block and in accordance with the majority vote amongst those shareholders in a pre-meeting[54]. Shareholders may agree with a third party about certain actions of the corporation (the sale of parts of its business) and they may also agree amongst themselves that they will appoint a new board, if required, in order to ensure proper performance under the agreement with this third party[55]. It is generally believed that other purposes for voting agreements may be valid as well, such as an agreement not to cast votes or to waive a vote under specific circumstances[56]. However, an outright sale of voting rights for consideration is generally perceived as prohibited and void[57].

Dutch law does not permit the formation of a voting trust. However, a similar result can be, and frequently is, achieved by the formation of a *stichting* (*see supra* Chapter 2.5.b) that holds title to the shares, subject to certain contractual obligations.

---

51 ASSER-MAEIJER 2, III, *supra* p. 2 at note 7, § 288.
52 Judgment of June 30, 1944, HR, 1944/1945 NJ No. 465.
53 BW arts. 2:120(1)/230(1).
54 Judgment of November 13, 1959, HR, 1960 NJ 472.
55 Judgment of February 19, 1960, HR, 1960 NJ 473. However, a voting agreement may not frustrate the statutory provision that any nomination for the appointment of a director can always be set aside by a majority of two-thirds of the votes cast, representing more than one-half of the issued capital (ASSER-MAEIJER 2, III, *supra* p. 2 at note 7, § 288). Likewise a voting agreement to distribute reserves to evade the thresholds for the applicability of the "large" company rules (*see infra* Chapter 7.1.b.ii) may under certain circumstances be void (Judgment in preliminary proceedings of December 15, 1976, Rechtbank [Rb.] (District Court) Alkmaar, 1978 NJ No. 319).
56 ASSER-MAEIJER 2, III, *supra* p. 2 at note 7, § 286.
57 ASSER-MAEIJER 2, III, *supra* p. 2 at note 7, § 288.

6.5 Inspection of Books and Records

Every corporation must keep books and records, and the management board must store these records for a period of at least ten years[58]. With the exception of the shareholders' register (*see supra* Chapter 5.2.b), shareholders are not entitled to inspect these books and records. Shareholders (or holders of depository receipts) representing either 10% of the issued shares or a nominal value of NLG 500,000 (or any lower percentage or amount as provided in the articles) may, under certain circumstances, request the Enterprise Chamber (a division of the Amsterdam Court of Appeal, *see infra* Chapter 9.1) to appoint one or more experts to investigate the conduct of the business (*see infra* Chapter 9.2.b). These court-appointed experts are entitled to full access to the books and records[59].

6.6 Information Rights of Holders of Depository Receipts

Holders of depository receipts issued with the support or concurrence of the corporation (*see supra* Chapter 5.5) enjoy the following rights on an equal basis with shareholders:
a the right to receive the agenda of the meeting[60];
b the right to attend meetings and to participate in discussions[61]. They do not, however, have the right to vote;
c the right to obtain the annual accounts and the annual report and the auditors' opinion (*see supra* Chapter 6.1.b)[62];
d the right to petition for a shareholders' meeting (*see supra* Chapter 6.2.a) or for an investigation into the affairs of the corporation (*enquête*, *see infra* Chapter 9.2.b).

---

58 BW art. 2:10; *see infra* Chapter 8.2.d for claims in bankruptcy upon non-compliance with these provisions.
59 BW art. 2:351. In a recent decision the Dutch Supreme Court ruled that the provisions of corporate law for obtaining information are not exhaustive and therefore do not preclude a minority shareholder obtaining information through a preliminary hearing of witnesses (Rv. art. 124) (Judgment of October 20, 1995, HR 1995 RECHTSPRAAK VAN DE WEEK [RvdW] No. 208). The court may also require the defendant to give the plaintiff access to its books and records (Judgment of November 7, 1997, HR 1997, RvdW No. 219c). This is particularly the case if the claim relates to books and records concerning the accounts of the company (WvK art. 8(1)).
60 BW arts. 2:113(1)/223(1), 2:114(1)/224(1).
61 BW arts. 2:117(2)/227(2).
62 BW arts. 2:102(1)/212.

7 DISTRIBUTION OF POWERS; MANAGEMENT OF BUSINESS AFFAIRS

7.1 Two-Tier System

a   General. Although Dutch corporate law is, in many respects, different from corporate law in other continental European countries, the same basic two-tier management system exists elsewhere. This consists of a management board (known in France as the *directoire*, and in Germany as the *Vorstand*) which performs executive functions, as well as a supervisory board (in France, the *conseil de surveillance*, in Germany, the *Aufsichtsrat*) which advises and supervises the management board. In the Netherlands, this system applies to both N.V.s and B.V.s. Each board has its own responsibilities, powers, and duties, and each is legally independent from the shareholders.

This two-tier system is mandatory for corporations that have qualified as "large" corporations (*see infra* Chapter 7.1.b) for more than three consecutive years. The status of "large" corporation can be adopted voluntarily[1]. This may result from negotiations with trade unions or the Works Councils in merger or other situations. This voluntary "large" corporation status is only available if the corporation or a corporation controlled by it has a Works Council (*see infra* Chapter 12)[2].

In an N.V. and a B.V., the shareholders have identical powers (and limitations thereto), and the management board (*directie* or *bestuur*) and, where applicable, the supervisory board (*raad van commissarissen*) have the same responsibilities. The concept of an "officer" is unknown in Dutch corporate law.

The management board is the executive body and may be made up of individuals and corporations[3]. The management board is responsible for the management of the corporation and for its representation, *i.e.*, the actions of the corporation towards third parties (*see infra* Chapter 7.2.d.iii)[4]. The Dutch management board combines the functions of inside managing directors and senior officers in an American corporation. Consequently,

---

1   BW arts. 157(1)/267(1).
2   *Id.*
3   For the fiduciary duties of managing directors, *see infra* Chapter 8.1.a.
4   BW arts. 2:129/239, 2:130(1)/240(1).

there is no position equivalent to that of chief executive officer. The management board may, however, consist of a sole member, in which case that person is customarily called the managing director or the general managing director (*algemeen directeur*). If the management board has more than one member, each can have different responsibilities and powers (*see infra* Chapter 7.2.a.i)[5].

The supervisory board is distinct from the management board and the same persons cannot serve on both boards. The supervisory duties are not necessarily similar to the duties of outside managing directors in an American corporation. The supervisory board has a primarily supervisory and advisory function[6]. The articles may give it more specific powers, but the supervisory board cannot exercise executive functions. The supervisory board is *not* empowered to give specific instructions to the management board, determine the business policy of the corporation, or appoint or remove managing directors. The precise duties and responsibilities of the supervisory board may vary, and depend on the articles. The actual duties of the supervisory board often reflect the degree of delegation of power by the shareholders (*see infra* Chapter 7.3). The shareholders are free, except in the case of a "large" corporation, to provide in the articles that there will be a management board only.

If the N.V. or B.V. is a "large" corporation, the supervisory board has a much more prominent position in the corporate hierarchy (*see infra* Chapter 7.3.a.ii). In neither case, however, does the supervisory board have the power to manage the business or negotiate and conclude contracts (except when the management board has a conflict of interest with the corporation, *see infra* Chapter 7.3.a.i).

Furthermore, the shareholders are not the supreme authority within the corporation. They have certain statutory powers, and the articles may to some extent increase their authority to determine the general policy of the corporation[7]. In "large" corporations, particularly, the shareholders have limited powers.

b   **"Large" Corporations (*Structuurvennootschappen*)**

i   *Extended Powers of the Supervisory Board.* If over a period of three years an N.V. or a B.V. meets the statutory definition of a "large" corporation (*see* ii below) and is not fully "exempt" (*see* iv below), the law

---

5   BW art. 2:9.
6   BW arts. 2:140(2)/250(2).
7   BW arts. 2:107(1)/217(1); RICHTLIJNEN, *supra* p. 36 at note 142, § 9.

requires it to have a supervisory board with broad powers[8]. Following initial appointment in the deed of incorporation by the shareholders, the supervisory directors are appointed as from the date the "large" company rules become applicable (*see* ii below) by the supervisory board itself. In addition, the supervisory board of a "large" corporation is charged with three other basic functions: appointment of the management board, adoption of the annual accounts, and approval of certain important decisions of the management board (*see infra* Chapter 7.3.a.ii). This mandatory two-tier system, intended to reduce the power of the shareholders and increase the power of the employee-based Works Council is the Dutch alternative to the more direct form of employee participation in management that exists, for example, in Germany (*Mitbestimmung*). Additional rules applicable to "large" corporations are described in Chapter 7.2 and Chapter 7.3.

ii *Definition of "Large".* In order to determine whether a corporation qualifies as "large", the following three *cumulative* tests apply[9]:

a The corporation's issued capital plus reserves, including its retained earnings, equal at least NLG 25,000,000; and

b The corporation or a "dependent company" (*see* below) has established a Works Council, as required by law (*see infra* Chapter 12.1); and

c The corporation, together with its dependent companies, normally employs one hundred or more persons in the Netherlands.

In addition to the requirement that it has a supervisory board, a corporation that by law qualifies as "large" or has adopted this status voluntarily (*see supra* Chapter 7.1.a) is subject to a number of special rules in a variety of areas. These are discussed where applicable throughout this paragraph.

A "dependent company" (*afhankelijke maatschappij*) as defined in the Dutch Civil Code, is (i) a legal person in which the corporation, or any of its dependent companies, solely or jointly and for their own account, contributes at least half of the issued capital, and (ii) a partnership with a business enterprise registered with the Commercial Register in which the corporation or a dependent company is a fully liable partner towards third parties[10]. Dutch law contains special rules for the qualification of "large" in case of a general partner in a limited partnership.

---

8   BW arts. 2:154(1)/264(1).
9   BW arts. 2:153(2)/263(2).
10 BW arts. 2:152/262.

iii *Notification to Commercial Register.* A corporation that qualifies as a "large" corporation and is not fully exempt (*see* iv below) must notify the Commercial Register (*see infra* Chapter 11.2) thereof within two months after the shareholders' meeting adopting or approving the annual accounts, as the case may be, for the year in which the corporation meets the statutory criteria[11]. Three years of uninterrupted registration automatically render the rules for "large" corporations applicable[12]. Before the end of the three-year period the articles must be amended to comply with the "large" corporation rules[13]. If the corporation no longer meets the statutory test of a "large" corporation, and it is expected that it will not do so again in the near future, it will be exempt until it qualifies as "large" again[14].

iv *Exemptions*

    A Fully Exempt "Large" Corporations (*Vrijgestelde Vennootschappen*)
An otherwise "large" corporation is *fully exempt* from the special rules and regulations, and need not notify the Commercial Register, if[15]:

    a the corporation is "dependent" (*see* ii above) on a legal person to which the special rules concerning a "large" corporation apply in full or in part (for partially exempt "large" corporations, *see* B below);

    b the corporation exclusively or almost exclusively restricts itself to the management and financing of group companies (*see supra* Chapter 3.1.b) and its own and their participation in other legal persons, provided, however, that the majority of the employees of this holding and finance corporation and all group companies are employed outside the Netherlands;

    c the corporation exclusively or almost exclusively renders management and financial services to a corporation as set forth under (b) above and to other companies of that group; or

    d at least one-half of the issued capital is held as a participation (*see supra* Chapter 3.1.b) under a mutual arrangement of co-operation between two or more "large" corporations or companies "dependent" on "large" corporations.

---

11   BW arts. 2:153(1)/263(1). Violation of this provision is a criminal offence, *see* WED art. 1(4).

12   BW arts. 2:154(1)/264(1).

13   BW arts. 2:154(3)/264(3).

14   Resolution of the Minister of Justice of April 1, 1987, 66 DE NAAMLOOZE VENNOOTSCHAP 30 (1988).

15   BW arts. 2:153(3)/263(3).

In practice, the exemptions under (b) and (c) above relate only to international groups of corporations with a Dutch-based holding or sub-holding company. In order to be exempted, the holding corporation must refrain from any activity other than the holding of shares and the financing of its group companies.

B   Partially Exempt "Large" Corporations (*Verlicht Regime*)
"Large" corporation rules apply only *partially* to (i) corporations controlled from outside the Netherlands or to (ii) international groups with a Dutch-based holding company[16]. This partial exemption sets aside the requirements that give the supervisory board special powers with respect to the appointment of the management board and the adoption of the annual accounts[17]. These powers then remain with the shareholders.

Control from outside the Netherlands is assumed or a Dutch-based holding corporation of an international group is deemed to exist (and therefore the "large" corporation rules apply only partially), if *at least one-half of the issued shares* of the corporation is held by:
a   a corporation or another legal person or its dependent companies, the majority of whose employees or the employees of their group companies are employed outside the Netherlands;
b   a joint venture formed by one or more corporations or other legal persons or their dependent companies that meet the criteria under (a) above; or
c   a joint venture formed by one or more legal persons that meet the criteria under (a) above and one or more fully or partially exempt "large" corporations.

However, the partial exemption is not available if the majority of the employees of the group to which the "large" corporation belongs, together with the employees of the legal persons or corporations referred to in (a), (b), and (c) above, are employed within the Netherlands[18].

---

16   BW arts. 2:155(1)/265(1).
17   BW arts. 2:155(1)/265(1).
18   BW arts. 2:155(2)/265(2).

7.2 The Management Board (*Bestuur*) and its Agents (*Procuratie-houders*)

a Powers of the Management Board

i *Regular N.V.s and B.V.s.* The members of the management board (often referred to as managing directors) have collective powers and responsibilities. The managing directors share responsibility for all decisions and acts of the management board and for the acts of each individual managing director. The management board is generally imputed to have knowledge of everything that each managing director knows or should know.

The management board may adopt, for internal purposes, a manual or set of regulations that describe in detail the duties, responsibilities, and powers of each managing director, as well as the rules applicable to board meetings. The articles may allow the supervisory board to adopt the regulations governing the management board, which may limit the powers of the management board[19]. Whilst these manuals and regulations have no external effect, they can be of practical use and may have a significant impact on the liability of a managing director towards the corporation for cases of mismanagement (*see infra* Chapter 8.2.b).

The law is not specific about the powers of the management board in undertaking "the management of the corporation[20]." This is generally understood to imply all powers of the management board, except for those expressly attributed to the shareholders or the supervisory board either by law or in the articles. The corporation's business policies must be determined by the management board within the confines of the corporate purposes and in the "interests of the corporation" (*see supra* Chapter 1.2). The management board oversees the implementation of its policies and the corporation's day-to-day affairs, in addition to implementing decisions of shareholders' meetings and of the supervisory board.

The management board prepares the annual accounts and the annual report (*see supra* Chapter 6.1.b). All members of the management board must sign the annual accounts (*see infra* Chapter 8.3.a). If a

---

19   HANDBOEK, *supra* p. 2 at note 7, § 233.
20   BW arts. 2:129/239.

managing director fails to sign, the reasons for his failure to do so must be stated[21]. The articles may empower the management board to create reserves and thereby allocate profits and consequently determine the amount of profits available to the shareholders for dividend distribution (*see supra* Chapter 6.1.b).

The management board is basically independent in the performance of its duties. It is not subordinate to either the shareholders or the supervisory board[22], nor can it be considered an executive committee of the supervisory board. The articles may, however, require the management board to obtain the prior approval of the supervisory board or shareholders with respect to decisions on matters set forth in the articles or determined by the supervisory board or the shareholders' meeting[23]. The articles may require that the management board comply with directives issued by the supervisory board or the shareholders concerning the general course of the corporation's financial, social and economic policy and personnel management which is especially relevant if the corporation is part of a group of companies[24]. Although the management board is not legally obliged to accept detailed instructions from any other corporate body, its refusal to do so could result in a serious conflict with the shareholders or the supervisory board, culminating in the suspension or removal of one or more managing directors. A managing director removed because of his refusal to follow detailed instructions may, however, be entitled to significant severance payments.

The Works Councils Act contains several provisions requiring the management board to seek the prior approval or advice of the Works Council for certain critical decisions. These provisions of the Works Council Act are strictly enforced and actions by the corporation that violate them are subject to judicial recourse (*see infra* Chapter 12.2.f).

The management board has no power to fill its own vacancies or to amend the articles. US-style bylaws do not exist in the Netherlands.

ii   *"Large" Corporations.* If an N.V. or B.V. is a "large" corporation, special rules govern the powers of the management board. These rules supple-

---

21   BW arts. 2:101(2)/210(2). A violation of these provisions is a criminal offence, *see* WED art. 1(4).
22   Judgment of January 21, 1955, HR, 1959 NJ No. 43.
23   RICHTLIJNEN, *supra* p. 36 at note 142, § 9.
24   *Id.*

ment the rules applicable to ordinary corporations and state that in case of a conflict, the special rules prevail. In a "large" corporation, the management board must obtain the approval of the supervisory board prior to undertaking any of the following[25]:

a   the issuance or acquisition of shares and debt instruments issued by the corporation or by a general or limited partnership in which the corporation is a general partner;

b   co-operation by the corporation in the issuance of depository receipts for shares in its capital;

c   an application for listing or withdrawal of a listing at a stock exchange of shares, debentures, bonds and depository receipts (for N.V.s only);

d   the commencement or termination of a major long-lasting co-operation of the corporation or dependent company (*see supra* Chapter 7.1.b.ii) with another corporation or partnership, or participation as a general partner in a general or limited partnership if this co-operation or the termination thereof is of major significance to the corporation;

e   any acquisition by the corporation or a dependent company of a participation (*see supra* Chapter 3.1.b) in another corporation that exceeds the amount of one-fourth of the participating corporation's issued capital and reserves as shown on its balance sheet and the notes thereto, and any substantial increase or decrease in any such participation;

f   any investment of an amount equal to at least one-fourth of the corporations' own issued capital and reserves as shown on the balance sheet and the notes thereto;

g   any proposal to amend the articles;

h   any proposal to dissolve the corporation;

i   the filing of a petition for bankruptcy or for a suspension of payments;

j   the termination of the employment of a significant number of employees of the corporation or of a dependent company, at the same time or within a short time span;

k   a substantial change in the employment conditions of a significant number of employees of the corporation or of dependent company; and

l   any proposal to reduce the issued capital.

The articles may further supplement these requirements.

---

25   BW arts. 2:164(1)/274(1).

If the management board enters into a transaction in violation of these provisions, the corporation is nevertheless bound. The violation may, however, form the grounds for removal of a managing director or for other legal actions (*see infra* Chapter 8.2.b.i).

The supervisory board cannot force the management board to take action on any of the matters set forth above. This initiative is at the sole discretion of the management board.

b   Structure of the Management Board. The management board may consist of individuals or corporations, either Dutch or foreign, resident or non-resident. The management board must have at least one member. Its size is determined by the articles and as the result of the appointment and removal of managing directors from time to time. The size of the board is not determined by the management board itself.

Most managing directors are employed full-time by the corporation. The concept of an "officer" does not exist in the Netherlands. The articles may assign special responsibilities (*e.g.*, financial affairs) to one or more members of the management board[26]. Frequently, the shareholders' meeting, the supervisory board or the management board itself assigns special responsibilities to an individual managing director. These delegated responsibilities remain within the power of the management board as a whole and are part of its general responsibility for corporate affairs. Consequently, the title of president or general director (*algemeen directeur*) does not always imply a legal position significantly more prominent than that of the other managing directors.

The articles may require certain qualifications or expertise for managing directors.

The managing director's name, residential address (or, if the director is a corporation, its head office address) and other particulars must be entered in the Commercial Register (*see infra* Chapter 11).

c   Appointment, Compensation, Suspension and Removal

i   *Appointment in Regular N.V.s and B.V.s.* The initial management board is appointed by the founders when the corporation is first incorporat-

---

26   BW art. 2:9.

ed[27]. Their names appear in the deed of incorporation. Thereafter, managing directors are appointed by the shareholders. The articles may also require the shareholders to consider a nomination from the supervisory board or from a particular type or class of shareholders (usually the holders of priority shares, *see supra* Chapter 5.1.c) or any other person or institution stated in the articles. This nomination can always be overruled by a qualified majority of two-thirds of the votes cast representing more than half of the issued shares[28]. Appointment by one class or type of share capital of all or part of the board (known as a classified board) is prohibited. Shareholders may, however, conclude a shareholders' agreement (*see supra* Chapter 6.4) requiring the parties thereto to vote in favour of a proposal made by holders of one class or type of shares.

If the corporation has a Works Council (*see infra* Chapter 12.1), the management board is required to give the Works Council prior notice of any proposed candidate for appointment to the board, in order to give the Works Council an opportunity to render non-binding advice before the appointment is made[29].

Managing directors are usually appointed for an indefinite period of time. Annual appointments or re-appointments are uncommon and, to the extent managing directors have an employment agreements with the corporation, are incompatible with Dutch labour law.

ii *Appointment in "Large" Corporations.* In the case of a non-exempt "large" N.V. or B.V., the members of the management board are appointed by the supervisory board[30]. This power cannot be made subject to a nomination by any class or type of shareholders, including priority shareholders (*see supra* Chapter 5.1.c). The shareholders must be notified prior to the appointment, although they cannot veto the appointment results. The Works Council (*see infra* Chapter 12.1) must also be notified and given the opportunity to render advice prior to the appointment[31].

In a partially exempt "large" corporation (*see supra* Chapter 7.1.b.iv) the appointment of managing directors is subject to the same rules as apply to regular corporations (*see* i above).

27   BW arts. 2:132/242.
28   BW arts. 2:133(2)/243(2).
29   WOR art. 30(1).
30   BW arts. 2:162/272.
31   WOR art. 30(1).

iii *Compensation; Employment Contracts.* Members of the management board are in most cases employed by the corporation. The terms of employment are determined by the shareholders, unless otherwise provided in the articles (*e.g.*, that the terms shall be fixed by the supervisory board)[32]. In a "large" corporation, whether or not partially exempt, the terms of employment are also determined by the shareholders, unless otherwise provided in the articles[33]. Although the corporation, in its capacity as employer, is managed by the management board, the management board cannot, by virtue of an employment agreement alone, give instructions to an individual managing director. Moreover, if the managing director is also employed by another corporation, *e.g.* a parent company, he might appear to be in an ambiguous position. Nevertheless, his responsibilities as a managing director cannot be subordinated to his employment relationship with either corporation.

A managing director's salary is often indexed to or subject to annual revision based on the cost of living. Fringe benefits such as a car, petrol, home telephone, travel expenses, out-of-pocket expenses, and moving costs can, if properly included in the employment agreement and if not excessive, be fully or partially exempt from personal income tax. Tax-free income can sometimes be arranged through the use of a share participation plan or a "phantom stock" plan. The combined salaries and fringe benefits of the managing directors must be disclosed in the annual accounts. The same applies to the compensation for supervisory directors.

iv *Suspension.* A managing director may be suspended from his powers and responsibilities at any time by a resolution of the shareholders' meeting (if the shareholders have the power to appoint managing directors). The supervisory board always has the power to suspend managing directors, unless otherwise stated in the articles[34]. In a "large" corporation that is not fully exempt this power to suspend is always vested in the supervisory board. A suspension may always be lifted by the shareholders, unless the suspended director was originally appointed by the supervisory board (which is the case in a "large" corporation that is not fully exempt). Suspension does not in itself terminate the director's employment contract with the corporation.

32   BW arts. 2:135/245.
33   ASSER-MAEIJER, 2, III, *supra* p. 2 at note 7, § 310.
34   BW arts. 2:147(1)/257(1).

An irregular or unreasonable resolution to suspend a managing director may be contested in court (*see infra* Chapter 9.2.c). Suspensions must be recorded at the Commercial Register (*see infra* Chapter 11).

v *Removal; Termination of Employment Contract.* The removal of a managing director requires a resolution of either the shareholders or the supervisory board, whichever has the power to appoint managing directors. In case of a "large" corporation, the supervisory board must first hear the shareholders' meeting[35]. In cases of mismanagement, the Enterprise Chamber (a division of the Amsterdam Court of Appeal, *see infra* Chapter 9.1) may also remove a managing director (*see infra* Chapter 9.2.b).

If the corporation has a Works Council (*see infra* Chapter 12.1), the management board must give the Council prior notice of an anticipated removal, in order to allow the Works Council time to render advice prior to the actual removal[36].

The articles may stipulate that any shareholders' resolution regarding the removal of a managing director requires a special quorum or qualified majority vote, or that no quorum or qualified majority will be required when the removal is proposed by a certain class or type of shareholders (*e.g.*, by priority shareholders) or by the supervisory board. A shareholders' resolution to remove a manager of the board can be voided by the court if the manager concerned has not been properly heard at the shareholders' meeting prior to the resolution[37]. The removal of a managing director must be recorded at the Commercial Register (*see infra* Chapter 11.2).

The employment contract of a managing director terminates, in most cases, on his removal from the board. The legal rules applicable to this termination of employment are similar to those that apply to the termination of other types of employees, except that no permit is required from the Regional Labour Market Agency (*Regionaal Bureau Arbeidsvoorziening* or RBA)[38]. Disputes and claims fall, in most

---

35   BW arts. 2:362/272.
36   WOR art. 30(1).
37   Judgment of January 29, 1943, HR, 1943 NJ 198; *see also* Judgment of May 18, 1990, Ger. Amsterdam, 1990 NJ 591.
38   Buitengewoon Besluit Arbeidsverhoudingen [BBA] (Decree on Labour Relations), art. 6(5), 1945 S. F214, *as amended*; Ministeriële Beschikking (Ministerial Decree) of December 10, 1954 Stcr. 242.

cases, under the jurisdiction of the District Court[39], rather than the Cantonal Court (which has jurisdiction over ordinary labour disputes), and the District Court cannot order the corporation to reinstate a managing director[40]. If the court finds that the termination was obviously unreasonable, the managing director may be entitled to a substantial severance payment from the corporation. In most cases, a settlement is reached with the board member whereby his employment is terminated with a so-called golden handshake.

d   Actions by the Management Board and Managing Directors

i   *Meetings.* Meetings are scheduled informally. There are no statutory notice requirements. Meetings are customarily held at the corporation's head office, but may be held elsewhere, even outside the Netherlands. The board's manual or regulations (*see supra* Chapter 7.2.a.i) may provide detailed rules concerning the scheduling of board meetings.

Although members of the management board, including the chairman, normally have equal powers and voting rights, the articles or board regulations may provide that a managing director with a defined function (*e.g.*, the chairman) has more votes or a casting vote. However, no managing director, including the chairman, may have a voting power that allows him to outvote all other managing directors. Managing directors may not vote by blank proxy. The articles may give the supervisory board or another corporate body a casting vote in the event of a deadlock[41].

ii   *Action without a Meeting.* The management board may take actions without a meeting if the managing directors unanimously agree to the action.

iii   *Acts of Individual Managing Directors.* Unless otherwise provided in the articles, each managing director has the authority to represent the corporation in respect of third parties (including appearing in court on behalf of the corporation). This authority does not require any specific action by the management board as a whole[42].

---

39   BW arts. 2:131/241.
40   BW arts. 2:134(3)/244(3).
41   RICHTLIJNEN, *supra* p. 36 at note 142, § 8.
42   BW arts. 2:130(2)/240(2).

The law prohibits any limitations on this basic power of an individual managing director to enter into transactions with third parties, except that either or both of the following may be imposed by the articles (assuming more than one managing director is in office)[43]:

a the corporation will be bound only if a minimum number of managing directors have acted jointly;

b the corporation will be bound only if one or more managing directors with defined functions have acted, either individually or jointly, with fellow managing directors or with designated agents of the corporation (*see infra* Chapter 7.2.d.iv).

However, it is not possible to limit in the articles the transactional power of managing directors to specific subject matters, or according to the size or nature of the transaction[44]. The limitation set out in (a) and (b) above may, however, be supplemented by a provision in the articles enabling a managing director to obtain a permanent power of attorney from the other directors. The power may then set forth certain limitations concerning the size or nature of the transactions allowed[45]. This power must be recorded at the Commercial Register (*see infra* Chapter 11.2). Third parties can then, by examining the corporation's filing at the Commercial Register, easily ascertain whether the managing director has the power he purports to have.

Certain matters fall within the exclusive statutory domain of the shareholders or the supervisory board (*e.g.*, adoption of the annual accounts) and may not be delegated. In these areas, the managing directors have no authority whatsoever.

Transactions with third parties which violate either the law or any of the acceptable limitations on the transactional powers of the management board are not enforceable against the corporation if the limitations are properly disclosed at the Commercial Register[46]. A managing director who lacks the required authority for his actions but implicitly or explicitly warrants that he has this authority may be liable to third parties for any resulting damages. If the unauthorised actions injure the corporation, the corporation may also be entitled to damages[47].

---

43   BW arts. 2:130/240.
44   RICHTLIJNEN, *supra* p. 36 at note 142, § 9.
45   BW arts. 3:60-79.
46   BW art. 2:6(2).
47   ASSER-MAEIJER 2, III, *supra* p. 2 at note 7, § 294.

When a managing director exceeds his authority by taking an action which should have been taken by others (*e.g.*, by the management board as a whole or jointly with one or more other managing directors, by the supervisory board, or by shareholders) the unauthorised act can be ratified through acquiescence or acceptance by the corporation of the benefits of the transaction with knowledge of the material facts.

The articles often contain other provisions limiting the power to transact with third parties. As discussed above, these provisions have no third party effect and serve only internal purposes. Transactions that violate these provisions are nevertheless binding on the corporation. The managing director involved may be liable to the corporation for non-compliance with the articles. Among these internal provisions are provisions requiring the management board to obtain prior approval for certain actions (*e.g.*, acquisition of property) from the shareholders or the supervisory board, including the approval required for the types of actions set forth above in "large" corporations (*see supra* Chapter 7.2.a.ii)[48], as well as provisions conferring certain management responsibilities on a specific managing director (*e.g.*, the finance director).

Apart from his individual power to bind the corporation, each managing director has a right of access to shareholders' meetings as well as the right to give his opinion on all matters under discussion[49]. This is of particular significance when an individual managing director disagrees with the majority position of the management board.

iv   *Managers and Agents (Procuratiehouders).* Dutch law does not recognise the concept of officers. All executive authority emanates from the management board[50], which may appoint persons who are not members of the board to certain management positions. These positions may involve the management of all or part of the corporation's routine affairs. The authority to delegate this power may be set forth in the articles. In the absence of a provision in the articles, the management board is free to appoint one or more managers. The management board then determines the scope of their powers, which determination may be subject to the prior approval of the supervisory board or the shareholders.

---

48   BW arts. 2:164(2)/274(2).
49   BW arts. 2:117(4)/227(4).
50   BW arts. 2:129/239.

The power of a person to act on behalf of the corporation with respect to third parties is, for the most part, controlled by ordinary agency principles[51]. The most significant difference, however, between ordinary agents and agents of corporations is the applicability of the *ultra vires* doctrine: the corporate agent cannot act beyond the scope of the corporation's purposes (*see supra* Chapter 3.6). Otherwise, the agent's power can be general, without any limitations. This general power excludes the power to appoint sub-agents, unless expressly granted[52]. Limitations on the authority of corporate agents should be clearly defined in a power of attorney. The powers of agents and the limitations on their authority to act for the corporation must be filed at the Commercial Register (*see infra* Chapter 11.2).

In addition to employees whose express authority is normally conferred in writing, corporate employees may have implied authority to engage the corporation in any act incidental to the employee's title or office. Thus, while a "sales director" may not be a managing director, he may nevertheless enter into sales transactions on the corporation's behalf which are concluded in the ordinary course of business. The use of titles for specific offices can therefore create corporate liability even though the holder of the office is not expressly empowered to bind the corporation. When the employee holds an executive office or title[53] and his course of conduct leads third parties to believe that he has the required power, third parties may rely on this apparent authority[54]. This is particularly true if the person has represented previously, with or without authority, the corporation in similar transactions which the corporation did not seek to challenge[55]. An effective means of advising third parties about the proper authority of corporate executives is by recording each power with the Commercial Register (*see infra* Chapter 11.2) and by strict enforcement. A corporate agent who is registered with the Commercial Register, but is not on the board, is referred to in Dutch as a *procuratiehouder*.

An agent who lacks the required authority for his actions but who implicitly or explicitly warrants that he has actual authority may be

---

51   BW arts. 3:60-79.
52   HANDBOEK, *supra* p. 2 at note 7, § 236.
53   The title *directeur* alone, or in combination with other designations, is often used for key employees, who are not managing directors, even though the Dutch word *directeur* literally implies board membership.
54   C. ASSER, 2, I VERTEGENWOORDIGING EN RECHTSPERSOON: DE VERTEGENWOORDIGING, § 27 (W.C.L. van der Grinten, 7th ed. 1990).
55   Judgment of March 19, 1942, HR, 1942 NJ No. 445.

liable to third parties for any resulting damages[56]. If the unauthorised actions cause injury to the corporation, the corporation may also be entitled to damages.

v   *Proof of Authority.* Dutch corporations do not have a secretary or other person capable of testifying to the authority of a person who transacts business with third parties on behalf of the corporation. Consequently, certificates of incumbency are unknown. However, as far as third parties are concerned, the corporation's filings at the Commercial Register (the corporation's unique registration number must be on the letterhead of the corporation, *see infra* Chapter 11.1.c) form conclusive evidence for the extent of the powers of each individual managing director, manager and agent, to sign on behalf of and thereby bind the corporation.

The Commercial Register will provide excerpts from registrations on request[57]. These excerpts are legal evidence and normally make it unnecessary to obtain the types of resolutions of the management board that are customary in other jurisdictions.

7.3   Supervisory Board (*Raad van Commissarissen*)

a   Powers of the Supervisory Board

i   *Regular N.V.s and B.V.s.* The members of the supervisory board (referred to individually as supervisory directors) have collective powers and responsibilities. The supervisory directors share responsibility for all decisions and acts of the supervisory board and for the acts of each individual supervisory director[58]. From a legal point of view the supervisory board is not subordinate to the shareholders and need not accept instructions from them. Its sole concern is the "interests of the corporation" (*see supra* Chapter 1.2) and its business enterprise. The management board is not hierarchically subordinate to the supervisory board and remains responsible for any action taken in response to a decision of the supervisory board[59].

---

56   BW arts. 3:70, 3:78, 3:79.
57   HrW 1996 art. 15; HrB 1996 art. 37.
58   BW arts. 2:140(2)/250(2).
59   BW arts. 2:151(2)/261(2).

The primary responsibility of the supervisory board is to supervise the policy of the management board and the general course of corporate affairs[60]. This supervision includes the power and duty to intervene, whenever necessary, and to take such corrective actions as may be required in the "interests of the corporation", always within the confines of the articles and the law. The management board must consult the supervisory board on all important matters including, but not limited to, any matters delineated in the articles. The supervisory board may also, on its own initiative, provide the management board with advice and request any information it deems appropriate. The articles usually provide for the right to inspect the books and records and for unrestricted access to the corporate premises. The management board has the statutory duty to provide the supervisory board in a timely fashion with the information necessary to carry out its responsibilities and perform its duties[61].

The articles may require the management board to obtain prior approval from the supervisory board for actions concerning matters set forth in the articles or in resolutions of the supervisory board. The management board may be required to comply with the supervisory board's directives on the general course of the corporation's financial, social and economic policy as well as its personnel management (*see supra* Chapter 7.2.a).

The articles may provide that, with respect to the appointment, suspension or removal of managing directors, the supervisory board, or some other person or institution as provided for in the articles, may make binding nominations that can only be rejected by the shareholders through a stipulated qualified majority. Any such nomination can always be overruled by a qualified majority of two-thirds of the votes cast representing more than half of the issued capital. The articles may give additional powers to the supervisory board, provided that these powers are not of an executive nature and do not affect the statutory powers of the shareholders.

Each supervisory director must sign the annual accounts. The reasons for any missing signatures must be stated[62]. Since annual accounts are normally open for public inspection (*see infra* Chapter 11.2), this statutory requirement emphasises the power that a supervisory director may be able to exercise by threatening to refuse to sign.

60   BW arts. 2:140(2)/250(2).
61   BW arts. 2:141/251.
62   BW arts. 2:101(2)/210(2).

Each supervisory director has access to all shareholders' meetings and may at all times state his opinion on matters on the agenda, whether or not he agrees with the position of the majority of the board[63].

The Works Council (*see infra* Chapter 12.1) meets twice annually with a managing director in what is known as a "consultation meeting" for the purpose of discussing general business affairs. At least one supervisory director usually attends this consultation meeting[64].

The supervisory board may acquire executive powers when the management board or any of its members has a conflict of interest with the corporation[65], unless the articles provide otherwise or the shareholders have appointed others to represent the corporation on such occasions. The articles may also grant executive powers to the supervisory board in the event that the members of the management board fail to act or are prevented from acting. The supervisory board is also responsible for retaining the auditor of the corporation if an audit of the accounts is required by law or the articles, but only if the shareholders' meeting fails to take the necessary action[66].

ii   *"Large" Corporations.* If an N.V. or a B.V. is a "large" corporation, special rules apply with regard to the powers of the supervisory board. These special rules supplement the rules for ordinary corporations. In the case of a conflict, the special rules prevail (*see supra* Chapter 7.1.b). The special rules must be incorporated into the articles within three years after the corporation gives notice to the Commercial Register that it qualifies as a "large" corporation (*see infra* Chapter 11.2).

The special powers of the supervisory board vary, according to whether the "large" corporation is non-exempt or partially exempt (*see supra* Chapter 7.1.b.iv). The supervisory board of a non-exempt "large" corporation has the following special powers:
a   the power to appoint, suspend and remove the managing directors (*see supra* Chapter 7.2.c.ii);
b   the power to adopt the annual accounts (*see supra* Chapter 6.1.b);
c   the power to approve or disapprove certain specified actions of the management board (*see supra* Chapter 7.2.a.ii); and
d   the power to fill its own vacancies (*see infra* Chapter 7.3.c.ii).

63   BW arts. 2:117(4)/227(4).
64   WOR art. 24.
65   BW arts. 2:146/256.
66   BW art. 2:393(2).

The special powers of the supervisory board of a partially exempt "large" corporation are limited to those set forth under (c) and (d) above. The powers of a supervisory board of a corporation that has adopted the "large" company status voluntarily (*see supra* Chapter 7.1.a) are at least equal to the powers of a supervisory board in a partially exempt "large" corporation. The appointment of managing directors and adoption of the annual accounts remain within the domain of the shareholders.

b   Structure of the Supervisory Board. Unlike the management board, which in the Netherlands may have corporate members, the supervisory board must consist of individuals[67]. Supervisory directors may be Dutch or foreign, resident or non-resident. The number of supervisory directors is determined by the articles or by a shareholders' resolution. The supervisory board may consist of a single supervisory director, unless it is a "large" corporation, in which case it must have at least three supervisory directors[68].

Although all supervisory directors, including the chairman of the supervisory board, have equal powers and duties, the articles may provide in certain cases for a "designated supervisory director" (*gedelegeerd commissaris*). This designated supervisory director represents the supervisory board in the period between meetings and supports the management board in its daily executive responsibilities.

In a "large" corporation, certain persons are ineligible for the office of supervisory director[69]. These include employees of the corporation or of other corporations in which the corporation holds at least half of the issued capital, as well as officials or employees of any trade union that is a party to a collective bargaining agreement covering any employees of the corporation. The supervisory directors' names, residential addresses, and other particulars must be entered in the Commercial Register (*see infra* Chapter 11.2).

c   Appointment, Compensation, Suspension and Removal

i   *Appointment in Regular N.V.s and B.V.s.* The initial supervisory board, if there is to be one, is appointed by the founders when the corpora-

---

67   BW arts. 2:140(1)/250(1).
68   BW arts. 2:158(3)/268(3).
69   BW arts. 2:160/270.

tion is incorporated[70]. Thereafter, supervisory directors are appointed by the shareholders. If the articles so provide, a maximum of one-third of the members of the supervisory board may be appointed by someone other than the shareholders[71]. The basic rules concerning nominations and qualifications for the appointment of members of the management board (*see supra* Chapter 7.2.c.i) apply equally to members of the supervisory board. The articles may, however, provide that holders of certain classes or types of shares, or other persons, have the power to nominate all or part of the supervisory board. However, any such nomination can be rejected by the shareholders through a two-thirds qualified majority vote representing at least half of the issued share capital[72]. A classified supervisory board is not allowed.

The proposal or nomination of a candidate for appointment to the board must state the candidate's age, his occupation, his ownership, if any, of shares in the corporation, other relevant positions currently or previously held, and the names of other corporations in which he serves as a supervisory director. The reasons for the proposal or nomination must be given[73].

Supervisory directors are usually appointed for a specific period of time, often between three and six years. When a term of office expires, the member may be re-appointed, unless the articles provide otherwise. The articles usually provide for a staggered supervisory board, whereby a proportion of the supervisory directors will be appointed over two or more years. No person is eligible to serve as a supervisory director beyond the age of 71[74].

ii   *Appointment in "Large" Corporations.* The supervisory directors of "large" corporations are appointed for a four-year term by the existing supervisory directors[75]. This rule does not apply at the incorporation stage, when the founders appoint the first supervisory directors, or in the initial three-year period during which the corporation qualifies as a "large" corporation but is not yet subject to the special statutory rules (*see supra* Chapter 7.1.b.iii)[76]. During this period, the shareholders retain the right to appoint supervisory directors.

---

70   BW arts. 2:142(1)/252(1).
71   BW arts. 2:143/253.
72   BW art. 2:142(2)/252(2), 2:133/243.
73   BW arts. 2:142(3)/252(3).
74   BW arts. 2:142(4)/252(4).
75   BW arts. 2:158(2)/268(2), 2:161(1)/271(1).
76   BW arts. 2:154/264.

The supervisory board can only appoint new supervisory directors after complying with the following procedure[77]. The supervisory board must first notify the shareholders, the management board and the Works Council (*see infra* Chapter 12.1) of an anticipated vacancy. In this way it solicits recommendations for candidates. After considering any recommendations, the supervisory board informs the shareholders and the Works Council of the candidate it intends to appoint. The shareholders or the Works Council may veto the appointment only if they were ill-informed or they believe that the candidate is unqualified to serve as a supervisory director or that as a result of the candidate's appointment, the supervisory board will not meet the test of being "properly constituted"[78]. The appointment by the supervisory board is not limited to those recommended by the shareholders, the management board or the Works Council. If the supervisory board insists on appointing its candidate, the veto of the shareholders or the Works Council may be submitted to the Enterprise Chamber, a division of the Amsterdam Court of Appeal (*see infra* Chapter 9.2.e), which may declare either that the veto is unfounded or that it should be upheld[79]. This appointment procedure cannot be made subject to nominations or other involvement in appointments by a specific class or type of shareholders.

iii   *Compensation.* A supervisory director is not considered an employee. This applies equally to a designated supervisory director (*see supra* Chapter 7.3.b), despite the fact that this office may in fact be a full-time position.

---

77   BW arts. 2:158/268.

78   Decision of September 27, 1983, Socio-Economic Council, 61 DE NAAMLOOZE VEN-NOOTSCHAP 233 (1983). The Works Council of Cyanamid prevailed in its claim that the supervisory board would not be properly constituted if the proposed person were appointed supervisory director. If the proposal had been confirmed, the supervisory board would have consisted of three supervisory directors, two of whom had never worked in the Netherlands, were therefore unaware of social relations in the Netherlands, and were employed by the parent company; Judgment of February 2, 1989, Ger. Amsterdam, 1990 NJ No. 86. The Works Council of Kodak prevailed in its claim that the supervisory board must be sufficiently independent *vis-à-vis* all interests and persons involved with the corporation, including interests and persons of the parent company. Officers of the parent companies and of other companies of the same group are not disqualified *per se* as supervisory directors, but a majority of such persons in the supervisory board may cause the board not to be "properly constituted".

79   Most vetos are filed by the Works Council. They purport to express the desire of the Works Council to have one or more persons on the supervisory board who have their special confidence.

Any remuneration paid to the supervisory board is determined by the shareholders unless the articles provide otherwise[80]. The supervisory directors are entitled to be reimbursed for their costs, including out-of-pocket expenses. The aggregate compensation for supervisory directors must be disclosed in the notes to the annual accounts[81].

iv   *Suspension and Removal.* Unless otherwise provided in the articles, the shareholders may suspend or remove a supervisory director at any time and without any compensation[82]. A supervisory director is also removed from his position by operation of law upon reaching the age of 72, but the articles may provide for his removal as of the date of the annual shareholders' meeting in the year that he attains the age of 72. In cases of mismanagement, a supervisory director may be removed by the Enterprise Chamber, a division of the Amsterdam Court of Appeal (*see infra* Chapter 9.2.b).

Any suspension or removal must be recorded at the Commercial Register (*see infra* Chapter 11.2). A supervisory director of a "large" corporation can only be suspended by the supervisory board[83]. The removal of a supervisory director of a "large" corporation prior to the end of his term of office falls under the exclusive jurisdiction of the Enterprise Chamber, and is based on a petition filed by the supervisory board, the shareholders, or the Works Council[84]. The grounds for removal are dereliction of duties or other serious reasons, or any drastic change of circumstances as a result of which the corporation cannot reasonably be required to keep the supervisory director in office.

d   Actions by the Supervisory Board. The rules concerning meetings of and actions by the management board (*see supra* Chapter 7.2.d) apply similarly to the supervisory board, except that individual supervisory directors cannot act on behalf of the supervisory board without specific authorisation (*see supra* Chapter 7.3.b).

80   BW arts. 2:145/255.
81   BW art. 2:383(1).
82   BW arts. 2:144/254.
83   BW arts. 2:161(3)/271(3).
84   BW arts. 2:161(2)/271(2).

8 DUTIES OF BOARD MEMBERS[1]

8.1 Introduction

a **Fiduciary Duties.** With regard to the fiduciary duties of directors, common law jurisdictions traditionally distinguish between the duty of care and the duty of good faith (also known as the duty of loyalty). In the Netherlands, the duty of care is expressed in terms of a duty to "properly perform" management or supervisory duties[2]. A breach of these duties may give rise to an action by the corporation. An action by the corporation may be instituted either by the supervisory board or another corporate body (or person) which is authorised to represent the corporation when the management board has a conflict of interest (*see supra* Chapter 7.3.a.i), by a subsequent management board, a moratorium trustee (*bewindvoerder*) (jointly with the managing directors), or a trustee in bankruptcy (*curator*). The duty of good faith is part of the reasonableness and fairness requirement that Dutch corporate law imposes on relationships among the management board, the supervisory board, shareholders and the Works Council[3] and that general contract law imposes on the parties to a contract.

Good faith principles govern situations in which a board member obtains personal benefit at the corporation's expense, as well as those in which the management board denies shareholders, or the supervisory board, any powers, rights or benefits to which they are entitled. The first category includes transactions in which a director has a personal interest (self-dealing), in which he obtains "soft" loans from the corporation, or in which he is personally or through other business enterprises in competition with the corporation (corporate opportunity). The second category relates to the protection of minority shareholders, power struggles among managing directors or between managing directors and shareholders or supervisory directors, the validity of anti-takeover devices, and the proper use of pre-emption rights. Insider trading to the detriment of the corporation or the other shareholders can also be considered a breach of the duty of good faith.

---

1   This chapter was revised by Hans A. de Savornin Lohman of Loeff Claeys Verbeke, Rotterdam office.
2   BW arts. 2:9, 2:138/248, 2:149/259.
3   BW art. 2:8.

These actions may be based on specific statutory provisions concerning breach of contract or general tort liability. A breach of the duty of care may give rise to a cause of action for mismanagement (*see infra* Chapter 8.2). Current Dutch law does not provide for shareholders' derivative suits.

b   Creditor Protection. In the 1980s, the financial collapse of several large Dutch business empires, as well as considerable abuse of the corporate form (especially the B.V. form) provided impetus in the Netherlands to further protect the interests of creditors. This protection requires review of the prior records of prospective corporate founders (*see supra* Chapter 3.3.b.iv), and imposes personal liability on directors for acts of mismanagement (*see infra* Chapter 8.2), for non-compliance with critical rules concerning the formation of the corporation (*see infra* Chapter 8.3.b) or its capital structure (*see infra* Chapter 8.3.d), for failure to notify the corporation's inability to pay taxes and social security premiums (*see infra* Chapter 8.3.c) and for inadequate bookkeeping or disclosure of the annual accounts of the corporation (*see infra* Chapter 8.3.a).

c   Litigation. The Enterprise Chamber, a division of the Amsterdam Court of Appeal, has exclusive jurisdiction over disputes concerning financial reporting (*see infra* Chapter 9.2.d), as well as for specific proceedings for investigation into the affairs of the corporation (also called *enquête, see infra* Chapter 9.2.b), and has the power to force the corporation to take corrective action. The findings and actions of the Enterprise Chamber do not in themselves impose liability on directors, but very often form the basis for subsequent lawsuits. Liability actions are litigated in the courts of ordinary jurisdiction.

d   The Director-Corporation. In the Netherlands a corporation can be appointed managing director of another corporation. In these cases, which are not uncommon in group structures, the individual directors of the director-corporation may be personally liable, jointly with the director-corporation[4].

e   Foreign Corporations. In determining the nationality of a corporation, Dutch law follows the "incorporation theory". Foreign corporations can therefore operate in the Netherlands under their own national corporate laws (*lex societatis*). However certain Dutch statutory rules concerning directors' liability for mismanagement do apply to directors of

---

4   BW art. 2:11.

foreign corporations (*see infra* Chapter 8.2). For the draft statute that intends to counter the evasion of Dutch corporate formalities by foreign corporations operating in the Netherlands, *see supra* Chapter 2.2.d.

f   Supervisory Directors. Implicit in the two-tier system of management, which is mandatory for "large" corporations (*see supra* Chapter 7.1.b.ii), is the personal liability of supervisory directors. Liability may particularly be incurred when the supervisory board temporarily assumes the powers of the management board (*see supra* Chapter 7.3.a.i; *see also infra* Chapter 8.2.b.iv), or when the annual accounts are erroneous or misleading (*see infra* Chapter 8.3.a).

8.2   Liability for Mismanagement

a   General. The statutory requirement to "properly perform" management or supervisory duties, as the case may be, requires each director to discharge his duties with care, skill and diligence. His tasks include properly implementing the provisions of the law and the articles, as well as actions initiated by the shareholders. It is not sufficient for a board member to argue that he performed his tasks to the best of his ability. On the other hand, he is not expected to guarantee the success of his actions. Each individual action must be judged on its own merits. There is no general standard similar to the "business judgment rule" in the United States. However, courts are generally not inclined to second-guess actions that under similar circumstances could reasonably have been taken by other, well-informed and diligent executives in similar positions in similar types of industry or trade. In addition, the courts are not allowed to judge management conduct with the benefit of hindsight. Generally, legal theory distinguishes between liability towards the corporation and liability towards third parties.

b   Liability to the Corporation

i   *Proper Performance of Management Duties.* The duties assigned to the management board and to each of its members are only partially defined by law. Most of these duties emanate from business practices or from a board manual or regulation. In order for liability to arise there must be serious negligence[5]. As a general rule, the responsibility of the management board is of a collective nature (*see supra*

---

5   Judgment of January 10, 1997, HR, 1997 RvdW 16.

Chapter 7.2.a.i). Each managing director is also responsible to the corporation for the proper performance of the specific duties assigned to him. In-house manuals or regulations may have a significant impact on the distribution of powers and responsibilities within the board. If a matter falls within the scope of responsibility of two or more managing directors, they are jointly and severally liable, unless one can prove that any shortcoming is not attributable to him[6]. In his defence he must show first, that he was not personally negligent, and second, that he did not fail in his duty to take action to avoid or prevent the consequences of the mismanagement.

ii   *Discharge.* The managers of the board can be discharged from their liability towards the corporation. The managers can be discharged by an express shareholders' resolution, but the articles of most corporations contain a provision that adoption or approval (in case of a "large" corporation) of the annual accounts by the shareholders' meeting discharges the managing directors from their liability *towards the corporation* for the performance of their duties during that financial year. The discharge does not release the managing directors from their liability for unlawful actions towards third parties (including individual shareholders and the trustee in bankruptcy claiming the shortfall)[7].

Since the Dutch Civil Code does not contain provisions specifically dealing with discharge of managing directors, this subject is governed by case law.

The discharge obtained by the managing directors is limited to facts disclosed to the shareholders' meeting in the annual accounts and the annual report or otherwise[8]. The managing directors are not discharged from legal acts unknown to the shareholders' meeting if those actions are intentionally withheld by the managing directors and the shareholders had no reason to suspect such[9]. Recently the Supreme Court held that, as a general rule, a discharge does not release from liability for acts which the shareholders could reasonably have known[10]. However, if legal acts which could be harmful to the corporation were known by the shareholders' meeting and the managing

---

6   BW art. 2:9.
7   BW arts. 2:138(6)/248(6).
8   Judgment of January 10, 1997, HR, 1997 NJ 360.
9   Judgment of June 20, 1924, HR, 1924 NJ 1107.
10   Judgment of January 10, 1997, HR, 1997 NJ 360.

directors were discharged for those acts, they can invoke the discharge on the grounds of the good faith requirements[11]. The shareholders' resolution to relieve the managing directors of their liability towards the corporation can be voided by the court or by the Enterprise Chamber (a division of the Amsterdam Court of Appeal) following the investigation into the affairs of the corporation (*see infra* Chapter 9.2.b). An appeal against the discharge of the managing directors can result in the discharge being rejected on grounds of violation of the good faith requirements.

iii *Amount of the Claim.* The claim by the corporation or by the trustee of the bankrupt corporation based on internal liability is for damages suffered by the corporation as a consequence of the mismanagement. The amount of damages is determined according to ordinary rules of the Dutch law of remedies.

iv *The Supervisory Board.* Management of the corporation is the responsibility of the management board, and actions for mismanagement will therefore, in most cases, be directed against the managing directors. There are, however, circumstances under which the supervisory directors may be held liable[12]. This is particularly likely when supervisory directors instead of the management board act on behalf of the corporation, for example, in cases of a conflict of interest between the management board (or one of its members) and the corporation (*see supra* Chapter 7.3.a.i). The act of approving or authorising management decisions does not in itself constitute an act of management by the supervisory board[13]. A negligent or improper decision of the management board is not, therefore, automatically attributed to the supervisory board merely by reason of its approval. Adoption or approval of the annual accounts, as the case may be, will normally discharge the supervisory directors from their liability to the corporation for the performance of their supervisory duties during the relevant financial year (*see* ii above).

c **Liability for Non-Payment of Taxes and Premiums**

i *Grounds for Liability.* If certain taxes or premiums (*e.g.,* wage tax, value added tax, social security premiums and premiums for manda-

---

11   Judgment of October 20, 1989, HR, 1990 NJ 308.
12   BW arts. 2:9, 2:149/259.
13   BW arts. 2:151(2)/261(2).

tory old age pension funds) are not paid when due, the managing directors are personally liable for the full amount of taxes and premiums outstanding if non-payment is caused by the "apparent negligence" of the management board over the three-year period prior to the due date[14].

If the corporation is unable to pay its taxes or social security or pension premiums it must notify the tax collector or the social security agency within fourteen days after the due date of its inability to pay. The notice must give reasons for its inability to pay and subsequent inquiries must be answered. The notice of non-payment by the corporation is critical. In case of failure to notify the competent authorities the managing directors are jointly and severally liable for the taxes or premiums. An individual managing director can escape liability only by proving that the failure to notify was not his fault and if the failure to pay is not imputable to him. An individual managing director can exculpate himself for the lack of proper notification only if he was physically or mentally unable to give the notice.

ii *Scope of Liability.* The law focuses on the managing directors (the law does not apply to supervisory directors, unless they act as *de facto* managers) who were in office at any time during the three-year period prior to the due date, but any executives, shareholders or others who have *de facto* managed the corporation in that period may be held liable as well. Most legal commentators take the view that instructions by a parent to a subsidiary do not constitute "management" for this purpose. However, the statutory language is ambiguous and there is no case law on this issue. Managing directors of foreign corporations that are subject to Dutch taxes and premiums are also liable. Local managers of these foreign corporations may be held liable as if they were managing directors (*see supra* Chapter 8.1.e).

iii *Amount of the Claim.* The claim of the tax collector and the social security agency will be for the full amount of taxes and premiums due. The managing directors have the right to seek recovery from the corporation. To the extent they fail, they must share liability for the shortfall equally among themselves.

---

14 Invorderingswet 1990 (Tax Collection Act) [Inv.], arts. 36, 37, 55, 57, 1990 S. 221, *as amended*; Coördinatiewet Sociale Verzekeringen (Coordination Act Social Insurance) arts. 16c, 16d, 16g, 16h, 1966 S. 64, *as amended*; Wet betreffende Verplichte Deelneming in een Bedrijfspensioenfonds (Act on Mandatory Participation in a Pension Fund) arts. 18a, 18b, 18c, 1945 S. J121, *as amended.*

d   Liability upon Bankruptcy

i   *Grounds for Liability.* If the corporation is declared bankrupt[15], the members of the management board are personally liable for the deficit in bankruptcy, if the bankruptcy is, to a significant extent, caused by "apparent negligence" by the management board[16] during the three-year period prior to the date of bankruptcy. The law imposes the obligation to keep financial records such that all assets and liabilities can be determined at any time and that the annual accounts and other financial information are filed with the Commercial Register within thirteen months of the end of the financial year. If one of these obligations has not been fulfilled two statutory presumptions enter into effect:
a   the irrebuttable presumption that there has been apparent negligence; and
b   the rebuttable presumption that the apparent negligence is a significant cause of the bankruptcy[17].

ii   *Defence.* An individual managing director can exonerate himself only by showing that he himself was not negligent, and that he did not fail in his duty to take action to avoid or prevent the consequences of the mismanagement[18].

iii   *Scope of Liability.* The law imposes liability on managing and supervisory directors, as well as executives, shareholders, and others who have *de facto* managed the affairs of the corporation. Directors of foreign corporations that are declared bankrupt in the Netherlands and are subject to Dutch corporate income tax (whether or not any tax is actually owed) are also liable. Local managers of these foreign corporations may be held liable as if they were managing directors[19].

iv   *Amount of the Claim.* The claim will be for the full amount of the shortfall in the liquidation, all to the benefit of creditors rather than shareholders. The court may reduce the amount of the claim[20].

---

15   Bankruptcy in this sense is akin to "liquidation" as set forth in Chapter 7 of the US Bankruptcy Code.
16   BW arts. 2:138(1)/248(1).
17   BW arts. 2:138(2)/248(2).
18   BW arts. 2:138(3)/248(3).
19   BW art. 2:138(11).
20   BW arts. 2:138(4)/248(4).

8.3 Liability for Violation of other Statutory Provisions

a   Liability for Annual Accounts. If the annual accounts, including any interim figures that the corporation produces (*e.g.*, quarterly reports) or the annual report (*see supra* Chapter 6.1.b) are erroneous or misleading with respect to the state of affairs of the corporation, each managing director and, where applicable, supervisory director may be liable for damages incurred by third parties[21].

b   Defective Formation of the Corporation

i   *Corporation Declared Non-Existent.* If, due to a violation of the rules concerning formation of a corporation, the court declares that the corporation never came into existence, persons who acted in the name of the non-existent corporation will be personally bound to fulfil all of its agreements with third parties[22].

ii   *Formalities.* The managing directors must ensure that the following formalities are complied with[23]:
a   the filing with the Commercial Register is completed (*see supra* Chapter 3.3.b.v);
b   paid-in capital plus statutory reserves on the date of formation are at least equal to the amount of the minimum capital as prescribed by law (*see supra* Chapter 4.3.b); and
c   at least one-fourth of the issued capital must be paid in (*see supra* Chapter 3.3.b.v).

As long as these formalities have not been completed, the managing directors are jointly and severally liable for all obligations arising out of legal acts of the corporation.

c   Pre-Formation Transactions. The founders, their representatives, and others who entered into agreements with third parties on behalf of the corporation to be formed are, unless specifically agreed otherwise, personally bound by pre-incorporation transactions until the date of ratification by the corporation (*see supra* Chapter 3.4.b)[24]. If, following

---

21   BW arts. 2:139/249, 2:150/260.
22   BW art. 2:4(4)
23   BW arts. 2:69(2)/180(2).
24   BW arts. 2:93(2)/203(2).

ratification, the corporation fails to perform such obligations, the persons who acted on behalf of the corporation may be liable if they knew or ought to have known that the corporation would not be able to comply with these obligations. Knowledge of the corporation's inability to comply will be presumed if the corporation is declared bankrupt within one year of formation[25].

d   Capitalisation. As previously explained, the rules concerning capitalisation of the corporation are of critical importance (*see supra* Chapter 4). Non-compliance can result in personal liability of the managing directors for any shortfall and for damages incurred by third parties.

e   General Tort Provision. An important legal basis for directors' liability is tort[26]. Creditors of the corporation may hold a managing director liable in tort if he entered into a transaction on behalf of the corporation whereas he knew or should reasonably have known that the corporation would not be able to fulfil its obligations arising out of that transaction[27]. Directors may also incur liability in tort in case of environmental pollution, fraudulent conveyance of assets or a misleading prospectus.

8.4   Criminal Liability[28]

a   General. Dutch law accepts the theory that a corporation can commit a crime. The individual directly responsible for the corporation's criminal behaviour may face penalties as well. This criminal liability can occur if the individual concerned (despite being authorised and reasonably bound to do so) omits to take preventive measures and knowingly accepts the substantial risk that illicit behaviour will occur. There are numerous statutes that impose specific criminal sanctions on the directors of business enterprises and on those who authorise or are otherwise responsible for offences relating to import and export, hazardous products, pharmaceutical and edible products, fair trade, business practices, wage and price controls, transportation, antitrust, taxation, zoning, protection of the environment and insider trading.

---

25   BW arts. 2:93(3)/203(3).
26   BW art. 6:162.
27   Judgment of October 6, 1989, HR, 1990 NJ 286.
28   This paragraph was revised by Hendrik Jan Biemond of Loeff Claeys Verbeke, Amsterdam office.

b   Violations of Statutory Corporate Law. Civil liability for non-compliance with statutory corporate law has been supplemented by certain criminal sanctions. To the extent the violation constitutes an offence under the Act on Economic Offences, it may attract imprisonment, a penalty and several severe civil sanctions. Other punishable offences include the following:

a   intentionally publishing inaccurate annual accounts[29];

b   involvement of a managing or supervisory director of the corporation in situations that are illegal or in conflict with the articles, resulting in serious harm to the corporation[30];

c   prior to or during bankruptcy proceedings, disguising profits or losses, or fraudulently disposing of assets[31];

d   prior to or during bankruptcy proceedings, disposing of assets at significantly less than their value[32];

e   prior to or during bankruptcy proceedings, giving preferential treatment to certain creditors in a manner detrimental to other creditors[33];

f   prior to bankruptcy proceedings, failure, or gross neglect, by the corporation in keeping proper records[34]; and

g   borrowing money with the purpose of forestalling bankruptcy, with knowledge that bankruptcy is unavoidable[35].

8.5   Insurance; Indemnification

Insurance for civil liability claims against managing and supervisory directors is available in the Netherlands. The standard insurance policy available in the Netherlands to cover this liability (*Bestuurders en Commissarissen Aansprakelijkheids Polis*) contains many exclusions and limitations.

There are no statutory provisions or case law with regard to the validity and enforceability of indemnities by the corporation, whether contained in the articles, or in a contract between the corporation and the director. Indemnification clauses are rare because of their limited effectiveness[36].

---

29   Wetboek van Strafrecht [WvS] (Criminal Code) art. 336, 1996 s. 64 *as amended.*
30   WvS art. 347.
31   WvS art. 343(1).
32   WvS art. 343(2).
33   WvS art. 343(3).
34   WvS arts. 342, 343(4).
35   WvS art. 342(2).
36   For a more detailed analysis of directors' liability (including the insurance and indemnity aspects), *see* H.A. DE SAVORNIN LOHMAN, DUTIES AND LIABILITY OF DIRECTORS AND SHAREHOLDERS UNDER NETHERLANDS LAW, PIERCING THE CORPORATE VEIL, 1996, Kluwer Law International (London, The Hague, Boston).

9   CORPORATE LITIGATION

9.1   Jurisdiction

The Enterprise Chamber, a division of the Amsterdam Court of Appeal, has an important role in the resolution of various disputes arising within and concerning the corporation. The Enterprise Chamber is made up of five judges with expertise in corporate affairs. The three legally-trained judges are accompanied by two lay judges, who are experts in socio-economic and accounting matters[1]. The Enterprise Chamber has exclusive jurisdiction over disputes concerning the form and content of the annual accounts, over appeals by a Works Council against certain proposed actions of the management board, and over the composition of the supervisory board of "large" corporations (*see supra* Chapter 7.3.c.ii). It can further order a legal person to take corrective measures in cases of mismanagement (*see infra* Chapter 9.2.b). Any action taken by a corporation in violation of an order by the Enterprise Chamber is null and void.

Actions for damages, as well as most other types of disputes, fall under the jurisdiction of the District Courts, except for certain disputes with the Works Council that fall under the statutory jurisdiction of the Cantonal Judge.

9.2   Litigation Concerning a Legal Person and its Business Affairs

a   **Works Council.** Certain decisions by the management board that have a potentially major impact on the corporation or its employees must be submitted to the Works Council for its prior advice (*see infra* Chapter 12.2.d.iii)[2]. If the procedural rules are not properly complied with, or if the contemplated action by the management board could not reasonably have been taken if the board had "weighed all interests involved", the Enterprise Chamber may prohibit or order the reversal of the action by the management board[3]. Certain management decisions require the consent of the Works Council (*see infra* Chapter 12.2.d.iv). The Canton-

---

1   Wet op de Rechterlijke Organisatie [RO] (Act on the Judiciary) art. 72(2), 1827 S. 20, *as amended.*
2   WOR art. 25(1).
3   WOR art. 26(4).

al Judge may enforce this right of the Works Council by ordering that those decisions cannot be made or implemented without the approval of the Works Council[4].

b   Mismanagement. The law does not allow for derivative suits, whereby a shareholder plaintiff sues in a representative capacity on the basis of a cause of action belonging to the corporation, nor for class actions. Mismanagement actions brought by the corporation or, if the corporation is bankrupt, by the trustee in bankruptcy or by individual shareholders or creditors, are adjudicated by the District Courts.

However, claims that require an investigation into the affairs of the company (*enquête*) fall under the jurisdiction of the Enterprise Chamber. Upon request, the Enterprise Chamber may appoint one or more persons, usually accountants or lawyers, to investigate all or part of the policies of any company as well as the general course of its affairs. In addition, disputes between shareholders that obstruct the "interests of the corporation" (*see supra* Chapter 1.2) may fall within the jurisdiction of the Enterprise Chamber. A request can be filed by the Attorney General in the public interest, by the shareholders or holders of depository receipts representing the lower of either 10% of the issued shares or a nominal value of NLG 500,000 (or any lower percentage or amount provided in the articles), by a trade union with members employed by the company, or by any others who, by virtue of the articles or an agreement with the corporation, have been granted this right[5]. The petitioner must first submit its complaint in writing to the management board and, where applicable, the supervisory board, and allow the company to take appropriate steps[6]. The investigation is ordered by the Enterprise Chamber if there are well-founded reasons for assuming that there will be a finding of mismanagement[7]. The experts' report is open for public inspection only if so ordered by the Enterprise Chamber. The Enterprise Chamber may take the following actions on a finding of mismanagement[8]:
a   the suspension or nullification of a resolution of the management board, the shareholders' meeting or any other corporate body;
b   the suspension or removal of one or more managing directors or supervisory directors;

4   WOR art. 27.
5   BW arts. 2:346, 2:347.
6   BW art. 2:349(1). A trade union must first solicit the views of the competent Works Council as well (BW art. 2:349(2)).
7   BW art. 2:350(1).
8   BW art. 2:356.

c the temporary appointment of one or more managing directors or supervisory directors;
d the temporary deviation from such provisions of the articles as shall be specified by the Enterprise Chamber;
e the temporary transfer of shares to a nominee;
f the dissolution of the corporation[9].

At any stage of the proceedings the Enterprise Chamber may, upon request, take preliminary measures, irrespective of any preliminary relief proceedings before the President of the District Court[10].

Expenses involved, including the experts' fees, are initially chargeable to the company. If, however, a request is lodged without serious grounds, the petitioner may be liable for damages to the company and for the costs of the investigation, including the experts' fees. If the experts' report shows that the mismanagement or the unsatisfactory conduct of the company is attributable to any members of the management board or supervisory board or others employed by the company, they may be held responsible by the company for all these expenses[11].

c Violation of Good Faith Principles, the Articles and Procedures Required by Law. Mismanagement is generally caused by a failure of the management board to exercise proper care in managing the corporation's affairs or by failure of the supervisory board to exercise proper care in supervising the management board. This duty of proper care for the business must be distinguished from the duty to observe standards of good faith in taking actions that affect the interests of other managing directors, the shareholders, the supervisory board or the Works Council[12]. The actions of the shareholders and the supervisory board are also subject to good faith principles. Actions taken in violation of good faith principles may be voided by the court[13].

Actions by the board or the shareholders which are in violation of public order, substantive mandatory rules of law or provisions of the articles are void[14]. Certain corporate actions that are void in principle can be rati-

---

9   This latter sanction cannot be imposed if this would be contrary to the interests of the shareholders or the employees or be contrary to the public interest (BW art. 2:357(6)).
10   BW art. 2:349a(2).
11   BW art. 2:354.
12   BW art. 2:8(1).
13   BW art. 2:15(1)(b).
14   BW art. 2:14(1).

fied[15] by the competent corporate body with retroactive effect, provided interested parties that could have invoked their nullity considered such actions valid. When actions of shareholders or the board are subject to actions of other corporate bodies, the actions can be ratified by those other corporate bodies, but are otherwise void[16]. All other procedural deficiencies in the decision making process are voidable by order of the court, not void *per se*[17].

Transactions with a third party that were entered into without a valid action of the corporation will be enforceable against the corporation if the third party had no knowledge, actual or imputed, about the invalidity of that action[18].

d **Annual Accounts.** All disputes concerning the form and contents of the annual accounts, as well as the standards applied, are subject to the exclusive jurisdiction of the Enterprise Chamber (*see supra* Chapter 9.1). Actions concerning compliance with audit rules, the involvement of auditors[19], and the filing of the annual accounts[20] and other financial information, fall within the jurisdiction of the District Courts. Any interested party (*e.g.*, shareholders, Works Council, etc.) may bring the action before the District Court.

e **Composition of the Supervisory Board of a "Large" Corporation.** As explained above (*see supra* Chapter 7.3.b), the supervisory board of a "large" corporation must consist of qualified individuals, and must be "properly" constituted. A veto by the shareholders or the Works Council of a proposal by the existing supervisory board for the appointment of a new supervisory director (*see supra* Chapter 7.2.c.ii) may be reversed by the Enterprise Chamber (*see supra* Chapter 9.1)[21]. The removal of a supervisory director of a "large" corporation also requires an action by the Enterprise Chamber[22]. However, violations of statutory or other procedural rules for the appointment are brought before the District Courts.

15 BW arts. 2:15(6), 3:58(1).
16 BW art. 2:15(6).
17 BW art. 2:15(1)(a).
18 BW art. 3:35.
19 BW art. 2:393(7).
20 BW art. 2:394(7).
21 BW arts. 2:158(9)/268(9).
22 BW arts. 2:161(2)/271(2).

9.3   Litigation between Shareholders

a   General. Proxy solicitations and proxy battles are unusual in the Netherlands. Securities listed on the Amsterdam Stock Exchange (AEX) are traded invariably either in the form of bearer shares or in the form of bearer depository receipts (BDRs). All B.V. shares and certain N.V. shares are in registered form. The shareholders' register is open for inspection by all shareholders (*see supra* Chapter 5.2.b). Force-outs of unwanted shareholders by means of a merger are impossible. A minority of 5% or less can be forced out under a special procedure (*see supra* Chapter 5.4.d.ii). Disputes between shareholders may be the focus of attention in an investigation (*enquête*) conducted under the supervision of the Enterprise Chamber (*see supra* Chapter 9.2.b). The actions that the Enterprise Chamber can take to remedy mismanagement include dissolution of the corporation.

b   Intolerable Behaviour; Force-Out. Any one or more shareholders representing at least one-third of the issued capital of a B.V., as well as of certain N.V.s, may require another shareholder to sell and transfer his shares if the other shareholder by his conduct prejudices the "interests of the corporation" (*see supra* Chapter 1.2) to such an extent that his continued shareholding cannot reasonably be tolerated[23]. Likewise, any shareholder of a B.V. corporation or of certain N.V. corporations may require one or more other shareholders to acquire his shares if that other shareholder is prejudicing his rights or interests to such an extent that his continued shareholding cannot reasonably be expected from him[24]. The other shareholder may in turn require other shareholders to join him as a party in the proceedings. The shares shall be allocated by the court with due observance of any right of first refusal contained in the articles (*see supra* Chapter 5.4.c).

The price to be paid for the shares shall be determined by the court, which will appoint either one or three experts to assess the price, in accordance with the clause in the articles which restricts the transfer of shares.

If a pledge or life interest is created (*see supra* Chapter 5.3) it may be agreed that the voting rights of the shares are to be exercised by the pledgee or beneficiary. If the conduct of the pledgee or beneficiary prejudices the "interests of the corporation", and the exercise of his voting right can

---

23   BW art. 2:336(1).
24   BW art. 2:343(1).

not reasonably be tolerated, the voting rights may, by court order, be returned to the shareholder.

The District Court in the district in which the corporation has its seat shall have jurisdiction over these proceedings, with appeal only available to the Enterprise Chamber[25].

These provisions apply only to corporations of a closed nature, that is to B.V. corporations and to N.V. corporations which have registered shares, no depositary receipts, and a transfer restriction clause in their articles[26]. Moreover, these provisions do not apply when either the articles or a shareholders' agreement contain a clause providing for the resolution of shareholders' disputes[27].

25   BW art. 2:336(2).
26   BW art. 2:335.
27   BW art. 2:337.

10   MAJOR CORPORATE CHANGES: AMENDMENTS; STATUTORY MERGERS; STATUTORY SPLIT-UPS, DIVISIONS AND DEMERGERS; ADOPTION OF DIFFERENT LEGAL FORM; DISSOLUTION AND TRANSFER OF CORPORATE SEAT

10.1 General

A Dutch legal entity cannot be merged under the statutory procedure (*see infra* Chapter 10.3) with a legal entity formed under foreign law nor can a statutory split-up (*see infra* Chapter 10.4) be effected between Dutch and foreign legal entities, nor can a Dutch legal entity adopt another legal form than those available under Dutch law (*see infra* Chapter 10.5).

10.2 Amendments (*Statutenwijzigingen*)

The articles may be amended upon a vote of the shareholders and the subsequent execution of a notarial deed containing the amended provisions[1]. Any amendment requires a certificate of no objection from the Ministry of Justice (*see supra* Chapter 3.3.b.iv)[2]. The articles may contain provisions that restrict or exclude the right to amend all or certain provisions. An amendment of these provisions is nevertheless possible, by a unanimous vote of a meeting at which all shareholders are present or represented[3]. Unless the articles state otherwise, no qualified majority or quorum is required for the amendment of any other provision, including the provisions concerning the corporate name, capital, purposes, quorum requirements and distributions.

If the articles require a quorum, and at the first properly notified shareholders' meeting no quorum is present, a second meeting can, unless the articles provide otherwise, ignore the quorum requirement and take a valid vote, provided that the notice for the second meeting specifically refers to this objective[4].

No amendment can abrogate, without their consent, the rights of third parties under the articles[5]. For example, directors' bonus provisions

---

1   BW arts. 2:124(1)/234(1).
2   BW arts. 2:125(1)/235(1).
3   BW arts. 2:121(3)/231(3).
4   BW arts. 2:120(3)/230(3).
5   BW arts. 2:122/232.

contained in the articles cannot be changed without the approval of each managing director who is effectively or potentially entitled to a bonus payment thereunder (unless the articles provide otherwise).

Shareholders adversely affected by a shareholder's resolution cannot insist on receiving payment of the fair market value of their shares. They may, however, seek a court order invalidating the shareholders' resolution on the basis that the resolution violates good faith principles (*see supra* Chapter 9.2.c)[6].

If a proposed amendment appears on the agenda of a shareholders' meeting, this must be set forth in the notices to the meeting. The text of any proposed amendments must be made available to the shareholders in a timely fashion at the main office of the corporation, and copies thereof must be available upon request[7].

An amendment may be proposed by any party entitled to convene a shareholders' meeting (*see supra* Chapter 6.2.a). If the amendment involves a reduction of capital, special rules for the protection of creditors must be satisfied (*see supra* Chapter 4.3).

The amendment becomes effective upon execution of a notarial deed in the Dutch language[8]. The complete amended text of the articles must be filed with the Commercial Register. Only upon this filing will the amendment have effect with respect to third parties.

10.3 Statutory Mergers (*Juridische Fusies*) and Consolidations

a   Introduction

i   *Types of Statutory Mergers.* The statutory merger[9] is a means of obtaining control over other business operations. The same economic result can often be reached by framing the transaction in the form of a share acquisition or an asset acquisition. Statutory mergers may take place between N.V.s, B.V.s, associations, cooperations, mutuals and foundations (*see supra* Chapter 2.5.a and b), provided that, in

---

6   BW arts. 2:92(2)/201(2), 2:8, 2:15(1)(b).
7   BW arts. 2:123/233.
8   BW arts. 2:124(1)/234(1).
9   The provisions concerning the statutory merger were introduced into Dutch law to implement the Third EC Company Law Directive (*see supra* Chapter 1.3.c).

the latter three cases as a general rule, the merging entities must have the same legal form (*see supra* Chapter 2.5.a and b)[10]. Only the forms of statutory mergers involving N.V.s and B.V.s as constituent legal entities are discussed here. Under Dutch law, a statutory merger is not possible between a Dutch and a foreign legal person. Consequently, a Dutch statutory merger cannot be used as a device for changing the law governing the legal person.

A statutory merger can take several different forms. In one scenario, a corporation (the surviving corporation) absorbs another corporation, so that the second corporation ceases to exist as a distinct corporation by operation of law, and the shares of the absorbed corporation are exchanged for shares in the surviving corporation by operation of law[11]. An "upstream merger" is a species of this form, involving a parent corporation that absorbs a subsidiary, so that the subsidiary ceases to exist. Alternatively, in a "downstream merger", the subsidiary is the surviving entity and the parent corporation ceases to exist.

A triangular merger is slightly more complicated. The surviving corporation absorbs one or more corporations, which cease to exist by operation of law, and the shares of the absorbed corporations are, by operation of law, exchanged for shares in a third corporation (the acquiror) that belongs to the same group as the surviving corporation. All of the shares of the surviving corporation must be held by the acquiror, either alone or together with another corporation that is part of its group (*see supra* Chapter 3.1.b)[12]. Through the use of a triangular merger, a parent corporation can avoid the existence of minority interests in one of its subsidiaries.

In a consolidation, a new corporate entity is formed upon the merger of two or more constituent corporations that are absorbed by the new corporation, so that the absorbed corporations cease to exist[13]. References to statutory mergers include consolidations, and the same rules apply to both legal forms, unless otherwise indicated.

A "sister merger" is deemed to exist with respect to a statutory merger between two or more wholly-owned subsidiaries[14].

---

10 BW arts. 2:308(1), 2:310(1),(3). BW art. 2:310(4) provides an exception to this general rule.
11 BW art. 2:309.
12 BW art. 2:334.
13 BW art. 2:309.
14 BW art. 2:333(2).

For "short-form" mergers, with simplified procedures, *see infra* Chapter 10.3.e.

ii   *No "Merger Force-Outs".* Dutch law does not recognise the right to "force-out", "freeze-out" or "squeeze-out" unwanted shareholders by means of a merger (*see supra* Chapter 5.4.d.ii) for force-outs of small minorities), and a merger can be used only to a limited extent to compel certain shareholders to accept cash or notes for their shares[15]. A statutory merger is not, therefore, the appropriate mechanism for either eliminating public shareholders in a "going private" effort or for forcing shareholders to accept a tender offer on penalty of being "mopped up" later for a less attractive consideration subsequent to the merger of the target into the aggressor corporation (known in the US as a "front-end loaded" tender offer).

iii   *Trade Unions; Works Council.* The Merger Code applies to the acquisition of direct or indirect control over all or part of the activities of another enterprise, when any of the enterprises involved regularly employs more than fifty employees in the Netherlands[16].

If the Merger Code applies, the trade unions must be consulted[17]. The Works Councils Act requires prior consultation of the Works Council in several situations, including the transfer of control of all or part of the enterprise; the establishment, take-over or relinquishment of control of another enterprise; or the establishment, substantial modification or discontinuation of long-term co-operation with other enterprises, including a substantial financial participation by or on behalf of such an enterprise (*see infra* Chapter 12.2.d.iii)[18]. A merger almost invariably falls within the scope of these provisions. No merger can be effected before completion of the consultation process[19], which may take considerable time.

Collective bargaining instruments may also have independent provisions requiring prior consultation with the trade unions or the Works Council in the event of mergers and consolidations. Any written opi-

---

15   BW art. 2:325(1).
16   Sociaal-Economische Raad (SER) (Socio-Economic Council), SER Fusiegedragsregels (Merger Code) arts. 14,15 (1991). For a detailed discussion on the Merger Code, *see* M&A IN THE NETHERLANDS, *supra* p. 3 at note 14, Chapter 9.4.
17   Merger Code art. 18.
18   WOR art. 25(1).
19   WOR art. 25(2).

nion given by the Works Council or the trade unions must be disclosed to shareholders (*see infra* Chapter 10.3.d.ii).

iv *Tax Considerations.* The statutory merger is not an event recognised by the tax laws as having special consequences and implications. This is one of the reasons it is not favoured as an instrument for acquiring another corporation. Prior consultation with the competent tax authorities, and in some cases a ruling, may be required.

b Legal Effect. Upon the statutory merger taking effect, by operation of law:
a the absorbed corporation(s) cease(s) to exist[20];
b all of the assets and liabilities of the disappearing corporation(s) are absorbed by the surviving corporation, thereby becoming part of its own assets and liabilities[21];
c except in certain limited cases defined by law (*see infra* Chapter 10.3.c and e), the shareholders of the disappearing corporation(s) become shareholders of the surviving corporation[22].

c Consideration

i *Shares.* A statutory merger is essentially an exchange of shares, and cash is used only to account for exchange ratio discrepancies, such as when the value of each newly issued share in the share capital of the surviving corporation is less than the value of each share in the absorbed corporation. The total amount of cash or promissory notes involved in the transaction cannot exceed 10% of the aggregate nominal value of the newly issued share capital[23]. In making payments in cash to third party minority shareholders, the good faith requirements (*see supra* Chapter 9.2.e), in this context meaning the requirement of equal treatment of shareholders, should be applied to the extent possible[24]. This precludes the use of high nominal value shares exclusively to create a "merger force-out" of minority shareholders. Property cannot be used as consideration for these discrepancies.

---

20   BW art. 2:311(1).
21   BW art. 2:309.
22   BW art. 2:311(2).
23   BW art. 2:325(1).
24   ASSER-MAEIJER 2, III, *supra* p. 2 at note 7, § 576.

No shares in the capital of a surviving corporation will be received in case of a "sister merger", an "upstream merger" involving wholly-owned subsidiaries or a triangular merger (*see supra* Chapter 10.3.a.i)[25].

ii *Treasury Shares.* The merger deed (*see infra* Chapter 10.3.d.iv) may provide for a cancellation by the surviving corporation of treasury shares or other shares in the surviving corporation held by the absorbed corporation, but not in excess of the total nominal value of the newly issued share capital[26]. The detailed statutory provisions for a reduction of issued capital (*see* Chapter 9.4.6) are not applicable.

d Procedure

i *Plan of Merger.* The "plan of merger" is a joint proposal by the management boards of the absorbed and surviving corporations[27]. It forms the basis for the notarial deed that completes the merger procedure. The plan must be signed by all managing directors and approved and signed by all supervisory directors, where applicable. If a director fails to sign, a reasoned explanation of this refusal is required[28]. Drawing up a plan is a prerequisite to a statutory merger. The joint nature of the required plan makes a statutory merger inconceivable as part of a hostile acquisition.

The plan must describe in detail the proposed actions, including, as a minimum[29]:
a the legal form, name and statutory seat of the corporations to be merged;
b the articles of the acquiror in their then existing form and in their post-merger form or, if the acquiror is newly-established, the draft deed of incorporation;
c the rights or compensatory payments which are chargeable to the acquiror and which are granted to persons who, other than as shareholders, have special rights *vis-à-vis* the corporations ceasing to exist, such as profit rights or share subscription rights, and their effective date;
d the benefits in connection with the merger, conferred on managing directors, supervisory directors or other persons involved in the merger;

---

25 BW art. 2:311(2)
26 BW art. 2:325(2).
27 BW art. 2:312(1).
28 BW arts. 2:312(4), 2:326(2).
29 BW arts. 2:312(2), 2:326(1).

e   the proposed composition of the management board and the supervisory board, if there is to be one;

f   in respect of each of the corporations ceasing to exist, the effective date from which financial information shall be incorporated in the annual accounts or other financial accounts of the acquiror;

g   the proposed measures in connection with the transfer of the share ownership of the absorbed corporations;

h   the proposed continuation or discontinuation of the business activities of the absorbed corporations;

i   who must approve the merger resolution;

j   the proposed exchange ratio for the shares, and any cash consideration;

k   the date from which and extent to which the shareholders of the absorbed corporation will share in the profits of the surviving corporation;

l   the impact of the merger on the amounts in the balance sheet for goodwill, capital surplus and distributable reserves of the surviving corporation; and

m   the number of shares that will be cancelled (*see supra* Chapter 10.3.c.ii).

ii   *Supporting Documents.* The plan of merger must be supported by an explanatory memorandum prepared by the management boards of each corporation involved. This memorandum must describe the reasons for the merger and must comment on the legal, economic and employment ramifications of the merger[30]. It must also explain the method or methods applied in determining the exchange ratio for the shares, whether such method or methods are justified under the circumstances, the valuation resulting from each method applied, and, if more than one method has been applied, whether the relative weights attributed to the valuation methods applied may be considered generally acceptable, and whether there have been any particular difficulties on the valuation and the determination of the exchange ratio[31].

If more than six months of a corporation's financial year have lapsed by the time the plan of merger and accompanying documentation are filed at the Commercial Register (*see infra* Chapter 11.1.a), its management board must prepare either annual accounts or an interim statement of assets and liabilities, consistent with the applied valua-

---

30   BW art. 2:313(1).
31   BW art. 2:327.

tion methods, as of a date which is not earlier than the first day of the third month preceding the month of the filing[32].

Each corporation must retain an auditor to examine the plan of merger and certify whether in his opinion the exchange ratio for the shares is reasonable[33]. The auditor must also certify that the equity of the absorbed corporation is as a minimum equal to the aggregate nominal value of the shares that will be issued, plus any cash consideration. He must further render an opinion on the statements made in the explanatory memorandum with respect to the valuation method or methods[34]. The auditors must have access to the books and records of all corporations involved[35].

Each corporation must file with the Commercial Register the plan of merger, the annual accounts for the three preceding years together with the relevant auditors' opinions, the annual reports of the three preceding years, and any interim statements or annual accounts not yet adopted (*see* above). These documents, together with the explanatory memorandum, as well as any advice or recommendations of the Works Council and the trade unions, where applicable, must also be deposited at the corporations' head offices for inspection by shareholders and others who have a similar interest *vis-à-vis* the corporation. A notice that the filings have been made must be published in a daily newspaper with national circulation[36].

iii *Authorisation.* As a general rule, a merger vote must be taken by the shareholders' meeting[37]. No vote can be taken on the merger within the one-month period following the publication in a national newspaper referred to above under ii (for timing, *see* iv below)[38]. A merger vote is similar to a vote to amend the articles (*see supra* Chapter 10.2), except that if less than one-half of the issued capital is represented at the shareholders' meeting, a qualified majority of two-thirds of the votes is required[39]. The surviving corporation may authorise the merger by resolution of its management board, provided that this

---

32   BW art. 2:313(2).
33   BW art. 2:328(1).
34   BW art. 2:328(2).
35   BW art. 2:328(3).
36   BW art. 2:314.
37   BW art. 2:317(1). The shareholders' meeting does not have the right to amend the merger plan (BW art.2:317(2))
38   BW art. 2:317(2).
39   BW arts. 2:317(3), 2:330(1).

procedure is not opposed by shareholders representing 5% or more of the issued capital, and provided the articles so permit and the intention to do so has been stated in the notice of deposit referred to above under ii[40].

iv *Timing.* Creditors may oppose the proposed merger and require the posting of a bond. The Works Council, where applicable, and, if the Merger Rules apply, the trade unions have the right to be consulted well in advance of the vote or the authorisation (*see supra* Chapter 10.3.a.iii)[41]. Parties to contracts with the absorbed corporation who may be detrimentally affected by the merger may have their contracts amended or rescinded by court order, and damages may be awarded[42]. This cause of action does not arise until the merger is completed, but it may be prudent to attempt to avoid it in advance. Pledgees and beneficiaries of a life interest (*see supra* Chapter 3.3.d.iv) in shares of the disappearing corporation will, as a general rule, receive a similar right in shares of the surviving corporation[43]. If an amendment to the articles of the surviving corporation is required, a certificate of no objection (*see supra* Chapter 3.3.b.iv) must be obtained from the Ministry of Justice prior to the execution of the notarial deed of merger[44].

The merger is completed by the execution of a deed before a Dutch civil-law notary, effective the following day[45]. The deed must be executed within six months of the date of the notice of deposit referred to above under ii. The civil-law notary is responsible for compliance with the mandatory statutory requirements and the requirements of the articles and must render an opinion that all requirements have been satisfied[46]. Within an eight-day period following the execution of the merger deed, the surviving corporation must file a certified copy of the merger deed with each of the Commercial Registers (*see infra* Chapter 11.1.a) with which filings have been made by any of the corporations involved[47].

---

40   BW art. 2:331.
41   Their recommendations must be deposited for shareholder inspection (*see* ii above).
42   BW art. 2:322.
43   BW art. 2:319(1).
44   BW art. 2:332.
45   BW art. 2:318(1).
46   BW art. 2:318(2).
47   BW art. 2:318(3).

e   **"Short-Form" Merger.** A "short-form" merger, with simplified procedures, is available, *inter alia*, for upstream mergers of a corporation with a wholly-owned subsidiary and for "sister mergers", *i.e.* statutory mergers between two or more wholly-owned subsidiaries[48].

The simplified procedures for a "short-form" merger entail exemptions for: (i) the items in the merger plan mentioned above in paragraph d.i under (j) through (m); (ii) the approval of the plan of merger by the supervisory directors; (iii) the explanatory memorandum for the absorbed corporation[49]; (iv) the valuation statements in the explanatory memorandum; and (v) the auditors' reports (*see supra* Chapter 10.3.d.ii)[50].

10.4   Statutory Split-Ups (*Juridische Splitsingen*)[51]

a   **Introduction**

i   *General.* By the end of 1997 a statute was adopted[52] (hereinafter: the "Split-Up Act") amending *inter alia* the Civil Code with respect to the implementation of the Sixth Company Law Directive (*see supra* Chapter 1.3.f). This new legislation will come into force on February 1, 1998. In this paragraph references to articles are references to articles of the Civil Code.

Statutory split-ups may take place between N.V.s, B.V.s, associations, co-operatives, mutuals and foundations (*see supra* Chapter 2.5.a and b), provided that in the latter three cases as a general rule the parties to the split-up have the same legal form[53]. Only the forms of split-ups involving N.V.s and B.V.s as constituent legal entities are discussed here. Under Dutch law, a split-up involving Dutch and foreign legal persons is not possible.

---

48   BW art. 2:333(2).
49   This exemption does not apply if other parties than the surviving corporation have a special right *vis-à-vis* the corporation ceasing to exist, such as profit rights or share rights.
50   BW art. 2:333; 2:313(3)
51   This paragraph has been prepared by Jan-Erik Janssen of Loeff Claeys Verbeke, Amsterdam office.
52   Statute of December 24, 1997 S. 776
53   BW arts. 2:308, 2:334b(1),(3). BW art. 2:334b(4) provides for an exception to this general rule.

Although a statutory split-up can take several forms (*see* ii below), it basically entails the absorption of the whole or a distinct part of the business of a corporation by one or more other corporations (the recipient corporations) through the exchange of shares. For consideration other than in shares, *see infra* Chapter 10.4.c. By means of a statutory split-up economic groups can be restructured or broken-up and joint ventures formed or terminated by means of one single legal act whereby assets and liabilities are transferred by operation of law.

An amendment to the tax legislation that will *inter alia* provide for a roll-over exemption in the case of a split-up is pending before Parliament as well[54].

To a certain extent a statutory split-up is the mirror of a statutory merger. In particular, this is the case with respect to the prescribed procedure (*see infra* Chapter 10.4.d). Moreover, the consultation requirements with the trade unions and Works Councils (*see supra* Chapter 10.3.a.iii) are similarly applicable in the context of split-ups. However, whereas in a statutory merger one or more businesses are transferred in their entirety to one corporation, in a statutory split-up there may often be a transfer of part of the assets and liabilities of a corporation to more than one recipient corporation. This requires specific forms of protection for third parties (*see infra* Chapter 10.4.f).

ii   *Types of Statutory Split-Ups.* The Split-Up Act distinguishes between two different methods of a split-up: the division (*zuivere splitsing*) and the demerger (*afsplitsing*)[55].

In a division two or more recipient corporations absorb all assets and liabilities of an existing corporation (the dividing corporation), such that the dividing corporation by operation of law ceases to exist as a distinct corporation[56]. As a general rule, the shares of the dividing corporation are exchanged for shares in the recipient corporations (for exceptions, *see infra* Chapter 10.4.c). A species of this form is the "qualified division" whereby different shareholders of the dividing corporation receive shares in different recipient corporations[57].

---

54   No. 25709
55   BW art. 2:334a(1).
56   BW art. 2:334a(2).
57   BW art. 2:334cc.

In a demerger one or more recipient corporations absorb the whole, or a distinct part, of the assets and liabilities of an existing corporation (the demerging corporation), whereby the demerging corporation does *not* cease to exist as a distinct corporation (such corporation after the demerger hereinafter: the surviving corporation). In a demerger the shareholders of the demerging corporation receive shares in one or more of the recipient corporations or one more recipient corporations will be incorporated by the demerging corporation in the demerger[58]. For "short-form" demergers, with simplified procedures, *see infra* Chapter 10.4.e.

In a triangular split-up, the shares of the dividing or demerging corporation are by operation of law exchanged for shares in a third corporation that belongs to the same group (*see supra* Chapter 3.1.b) as the recipient corporation[59]. All of the shares of the recipient corporation must be held by the group company, either alone or together with another corporation in the group of the recipient corporation[60]. For "short form" demergers, with simplified procedures, *see infra* Chapter 10.4.f).

In both a division or a demerger, the recipient corporations can be existing corporations or can be incorporated at the time of the split-up. While the Split-Up Act defines the splitting, dividing or demerging corporation and every recipient corporation (with the exception of corporations that are incorporated at the time of the split-up) as a "party to the split-up"[61], hereinafter such parties to the split-up may also be referred to as "corporations involved".

b   **Legal Effects.** Upon the split-up taking effect, by operation of law:
a   the dividing corporation ceases to exist (by its nature only in case of a division)[62];
b   the transferred assets and liabilities of the dividing or demerging corporation are absorbed by the recipient corporation(s), thereby becoming part of its or their respective assets and liabilities[63];

58   BW art. 2:334a(3).
59   BW art. 2:334ii(1).
60   BW art. 2:334ii(2).
61   BW art. 2:334a(4).
62   BW art. 2:334c(1).
63   BW art. 2:334a(2),(3).

c except in certain limited cases defined by law (*see infra* Chapter 9.10.4.c) the shareholders of the splitting corporation become shareholders of (all) the recipient corporation(s)[64].

c   Consideration. A statutory split-up is essentially an exchange of shares, and cash is used only to account for exchange rate discrepancies, such as when the value of each newly issued share in the share capital of the recipient corporation(s) is less than the value of each share in the splitting corporation. The total amount of cash or promissory notes involved in the transaction cannot exceed 10% of the aggregate nominal value of the newly issued share capital[65]. In making payments in cash to third party minority shareholders, the good faith requirements (*see supra* Chapter 9.2.c), in this context meaning the requirement of equal treatment of shareholders should be applied to the extent possible (*cf. supra* Chapter 10.3.c.i).

No shares in the capital of a recipient corporation will be received for shares in the capital of a splitting corporation that are held by or on behalf of such recipient or splitting corporation[66]. Furthermore, the shareholders of the splitting corporation will not become shareholders of all the recipient corporations (a) in case the recipient corporations are incorporated at the time of the split-up and the splitting corporation will receive all their shares, (b) in case of a "qualified division" or (c) in case of a triangular split-up (*see supra* Chapter 10.4.a.ii)[67].

The split-up deed (*see infra* Chapter 10.4.d.iv) may provide for a cancellation by a recipient corporation of shares in its own capital that it holds or will receive pursuant to the split-up, but not in excess of the total nominal value of the newly issued share capital. The detailed statutory provisions for a reduction of issued capital (*see supra* Chapter 4.6) are not applicable here[68].

d   Procedure

i   *Split-Up Plan.* The "split-up plan" (*voorstel tot splitsing*) is a joint proposal by the management boards of the corporations involved[69]. It

---

64   BW art. 2:334e(1).
65   BW art. 2:334x(2).
66   BW art. 2:334e(2).
67   BW art. 2:334e(3).
68   BW art. 2:334x(3).
69   BW art. 2:334f(1).

forms the basis for the notarial deed that completes the split-up procedure. The plan must be signed by all managing directors and approved and signed by all supervisory directors, where applicable[70]. If a director fails to sign, a reasoned explanation of this refusal is required[71].

The plan must describe in detail the proposed actions, including, as a minimum[72]:

a   the legal form, name and statutory seat of the corporations involved and the corporations to be incorporated at the time of the split-up, where applicable;

b   the articles of the recipient corporations and the surviving corporation in their then existing form and in their form after the split-up or, if the recipient corporations are newly established, the draft deed of incorporation;

c   whether all assets and liabilities of the splitting corporation will be transferred or only part thereof;

d   a description on the basis of which it can be accurately determined which assets and liabilities of the splitting corporation will be transferred to each of the recipient corporations and, if not all assets and liabilities of the splitting corporation will be transferred, which assets and liabilities will remain with the surviving corporation, as well as a pro forma profit and loss account of the recipient corporations and the surviving corporation;

e   the value of the assets and liabilities that each of the recipient corporations will receive and of the assets and liabilities that will remain with the surviving corporation, as well as the value of the shares in the capital of the recipient corporations that the surviving corporation will receive in the split-up;

f   the rights or compensatory payments which are chargeable to the recipient corporations and which are granted to persons who, other than as shareholders, have special rights *vis-à-vis* the splitting corporation, such as profit rights or share subscription rights, and their effective date;

g   the benefits in connection with the split-up, conferred on managing or supervisory directors of the corporations involved or other persons involved in the split-up;

h   the proposed composition of the management boards and the supervisory boards of the recipient corporations and the surviving corporation, where applicable;

---

70   BW art. 2:334f(3),(4).
71   BW art. 2:334f(3),(4).
72   BW arts. 2:334f(2),(4), 2:334y.

i   the effective date from which financial information regarding the relevant parts of the assets and liabilities to be transferred shall be incorporated in the annual accounts of the recipient corporations;
j   the proposed measures in connection with the receipt by the shareholders of the splitting corporation of shares of the recipient corporations;
k   the proposed continuation or discontinuation of business activities;
l   who must approve the split-up resolution;
m the proposed exchange ratio for the shares, and any cash consideration;
n   the date from which and extent to which the shareholders of the splitting corporation will share in the profits of the recipient corporations;
o   the number of shares that will be cancelled (*see supra* Chapter 9.10.4.c);
p   the impact of the split-up on the amounts of goodwill and the distributable reserves of the recipient corporations and the surviving corporation.

In case of a "qualified division" the split-up plan also states which shareholders will become shareholders in the respective recipient corporations[73].

ii   *Supporting documents.* The split-up plan must be supported by an explanatory memorandum prepared by the management boards of each corporation involved. This memorandum must describe the reasons for the split-up and must comment on the legal, economic and employment ramifications of the split-up[74]. It must also explain: the method or methods applied in determining the exchange ratio for the shares[75]; whether such method or methods are justified under the circumstances; the valuation resulting from each method applied, and, if more than one method has been applied, whether the relative weights attributed to the valuation methods applied may be considered generally acceptable; and whether there have been any specific difficulties in the valuation and the determination of the exchange ratio[76]. In case

---

73   BW art. 2:334cc sub a.
74   BW art. 2:334g(1).
75   In case shares, or depository receipts issued therefor, of a splitting corporation are listed on a stock exchange, the exchange ratio may be made dependent on the price of the shares (or depository receipts) on that exchange at one or more dates preceding the split-up date and determined in the split-up proposal (BW art. 2:334x(1)).
76   BW art. 2:334z.

of a "qualified division" the memorandum also states the criteria for the allocation of the shareholders between the respective recipient corporations[77].

If more than six months of a corporation's financial year have lapsed by the time the split-up plan was filed at the Commercial Register (*see infra* Chapter 11.1.a), its management board must prepare either annual accounts or an interim statement of assets and liabilities as of a date which is not earlier than the first day of the third month preceding the month of filing[78].

Each corporation must retain an auditor to examine the split-up plan and certify whether in his opinion the exchange ratio for the shares is reasonable[79]. In case of a demerger the auditor must also certify that the value of the assets and liabilities that shall remain with the surviving corporation, together with the value of the shares in the capital of the recipient corporations to be received pursuant to the demerger, is as a minimum equal to the issued and called up part of the capital, increased by the reserves that the corporation must have by law or the articles immediately following the demerger[80]. The auditor must further render an opinion on the statements made in the explanatory memorandum with respect to the valuation method or methods[81]. The auditors must have access to the books and records of all parties to the split-up[82]. In case of a "qualified division" the auditor must also certify that the allocation of the shareholders of the dividing corporation between the respective recipient corporations is reasonable[83].

Each corporation involved must file with the Commercial Register (*see infra* Chapter 11.1.a) the split-up plan, the annual accounts for the three preceding years together with the relevant auditors' opinions, the annual reports for the three preceding years, and any interim statements or annual accounts not yet adopted (*see* above)[84]. These documents, together with the explanatory memorandum, as well as any advice or recommendations of the Works Council and the trade unions, where applicable, must also be deposited at the corpo-

---

77   BW art. 2:334cc sub b.
78   BW art. 2:334g(2).
79   BW art. 2:334aa(1).
80   BW art. 2:334aa(2).
81   BW art. 2:334aa(3).
82   BW art. 2:334aa(5).
83   BW art. 2:334cc sub c.
84   BW art. 2:334h(1).

rations' head offices for inspection by shareholders and others who have a special right *vis-à-vis* the corporation[85]. A notice that the filings have been made must be published in a daily newspaper with national circulation[86].

iii *Authorisation.* As a general rule, a split-up vote must be taken by the shareholders' meeting[87]. No vote can be taken on the split-up within the one-month period following the publication in a national newspaper referred to above under ii (for timing, *see* iv below)[88]. A split-up vote is similar to a vote to amend the articles (*see supra* Chapter 10.2), except that if less than one-half of the issued capital is represented at the shareholders' meeting, a qualified majority of two-thirds of the votes is required[89]. A split-up vote for a "qualified division" can only be taken by a majority of three-fourths of the votes cast in a meeting where at least 95% of the issued capital is represented[90].

A recipient corporation may authorise the split-up by resolution of its management board, provided that this procedure is not opposed by shareholders representing 5% or more of its issued capital, and provided the articles so permit and the intention to do so has been stated in the notice of deposit referred to above under ii. The same applies to a demerging corporation, provided all recipient corporations are incorporated at the time of the demerger and the demerging corporation will become their sole shareholder[91].

iv *Timing.* The Works Council, where applicable and, if the Merger Rules apply, the trade unions have the right to be consulted well in advance of the vote or the authorisation (*see supra* Chapter 10.3.a.iii)[92].

The split-up is completed by the execution of a deed before a Dutch civil-law notary, effective the following day[93]. If an amendment to

---

85 BW art. 2:334h(2),(4).
86 BW art. 2:334h(3).
87 BW art. 2:334m(1). The shareholders' meeting does not have the power to amend the split-up plan (*id.*)
88 BW art. 2:334m(2).
89 BW arts. 2:334m(3), 2:334ee(1).
90 BW art. 2:334cc sub d.
91 BW art. 2:334ff.
92 Their recommendations must be deposited for shareholder inspection (*see* ii above).
93 BW art. 2:334n(1). The description of assets and liabilities referred to in paragraph i under (d) above is attached to the deed (BW art. 2:334n(2)).

the articles of the recipient corporations is required, a certificate of no-objection (*see supra* Chapter 3.3.b.iv) must be obtained from the Ministry of Justice prior to the execution of the notarial split-up deed[94].

The deed cannot be executed until any creditor opposition (*see infra* Chapter 10.4.f) has been withdrawn or upon a court order setting aside such opposition has become enforceable[95]. The notarial deed must be executed within six months after the notice of deposit referred to above under ii or, in case this in not allowed as a result of creditor opposition, within one month following the withdrawal or setting aside of such creditor opposition[96]. The civil-law notary is responsible for compliance with the mandatory statutory requirements and the requirements of the articles and must render an opinion that all requirements have been satisfied[97]. Within an eight-day period following the execution of the split-up deed, each of the recipient corporations and the surviving corporation, where applicable, must file a certified copy of the split-up deed with the competent Commercial Registers (*see infra* Chapter 11.1.a)[98].

e   "Short-Form" Demerger. A "short-form" demerger, with simplified procedures, is available for demergers in which all recipient corporations are incorporated at the time of the demerger and the demerging corporation will become their sole shareholder pursuant to the demerger[99].

The simplified procedures for a "short-form" split-up entail exemptions for: (i) the items in the split-up plan mentioned above in paragraph d.i under (m) through (o); (ii) the approval of the split-up plan by the supervisory directors; (iii) the valuation statements in the explanatory memorandum; and (iv) the auditors' reports[100].

f   Third Party Protection. To a large extent third parties derive protection from the detailed procural rules for a split-up. However, the Split-

---

94 BW art. 2:334gg.
95 BW art. 2:334l(3).
96 BW art. 2:334n(1).
97 BW art. 2:334n(2).
98 BW art. 2:334n(3). With respect to the corporation that has disappeared as a result of a division, this obligation lies on each of the recipient corporations.
99 BW art. 2:334hh.
100 BW art. 2:334hh.

Up Act contains specific additional provisions with respect to third party protection.

Firstly, contractual relations whereby the splitting corporation is a party can only be transferred in their entirety[101]. However, if a contractual relation is inherent to assets or liabilities that will be transferred to different recipient corporations, the contractual relation may be split between the recipient corporations pro rata to its connection with the assets and liabilities that each recipient corporation will receive[102].

Secondly, upon request of a creditor of one of the parties to the split-up, at least one of the corporations involved must provide security for, or otherwise guarantee, the payment of his claim. This is not required if the payment of the creditor's claim is sufficiently secured or if the financial condition of the debtor after the split-up does not provide less security for the payment of the claim[103]. During a one-month period following the notice of deposit by the corporations involved (*see supra* Chapter 10.4.d.ii), a party to a contract with any of them may, by filing a petition with the District Court, oppose the split-up proposal on the grounds that it infringes the allocation rules with respect to his contractual relation or that the requested security or guarantee was not given[104].

Thirdly, pledgees and beneficiaries of a life interest in shares of the splitting corporation will, as a general rule, receive a similar right in shares of the recipient corporations[105]. Alternatively, a person who, other than as a shareholder, has a special right *vis-à-vis* a splitting corporation, such as profit rights or share subscription rights, must either receive (i) rights in the recipient corporations that, together with the rights *vis-à-vis* the surviving corporation (where applicable), are equivalent to his rights prior to the split-up, or (ii) compensation[106].

---

101 BW art. 2:334j(1).
102 BW art. 2:334j(2). The same principle applies to contractual relations that are partly connected to assets and liabilities that will remain with the surviving corporation (BW art. 2:334j(3)).
103 BW art. 2:334k.
104 BW art. 2:334l(1). Prior to its ruling, the court may enable the corporations involved to amend their split-up proposal (and publish the same in accordance with the publication requirements discussed above in Chapter 10.4.d.ii) or to give a security or guarantee (BW art. 2:334l(2)).
105 BW art. 2:334o(1). In case of a surviving corporation, the existing pledge or life estate will remain in place (*id.*)
106 BW art. 2:334p(1).

Fourthly, parties to contracts with a party to the split-up may have their contracts amended or rescinded by court order and damages may be awarded[107].

Fifthly, the Split-Up Act contains detailed rules in case the description of assets and liabilities is not clear about their allocation. In case all the assets and liabilities of the splitting corporation have been transferred, the recipient corporations are jointly entitled to the assets and jointly and severally liable for the debts[108]. With respect to the assets the entitlement of each recipient corporation is proportional to the value of its part of the assets and liabilities received. In case not all the assets and liabilities have been transferred, the entitlement to the assets lies with the surviving corporation[109].

Finally, the Split-Up Act provides that the recipient corporations and the surviving corporation are jointly liable for the performance of the obligations of the surviving corporation at the time of the demerger[110]. For indivisible obligations this liability is several[111]. For divisible obligations either the recipient corporation or the surviving corporation, depending on whom the obligation was transferred to, is liable for the whole[112]. For other corporations, liability for divisible obligations is limited to the value of the assets and liabilities received or retained in the split-up[113].

10.5 Adoption of Different Legal Form (*Omzetting*)

An N.V. can be converted into a B.V. and a B.V. into an N.V. by amending the articles[114]. The required certificate of no objection from the Ministry of Justice (*see supra* Chapter 3.3.b.iv) concerns the conversion and the amendments of the articles[115]. The amendment must incorporate all statutory provisions specifically required for the newly-adopted corporate form. The conversion does not in any way affect the identity or contin-

---

107 BW art. 2:334r(1),(3).
108 BW art. 2:334s(2),(4).
109 BW art. 2:334s(3).
110 BW art. 2:334t(1).
111 BW art. 2:334t(2).
112 BW art. 2:334t(3).
113 BW art. 2:334t(3). These other corporations are required to perform these obligations only upon failure of the recipient corporation or the surviving corporation to do so (BW art. 2:334t(4)).
114 BW arts. 2:18(1),(2), 2:72(1)/183(1).
115 BW arts. 2:72(1)(a)/183(1)(a), 2:72(2)(a)/183(2)(a).

ued existence of the corporation[116], and it continues to have the same assets and liabilities, tax status, managing directors, and, where applicable, supervisory directors. Associations, co-operatives, mutuals and foundations (*stichtingen*) can also be converted into N.V.s or B.V.s, and *vice versa*. For the conversion of a *stichting* to another legal entity, the conversion of another legal entity to a *stichting*, and the conversion of an N.V. or B.V. to an association, the conversion is subject to court approval[117].

For a conversion of an N.V. to a B.V., and *vice versa*, the law requires an opinion of a Dutch registered accountant that confirms that the equity on a date within the five-month period preceding the conversion date was equal or in excess of the issued and called up capital[118]. A similar provision exists for all other types of conversions[119].

10.6 Sale of Assets; Dissolution; Winding Up

a   Sale of Assets. A sale of all or substantially all of the corporation's assets may preclude the corporation from continuing the business it has been operating. There is no statutory provision covering this specific event, but certain legal commentators consider it a matter outside of the realm of powers of the management board and consider this an action equivalent to dissolution of the corporation, which requires a shareholders' resolution[120]. The question as to whether the transfer conflicts with the corporation's purposes has limited importance in practice, as an action on the basis of *ultra vires* (*see supra* Chapter 3.6) can only be instituted by the corporation itself. However, any minority shareholder of the seller may challenge the sale of the seller's business to an acquiror on the basis of an alleged violation of the good faith requirements (*see supra* Chapter 9.2.c). Such claim is more likely to be successful if the majority shareholder has a special relationship with the acquiror that would benefit from a sale on terms other than at arm's length. To avoid legal disputes, it may be advisable to have the business to be transferred appraised by an independent expert.

---

116 Judgment of July 17, 1980, Ger. Amsterdam, 1981 NJ No. 214.
117 BW art. 2:18(4).
118 BW arts. 2:72(1)(b)/183(1)(b).
119 BW arts. 2:72(2)(b)/183(2)(b).
120 ASSER-MAEIJER 2, III, *supra* p. 2 at note 7, §§ 258, 259; HANDBOEK, *supra* p. 2 at note 7, § 231.

b   Dissolution

i   *Voluntary Dissolution.* Shareholders may vote to have the corporation dissolved[121], with the result that the liquidation proceeds will be distributed to shareholders in accordance with the articles. Certain shareholders, usually owners of preference shares, may have preferential rights to these distributions. Unless the articles require a qualified majority, any affirmative vote of the shareholders' meeting is sufficient to bring the corporation into a state of dissolution. The action is irreversible. There are no special statutory notice or quorum requirements. For an N.V. or B.V. that is not "large", no authorisation by the management board or the supervisory board is required, unless the articles provide otherwise. "Large" corporations can only be dissolved upon approval of the supervisory board[122].

ii   *Involuntary Dissolution.* The law does not require a corporation to be dissolved once it becomes insolvent[123]. However, any creditor, or the corporation, may file for bankruptcy once the corporation fails to pay two or more of its creditors[124]. Unless the articles provide otherwise, the management board requires an affirmative vote of the shareholders, authorising it to file for bankruptcy (in the sense of a liquidation)[125]. This shareholders' vote is also required when the corporation has the status of a "large" corporation (*see supra* Chapter 7.2.a.ii), in which case the prior approval of the supervisory board must also be obtained[126]. For the liability of managing directors and supervisory directors in case of bankruptcy, *see supra* Chapter 8.2.d. Bankruptcy (in the sense of liquidation) has the effect of dissolving the corporation.

A court may also order the dissolution of a corporation in an action brought by the public prosecutor in the event that the corporation has an illegal purpose[127], and also by an action of an interested party, if, *inter alia*, its articles do not comply with the statutory requirements or the corporation is grossly violating either its articles[128] or the critical

---

121   BW art. 2:19(1)(a).
122   BW arts. 2:164(1)(h)/274(1)(h).
123   Once the equity of an N.V. falls below 50% of its issued capital, the management board must convene a shareholders' meeting to discuss appropriate steps (BW art. 2:108a).
124   Faillissementswet [Fw.] (Bankruptcy Act) art. 1, 1983 S. 140, *as amended.*
125   BW arts. 2:136/246.
126   BW arts. 2:164(1)(i)/274(1)(i).
127   BW art. 2:20(2).
128   BW art. 2:21(1).

rules concerning the preservation of capital or the rules concerning the minimum capital (*see supra* Chapter 4.3.b)[129], or if the corporation is no longer in a financial position to conduct business in accordance with its purposes, or is no longer in business[130]. This latter provision is of particular importance in view of the current trend of dissolving "dormant" corporations, thereby precluding founders from using corporate vehicles which have not been properly screened through the process of obtaining a certificate of no objection (*see supra* Chapter 3.3.b). The public prosecutor will notify the competent Chamber of Commerce of its intention to bring an action for dissolution of the company[131]. This provision intends to co-ordinate actions by the public prosecutor and the Chamber of Commerce, which has recently been given the power to dissolve dormant companies by an administrative decision in order to combat fraud and clean-up its registers.

The Chamber of Commerce (*see infra* Chapter 11.1.a) must dissolve a corporation, co-operative or mutual upon the occurrence of two or more of the following conditions[132]:

a the legal entity has not paid its filing fees for one year or more after registration;

b the legal entity has not registered any managing directors for one year or more, or the managing director has deceased, could not be reached for one year or more at the address registered with the Commercial Register, nor at the register of his municipality, or his address was not registered at all with the Commercial Register for one year or more;

c the legal entity has not published its annual accounts in accordance with the law; or

d the legal entity has not complied with the obligation to file a return for corporate income tax for one year or more.

For registered associations or foundations that do not conduct a registered business enterprise (*see supra* Chapter 2.5.a.vii and Chapter 2.5.b), the non-payment of the respective filing fees in combination with one of the events mentioned above under (b) will trigger an action for dissolution by the Chamber of Commerce[133]. The Chamber of Commerce must notify the legal entity and its registered managing directors of its intention to take the dissolution action, including the

129 BW arts. 2:74(2)/185(2).
130 BW arts. 2:74(1)/185(1).
131 BW arts. 2:75(1)/185(1).
132 BW art. 2:19a(1).
133 BW art. 2:19a(2).

grounds for such action and will publish this notification in the Government Gazette. If the legal entity has not properly registered any managing directors for a period of one year or more, as outlined under (b) above, the Chamber of Commerce will also publish this event in the Government Gazette[134]. Unless the grounds for dissolution have been remedied timely, the Chamber of Commerce will dissolve the legal entity by administrative decision after a period of eight weeks following the date of notification[135]. The administrative decision can be appealed against at the Court of Appeal from Decisions of the SER, Product and Trade Boards (*College van Beroep voor het bedrijfsleven*)[136].

The public prosecutor, or an interested party, may also petition the court to order dissolution if the corporation was formed in violation of the rules concerning the formation of corporations[137] or to order nullification of a purported corporation if business was conducted in the name of a corporation that was never formed[138]. The Enterprise Chamber can also order the corporation dissolved if an investigation into the affairs of the corporation shows mismanagement and the Chamber deems dissolution the most appropriate solution (*see supra* Chapter 9.2.b)[139].

c   **Winding Up.** Upon dissolution other than in the context of bankruptcy, the corporate affairs must be wound up by a receiver. In case of a voluntary dissolution, the articles will usually empower the shareholders' meeting to appoint the receiver in charge of the winding up process. (*see supra* Chapter 10.6.b.i). If no receiver is appointed or designated, the managing directors will serve as receivers of the estate of the dissolved company[140]. If no receivers can be appointed or designated on the basis of the above, the Chamber of Commerce will serve as the receiver[141]. The estate of a company dissolved by court order (*see supra* Chapter 10.6.b.ii) will be wound up by one or more receivers appointed by the court[142]. If the corporation is dissolved by court order, the receiver will be designated in the order.

---

134 BW art. 2:19a(3).
135 BW art. 2:19a(4). The administrative decision will be notified to the legal entity and its registered managing directors, if any (BW art. 2:19a(5)).
136 BW art. 2:19a(8).
137 BW art. 2:21(1)(a).
138 BW art. 2:4(1),(3).
139 BW art. 2:356(f).
140 BW art. 2:23(1).
141 BW art. 2:19a(7).
142 BW art. 2:23(1).

After discharging all liabilities of the corporation, or making adequate provisions for discharge, the corporation may distribute the remainder of its assets to its shareholders[143]. In the event of disputed creditors or claims, and unidentifiable shareholders, the receiver may, after a certain period of time, deposit funds with the court that are adequate to meet these claims to the extent they are entitled to share in the distribution[144].

The receiver must file a plan of distribution at both the offices of the corporation and the Commercial Register (*see infra* Chapter 11.1.a) and announce the filings in newspapers and, if required by the court, in the Government Gazette[145]. No distribution to creditors can be made before expiration of a two-month period after filing, during which time any interested party may object to the planned distribution[146]. Anticipated distribution may be suspended until the court rules on the objection[147].

The final accounting by the receiver must be filed and announced similarly in the plan of distribution[148]. If there is no objection to the final accounting, it is deemed approved. Objections are submitted to the jurisdiction of the District Court. After the final accounting has been approved, the corporation continues to exist to the extent necessary for the winding up process[149] and it remains open to suit[150].

10.7   Transfer of Seat (*Zetelverplaatsing*)

a   Extraordinary Events. Under Dutch law, the seat of a corporation must be in the Netherlands in order for it to be recognised as a Dutch corporation[151]. Normally, the transfer of the seat of a Dutch corporation to another country is not possible under Dutch law. However, upon the occurrence of certain "extraordinary" events, such as war, immediate danger of war, revolution and similar situations, a "transfer of seat" is possible

---

143   BW art. 2:23b(1).
144   BW art. 2:23b(8).
145   BW art. 2:23b(4). A violation of these provisions is a criminal offence, *see* WED art. 1(4).
146   BW art. 2:23b(5).
147   BW art. 2:23b(7).
148   BW art. 2:236(4).
149   BW art. 2:19(5).
150   BW art. 2:23c.
151   BW arts. 2:66(3)/177(3).

to other parts of the Kingdom, *i.e.*, the Netherlands Antilles and Aruba[152], or to other countries[153]. For a transfer of seat, the anticipated transfer must also be in "the interests of the corporation" (*see supra* Chapter 1.2)[154].

b   Transfer of Seat to Other Parts of the Kingdom of the Netherlands. The legal effect of this transfer of seat is somewhat similar to a conversion from an N.V. into a B.V. (*see supra* Chapter 10.5). The Dutch N.V. or B.V. becomes an Antillean N.V. or Aruban N.V., and from that moment is governed by the laws of the Netherlands Antilles or Aruba[155]. It continues, however, to be the same corporation and retains all of its assets and liabilities.

The procedure for this transfer of seat basically involves an amendment to the articles, subject to significantly different rules as compared to ordinary amendments (*see supra* Chapter 10.2). Whereas an ordinary amendment requires a certificate of no objection (*see supra* Chapter 3.3.b.iv), a transfer of seat requires either the "approval" of the Minister of Justice in the Netherlands prior to the execution of the transfer of seat deed, or the "confirmation" of the duly executed transfer of seat deed by the Minister of Justice in the Netherlands Antilles or Aruba, as the case may be[156]. The procedure for obtaining this governmental approval or confirmation is discussed below. The power to make the amendment is also different. While a regular amendment requires the authorisation of the shareholders' meeting[157], a resolution to transfer the seat may come from any of the following corporate bodies, at their option and without any specific provision to that effect being required in the articles: the shareholders' meeting, the management board[158], any person designated for the purpose by the shareholders' meeting or the management board[159], and each individual managing director[160].

The amendment must be incorporated in a transfer of seat deed which also restates the articles of the corporation under the laws of the Nether-

---

152 Rijkswet vrijwillige zetelverplaatsing van rechtspersonen [RVZ] (Act on Voluntary Transfer of Seat) art. 1(2), 1967 S. 161, *as amended.*
153 Wet vrijwillige zetelverplaatsing derde landen [WVZ] (Act on Voluntary Transfer of Seat to Third Countries) art. 1(1), 1994 S. 800.
154 RVZ art. 6(1)(a).
155 RVZ art. 18(1).
156 RVZ art. 3(1).
157 BW arts. 2:121(1)/231(1).
158 RVZ art. 1(2).
159 RVZ art. 1(3).
160 RVZ art. 1(6).

lands Antilles or Aruba[161]. The deed can also state who will be the managing directors upon the transfer of seat[162]. The seat transfer becomes effective upon the notarial execution of the transfer of seat deed, on the effective date stated in the deed, or on the occurrence of a certain condition specified in the deed[163]. The deed must be executed by a notary in either the Netherlands, the Netherlands Antilles, or Aruba[164]. The tax effects require close attention.

If at the time of the application for the approval no events have occurred that qualify as extraordinary events justifying the transfer (*see supra* Chapter 10.7.a), the approval of the Dutch Ministry of Justice may be granted conditionally, subject to the occurrence of such event[165]. A serious drawback of this approval procedure is that approval might subsequently be cancelled or revoked by any revolutionary government or a government that is under pressure from foreign political powers[166]. The alternative to the approval procedure is a confirmation by the Minister of Justice of the Netherlands Antilles or Aruba, as the case may be, that an extraordinary event has occurred. The application for confirmation must be made subsequent to the execution of the transfer of seat deed, and within thirty days after the occurrence of one or more of the extraordinary events[167]. If the confirmation is not obtained, the seat will automatically return to the Netherlands[168].

c **Transfer of Seat to Third Countries.** The procedure for the transfer of seat to countries outside the Kingdom of the Netherlands is similar to the procedure mentioned above in Chapter 10.7.b. The procedure can be applied by corporations, co-operatives, mutuals and foundations (*stichtingen*)[169]. No provisions with respect to the legal implications of the transfer of seat to third countries are given. The action to transfer the seat may come from the shareholders' meeting, the management board or any person designated for that purpose by the shareholders' meeting or the management board by means of a deed executed before a Dutch civil-law notary[170]. The action is subject to an extraordinary event referred to in

161 RVZ art. 8(1).
162 RVZ art. 1(8).
163 RVZ arts. 2(2), 21.
164 RVZ arts. 2(1), 21(1).
165 RVZ art. 6(1)(a), 6(3).
166 RVZ art. 7(1).
167 RVZ art. 5(1).
168 RVZ art. 5(2).
169 WVZ art. 1(1).
170 WVZ art. 2(1).

Chapter 10.7.a above. Any such action must either be in the form of a deed executed before a Dutch civil law notary, or be in compliance with such formalities required in the host country for an amendment of the articles. Upon transfer of seat, the legal person becomes a similar type of legal person in the country to which it has transferred its seat and is governed by the laws of that host country[171]. No approval of the Minister of Justice in the Netherlands is needed for the transfer to a third country. If the seat of the legal person is transferred back to the Netherlands, the legal person has to re-register in the Commercial Register and has to take on the same legal personality as it had prior to the transfer of seat[172]. The resolution to transfer of seat back to the Netherlands must be approved by the Minister of Justice. This approval will be refused only if (a) the re-transfer action is not in compliance with applicable law, (b) the articles violate Dutch corporate law, and (c), in case of an N.V. or B.V.: (i) the corporation does not meet the minimum capital rules (*see supra* Chapter 4.3.b), or (ii) there is danger, in light of the prior records of those who will determine or take part in the determination of the corporate policy, that the corporation will be used for unlawful activities, or that creditors will be prejudiced by its activities. The notarial deed containing the articles that will apply upon the re-transfer to the Netherlands must be executed before a Dutch civil-law notary[173].

171 WVZ art. 3(2).
172 WVZ art. 5(2).
173 WVZ art. 5(3).

11 COMMERCIAL REGISTER; PUBLIC FILINGS[1]

11.1 The Commercial Register

a   Introduction. The Netherlands is divided into districts, each having its own Chamber of Commerce and Industry, a non-governmental agency established under the Chamber of Commerce and Industry Act[2].

Each Chamber maintains an on-line Commercial Register. All Dutch and foreign-owned business organisations, corporations, EEIGs with their statutory seat in the Netherlands, general and limited partnerships, commercial agents, distributors and other commercial representatives meeting the requirements set forth in the Commercial Register Act 1996[3] must register and disclose an extensive amount of information. Corporations, mutuals, co-operatives, certain associations and foundations that conduct a business enterprise (*see supra* Chapter 2.5.a.vii and Ch 2.5.b) and limited partnerships, whose fully liable partners are foreign corporations, must also file their annual accounts[4]. The criteria vary, depending on the legal form in which the business is conducted or the agent is operating, but essentially all business forms, agents and representatives are subject to the registration requirements once they have an address in the Netherlands. The legal and commercial effects of these disclosures are significant. Third parties acting in good faith may rely on the filed statements, even if the filings are erroneous, or filed without proper corporate authority. The commercial effect is that disclosure makes it possible to analyse the financial strength of public and non-public corporations, including competitors, and that for almost every business operation, basic corporate information is freely accessible to outsiders.

b   Where to File. As a general rule, under the Commercial Register Act 1996, a legal person can suffice with a single filing in the district in which it has its official seat or its principal place of business[5].

---

1   This chapter was revised by Jan-Erik Janssen of Loeff Claeys Verbeke, Amsterdam office.
2   Wet op de Kamers van Koophandel en Fabrieken (Chambers of Commerce and Industry Act), 1963 S. 286, *as amended.*
3   HrW 1996 arts. 1,3,4.
4   BW arts. 2:394(1), 2:360.
5   HrW 1996 art. 6(1).

The information filed may be viewed at nominal cost by any person, without any requirement that a particular interest be demonstrated[6]. Copies of the filings and extracts from the filings of certain corporate information can also be obtained at nominal cost[7].

c   Registration Number on Letterhead. Each business organisation must state its registration number on its letterhead stationery, invoices, order forms, as well as any offering and tender documents[8].

d   Duty to Register. Each managing director, owner of a business enterprise, person responsible for the Dutch business or branch of a foreign organisation[9] is under a statutory duty to make filings within one week after the occurrence of any event that triggers the filing requirement[10].

The Chamber may also, at its own initiative, amend certain registrations concerning a business enterprise[11]. The Chamber of Commerce and every interested party may also petition the Cantonal Judge to rectify a registration[12].

In addition, the Enterprise Chamber may, at its own initiative or at the request of any interested person, require certain registrations to be made (*see supra* Chapter 9.2b). Compliance with the registration requirements is enforced by the Chamber of Commerce, and a violation of the provisions of the Commercial Register Act is a criminal offence[13].

11.2   Information to be Disclosed

Disclosures are made in the form of registrations and filings at the competent Commercial Register and in the form of publications that the Chamber makes in the Government Gazette. The publications in the

---

6   HrW 1996 art. 14; HrB 1996 art. 36.
7   HrW 1996 art. 15; HrB 1996 arts. 37,38.
8   HrW 1996 art. 25(1). A violation of this provision is a criminal offence, *see* WED art. 1(4).
9   HrW 1996 art. 5.
10   HrW 1996 art. 9.
11   HrW 1996 arts. 10,11. The Chamber must notify the person having the primary responsibility for filing thereof (HrW 1996 art. 10(4)).
12   HrW 1996 art. 23.
13   WED art. 1(4).

Government Gazette refer to the vast majority of the data that a corporation must file[14].

The information that must be registered and filed differs for the various legal forms in which a business enterprises can be conducted, and agents, distributors and other legal representatives are likewise subject to their own requirements.

For each business enterprise, principle place of business or Dutch branch of a foreign company, the following information must be filed[15]:

a trade name(s);

b address and, where applicable, post address (including, if possible, postal code), as well as the address of authorised trade agents representing the business enterprise in the Netherlands;

c telephone number, as well as, where applicable, facsimile number and e-mail address;

d summary of business activities;

e the commencement date of trading;

For business enterprises conducted in the form of corporations, the following additional information must be provided[16]:

a the name of the corporation and its statutory seat;

b personal data for each managing director and supervisory director, including the date on which these positions were obtained and whether the managing directors are solely or jointly authorised to represent the corporation (*see supra* Chapter 7.2d.iii);

c personal data for persons other than managing directors who have been granted the authority to represent the corporation, as well as the terms of such powers (*see supra* Chapter 7.2.d.iv);

d the authorised capital, as well as, at least once a year, the amount of the issued capital and the paid-up part thereof, divided by type of shares, where applicable;

e in case of issued shares that have not been fully paid-up: personal data for the holders of such shares, including the number of shares held by each such holder and the amounts contributed to such shares (changes in this information must be filed at least once a year);

f in case of an investment company with variable capital (*see supra* Chapter 3.1.c), changes in the registered capital must be filed at least once a year;

14   HrW 1996 art. 17(1).
15   HrB art. 9(1)
16   HrB art. 14(1)

g personal data for the holders of all shares in the capital of the corporation, disregarding the shares held by the corporation itself or any of its subsidiaries;

h where applicable, that the articles of the corporation are in conformity with the articles for a "large" corporation.

11.3 Legal Effect

Disclosures in the Commercial Register and the Government Gazette create a high degree of certainty about what third parties are presumed to know[17]. This statutory presumption is nevertheless subject to limitations. Information required to be disclosed may not be asserted against third parties who were not aware of it until this information is actually disclosed in accordance with the Commercial Register Act[18]. Furthermore, if a required publication was made in a Government Gazette that the third party could not possibly have read (*e.g.*, due to a postal strike), then the statutory presumption has no effect with respect to events that occurred during the fifteen days following the date of publication[19]. The corporation or owner of a business organisation cannot validly argue that a third party should not have relied on disclosed information that turns out to be erroneous or incomplete[20].

11.4 Filing Fees

The Chambers of Commerce are largely self-supporting as a result of which the Commercial Registers are dependent on registration fees from the parties making the filings, fees from third parties requesting information and annual registration levies[21]. The annual registration levies differ per Chamber, but remain within limits determined by Government Decree[22]. All relevant publications in the Government Gazette are made by the Chamber at the expense of the corporation concerned[23].

17   BW art. 2:6(4)
18   HrW 1996 art. 18(1), BW arts. 2:6(2), 3:61(3).
19   HrW 1996 art. 18(2).
20   HrW 1996 art. 18(3); BW art. 3:6(3).
21   HrW art. 22(1).
22   HrW 1996 arts. 19-22, HrB 1996 arts. 39-52.
23   HrW art. 30a(2).

12   EMPLOYEE PARTICIPATION, WORKS COUNCILS

12.1   General

Dutch law does not entitle employees to representation on the management board of an enterprise (no *Mittbestimmung*), nor does it entitle employees to determine the allocation of profits[1].

The most important body through which labour participation is exercised on an enterprise level is the Works Council, which possesses the powers vested in it by the Works Councils Act (WOR). An amendment[2] to the Works Councils Act is currently pending before Dutch Parliament and is expected to be adopted shortly. In this chapter references to the Works Councils Act are references to the amended Works Councils Act, assuming that the draft statute dated September 2, 1997 had been implemented. The Works Council is an integral part of corporate governance, and its mandatory involvement in decision-making processes makes it part of the Dutch laws of business organisations (*ondernemingsrecht*). A Works Council is mandatory for each enterprise in the Netherlands, regardless of its legal form or nationality, which has fifty or more employees[3].

The Dutch legislature has implemented the Directive for the European Works Council (*see supra* Chapter 1.3.g). A company having a Community-scale dimension may, instead of forming a European Works Council, comply with this directive by instituting certain information and consultation procedures, negotiated between that company and a so-called Special Negotiating Body (*see infra* Chapter 12.3.c). Compared with the powers of the Dutch Works Council, the powers of a statutory European Works Council are restricted (*see infra* Chapter 12.3.d.ii).

---

1   Reference is made to the following English language publications: E.P. JANSEN, "Labour", in: DUTCH BUSINESS LAW, *supra* p. 1 at note 3, Chapter 12 and L.G. VERBURG, Employee Participation; Works Councils in: DUTCH BUSINESS LAW, *supra* p. 1 at note 3, Chapter 11.
2   No. 24615.
3   WOR art. 2.(1) Currently, this threshold is set at 35 employees who are working more than one-third of the normal working hours in the relevant business enterprise.

12.2 Works Councils

a   Scope

i   *General.* The "entrepreneur", defined as the natural or legal person that maintains the qualifying business enterprise, must institute a Works Council[4]. For an incorporated business enterprise, the entrepreneur for purposes of the Works Councils Act is the corporation, represented by its management. For purpose of convenience, below we will refer to "management" or "the company" whenever a reference under the Works Councils Act is made to the "entrepreneur".

The Works Councils Act defines "enterprise" as: every organisation operating as an independent organisation in which work is performed on the basis of an employment agreement[5] or an appointment as civil servant (for this purpose, including persons employed by any governmental instrumentality on a contractual basis)[6]. Consequently, governmental agencies and non-profit organisations must also apply the Works Councils Act. Hereinafter, the term "enterprise" is confined to business enterprises only.

ii   *Applicability to Foreign Companies.* A Dutch enterprise may be owned by a Dutch company, or a foreign company through its Dutch branch office.

In conformity with the Dutch rules for the conflicts of law, only enterprises located in the Netherlands fall within the scope of the Works Councils Act; activities of a Dutch enterprise outside the Netherlands may be taken into account for the applicability of the Works Councils Act only if they are managed directly by the Dutch organisation and are considered activities inherently connected with the Dutch labour organisation[7].

---

4   WOR art. 1(1)(d).
5   Every person, that is not a civil servant, employed under Dutch law, under a contract or otherwise, is deemed to have an employment agreement, with the exception of temporary employees, contractors and independent consultants.
6   WOR art. 1(1)(c).
7   However, the Works Council of a Dutch enterprise has the right to render advice on proposed management actions relating to the establishment, takeover or relinquishment of control over a foreign enterprise, or to important modifications in the co-operation with or participation in such foreign enterprise, if it can reasonably be anticipated that the proposed action will have significant implications for the Dutch enterprise (WOR art. 25(1)(b); *see infra* Chapter 12.2.d.iii).

b   Joint, Group and Central Works Councils. If a company or a group of affiliated companies owns two or more enterprises employing fifty employees or more, it must set up a Joint Works Council for all or several of these enterprises "if this would advance the proper implementation of the Works Councils Act"[8]. Alternatively, the management of an enterprise with 100 employees or more must set up a separate Works Council for any substantial part of that enterprise if it would advance the proper implementation of the Works Council Act within its enterprise[9].

For the proper implementation of the Works Councils Act, the company or group which has established two or more Works Councils: (a) must establish a Central Works Council for the enterprises involved; and (b) in the case of more than two Works Councils within the same divisional structure of the enterprise, must establish a Group Works Council[10]. The Central or Group Works Council only handles matters which are of common interest to the enterprises they represent, irrespective of any powers of the Works Councils with respect thereto[11]. Any powers of the individual Works Councils with regard to matters of common interest are by operation of law vested in the Central or Group Works Councils, with the Group Works Councils in turn being subordinate to the Central Works Council[12].

This distribution of powers over Works Councils on the different levels of the corporate hierarchy has in the past lead to various conflicts between them[13].

c   Organisation

i   *Composition, Committees and Experts.* The Works Council consists of elected employees only, with a minimum of three members where

---

8   WOR art. 3(1),(2).
9   WOR art. 4(1).
10   WOR art. 33.
11   WOR art. 35(1).
12   WOR art. 35(2).
13   For example, in the case of an anticipated acquisition, the Central Works Council of the target may be inclined to give positive advice (*see infra* Chapter 12.2.d.iii) on the ground that the acquisition would be beneficial to the group of enterprises as a whole, while an individual Works Council of a certain enterprise may try to oppose the acquisition on the ground that the acquisition would be disadvantageous to that enterprise (*see* Judgment of August 30, 1984, Ger. Amsterdam (Enterprise Chamber), 1985 NJ No. 475). For the delineation of powers between the Works Councils, Group Works Councils and Central Works Councils, *see* Judgment of May 10, 1990, Ger. Amsterdam (Enterprise Chamber), 1992 NJ No. 126.

there are fewer than 50 persons employed by the enterprise, and a maximum of twenty-five members where there are 7,000 or more employees[14].

The Works Council may establish standing committees to address matters involving such groups of employees or issues as it may designate, committees for separate locations of the enterprise and committees to prepare certain issues to be dealt with by it[15].

The Works Council may invite one or more experts to attend a meeting[16].

ii *Election.* The members of the Works Council are elected by and must be employees of the enterprise[17]. They are elected from a list of candidates, which may be submitted by[18]:
    a a trade union which has among its members persons employed in the enterprise and qualified to vote; or
    b the lesser of thirty persons or one-third of the number of employees entitled to vote, who are not members of a trade union that have submitted a list of candidates as described under (a) above.

iii *Job Protection.* Except for "urgent cause", an employee who is a member of the Works Council, or who has a special relationship with the Works Council can not be dismissed without the approval of the Cantonal Court[19]. The court shall ensure that the reason for the dismissal shall not relate to the membership of the Works Council or any candidacy to be elected thereto.

iv *Secrecy.* The members of the Works Council, as well as its committees or experts retained (*see* i above), are under a strict obligation of secrecy[20]. The enforcement of this rule may depend on the traditions of the relevant Works Council and the actions that the management took on previous occasions to counter any secrecy infringements.

---

14 WOR art. 6(1).
15 WOR art. 15.
16 WOR art. 16(1).
17 WOR art. 6(1). The members of the Works Council are elected by employees of at least six months' standing (WOR art. 6(2)). Membership is open only to employees with at least one year's standing (WOR art. 6(3)).
18 WOR art. 9(2).
19 WOR art. 21
20 WOR art. 20(1).

d   Powers of the Works Council

i   *General.* The Works Council and its committees are entitled to receive from management all information reasonably required for the performance of their duties, including financial and business information and information on social policies[21].

ii   *Consultation Process.* Consultations between management and the Works Council take place at consultation meetings within two weeks following a request thereto of either the management or the Works Council[22]. The general business of the enterprise must be discussed at least two times per calendar year[23]. At these meetings, management must inform the Works Council about any actions that are being prepared with respect to matters requiring prior consultation with, or consent of, the Works Council (*see* iii and iv below). It shall be agreed at what moment and in which manner the Works Council shall be engaged in decision-making with respect thereto[24].

iii   *Matters Requiring Prior Consultation.* Management must give the Works Council the opportunity to render *advice* on any proposed action[25] involving[26]:

a   the transfer of control over the enterprise or any part thereof;

b   the establishment, take-over or relinquishment of control over another enterprise or the formation, substantial modification, or discontinuation of any long-term co-operation with other enterprises, including the formation, substantial modification or discontinuation of a substantial financial participation by or on behalf of such enterprise;

c   the discontinuation of the activities of the enterprise or of a major part of these activities;

d   a substantial change in the activities of the enterprise;

e   a substantial change in the organisation of the enterprise or in the allocation of responsibility within the enterprise;

---

21   WOR art. 31(1).
22   WOR art. 23(1). Management is represented by "the person who either alone or jointly with others in an enterprise, directly exercises the highest authority in the management of the work" (WOR arts. 1(1)(e), 23(4)).
23   WOR art. 24(1).
24   WOR art. 24(1)
25   The WOR specifically refers to "proposed decisions" of management. The term decisions in fact includes actions, whether or not formalised, for which management is responsible.
26   WOR art. 25(1).

f   a change of the location at which the enterprise carries on its activities;
g   the recruitment or subcontracting of groups of workers;
h   any major capital investment on behalf of the enterprise;
i   the seeking of substantial credit on behalf of the enterprise;
j   the granting of substantial credit and providing security for substantial debts of another company, unless within the ordinary course of business of the enterprise;
k   the introduction or modification of a major technological facility;
l   major measures of the enterprise regarding care for the environment, including introducing or modifying any policy and any organisational or administrative facility relating to the environment; and
m   the retention of and the terms of reference for any outside expert to provide advice on any of the foregoing matters.

In addition, management and the Works Council may, by an agreement to that effect (*see infra* Chapter 12.2.g), expand the list of matters that require the advice of the Works Council and the provisions of the Works Council will apply accordingly to these additional matters[27].

The substantiality test depends, *inter alia*, on the size and nature of the enterprise[28]. The provisions under (b) and (m) above, insofar as the latter relates to any matter referred to under (b), are not applicable if the other enterprise is or is to be established abroad, and if it can not be reasonably expected that the proposed management action will lead to changes under paragraphs (c) through (f) above with regard to an enterprise in the Netherlands (*see supra* Chapter 12.2.a.ii)[29].

Management must also seek the advice of the Works Council prior to any action involving the appointment or removal of a managing director of the enterprise[30]. However, the Works Council is not formally entitled to appeal against a decision by the entrepreneur to appoint or remove a managing director contrary to the Works Council's advice.

---

27   Judgment of March 17, 1993, HR, 1993 NJ No. 366.
28   A change in the activities of the enterprise that does not entail important and direct consequences may nevertheless be considered "substantial" for this purpose because of its long-term structural consequences (Judgment of February 19, 1981, Ger. Amsterdam (Enterprise Chamber), 1982 NJ No. 244).
29   WOR art. 25(1).
30   WOR art. 30(1).

Any request for advice must be made in writing and sufficiently early so that the advice may have a significant influence on the proposed action[31].

In practice, the decision as to when the Work Council's advice should be requested is not always an easy one. In the case of an anticipated acquisition or joint venture, advice must be sought prior to initialling or signing a binding letter of intent. However, the advice should not be requested too early either, as would be the case if the proposed action is not sufficiently clear and its consequences cannot be sufficiently assessed[32].

The request for the Works Council's advice must be accompanied by a detailed summary of the reasons for the proposed action, the anticipated consequences thereof to the employees of the enterprise and the proposed measures to be taken in relation thereto[33].

The Works Council may not render its advice until there has been at least one consultation meeting on the subject[34]. The Works Council must render its advice within a "reasonable" time, depending, *inter alia*, on the complexity of the matter, the urgency involved, and the speed with which the information had been provided by the entrepreneur.

Only following the date the Works Council has rendered its advice may the management take the proposed action. The Works Council must be notified promptly thereof in writing. If the Works Council's advice is not followed or is only partially followed, the Works Council shall be informed as to the reason why its advice was not followed[35]. In the latter case, the implementation of the action must be suspended for one full month following the notice[36]. During this one-month period, the Works Council is entitled to appeal against the action (*see infra* Chapter 12.2.f).

31   WOR arts. 25(2), 30(2).
32   Judgment of April 25, 1991, Ger. Amsterdam, 1992 NJ No. 271.
33   WOR art. 25(3). With respect to the proposed appointment or removal of a managing director, the entrepreneur must provide the Works Council with the reasons for the decision and, in the event of an appointment, with information on the basis of which the Works Council can form an opinion about the person involved with regard to his future position within the enterprise (WOR art. 30(3)).
34   WOR art. 25(4).
35   WOR art. 25(5).
36   WOR art. 25(6). Non-compliance with this suspension requirement is a criminal offence, *see* WED art. 1(4).

iv *Matters Requiring Prior Consent.* There are a number of matters that cannot be undertaken by management without the prior *consent* of the Works Council. These include the introduction, modification or repeal of[37]:

a arrangements involving pension funds, profit-sharing plans or savings plans;

b rules pertaining to working hours or vacation policy;

c remuneration or job classification systems;

d rules pertaining to safety, health or welfare in connection with work or absence through illness;

e rules pertaining to hire, dismissal or promotion policies;

f rules pertaining to employee training;

g rules pertaining to employee performance review;

h rules pertaining to industrial social work;

i rules pertaining to work consultation;

j rules pertaining to the handling of complaints;

k rules pertaining to the registration, use and protection of personal data of the enterprise's employees;

l rules pertaining to the facilities aimed at or suitable for observation or control of presence, behaviour or performance of the employees; and

m rules pertaining to the position of minors in the enterprise.

However, the Works Council is not required to approve matters if and to the extent that those matters which would ordinarily require the consent of the Works Council have already been covered by a collective bargaining agreement[38].

e   **Employee Participation in Small Enterprises**

i *Enterprises With Fewer Than 50 But At Least 10 Employees.* The management of an enterprise with ten or more, but fewer than fifty employees, and for which no Works Council has been established, is required to set up bi-annual meetings with its employees as a minimum[39].

Management must give the employees an opportunity to render advice on any proposed action that may lead to: (i) the loss of jobs, or (ii) an important change in the nature of work, the working conditions, or

---

37   WOR art. 27(1).
38   WOR art. 27(3).
39   WOR art. 35b.

the circumstances under which the work is performed for one-quarter or more of the employees[40].

If management takes action contrary to the advice of its employees, it is not required to suspend the implementation of the action Moreover, the employees may not appeal against any such management action.

The Works Councils Act provides for an optional adoption of a body for employee representation (*personeelsvertegenwoordiging*), consisting of a minimum number of three persons[41]. However, at the request of the majority of the employees, management must institute such body[42]. The *personeelsvertegenwoordiging* must consent to any introduction, modification or repeal of rules pertaining to (a) working hours or vacation policy, and (b) safety, health or welfare in connection with work or absence through illness (*see supra* Chapter 12.2.d.iv under (b) and (d))[43].

The WOR provides for a statutory basis for the granting of additional powers to the *personeelsvertegenwoordiging*[44].

ii *Enterprises With Fewer Than 10 Employees.* The management of an enterprise with fewer than 10 employees and for which no Works Council has been established may institute a *personeelsvertegenwoordiging* as discussed above under i. Any *personeelsvertegenwoordiging* must consent to any introduction, modification or repeal of rules pertaining to working hours or vacation policy (*see supra* Chapter 12.2.d.iv under (b))[45].

The WOR provides for a statutory basis for the granting of additional powers to any *personeelsvertegenwoordiging*[46].

f   Appeal and Risks of Non-Compliance

i *Appeal Regarding Consultation Matters.* If management has decided to pursue an action involving one of the matters requiring formal consultation of a Works Council (*see supra* Chapter 12.2.d.iii) that is

40 WOR art. 35b(5).
41 WOR art. 35c.
42 WOR art. 35c(2).
43 WOR arts. 27(1), 35c(3).
44 WOR arts. 32, 35c(3).
45 WOR arts. 27(1), 35d(2).
46 WOR arts. 32, 35d(2)

contrary to the advice rendered by that Works Council, or if facts or circumstances become known which, had they been known to the Works Council at the time its advice was rendered, might have led to a different result, the Works Council may appeal to the Enterprise Chamber within one month following management's written notice of its action (*see supra* Chapter 9.2.a)[47].

During this one-month period management must suspend the implementation of its proposed action.

The only available ground for appeal is that management "could not reasonably have reached the decision had it weighed the interests involved"[48]. Because of this limited scope of appeal, appeals are not easily granted on substantive issues, but rather on procedural inadequacies which will almost invariably lead to the conclusion that the interests have been improperly weighed. If the Enterprise Chamber sustains any claim it may, *inter alia*, give an order requiring the entrepreneur to repeal the action, in whole or in part, and to reverse any specific effects of that action, with due respect to the acquired rights of third parties acting in good faith[49].

ii   *Non-Compliance with Consent Requirement.* Subject to any action to that effect by the Works Council, any management action with respect to any consent matters (*see supra* Chapter 12.2.d.iv) without the prior approval of the Works Council shall be null and void by operation of law[50].

g   Agreements with the Works Council. Management and the Works Council may conclude agreements, generally known as *convenanten*, for a variety of purposes[51]. However, such agreements may not limit or restrict the statutory powers of the Works Council pursuant to the Works Councils Act. Many such agreements have been concluded in the restructuring of enterprises or in the merger or joint venture context.

---

47   WOR art. 26(1). Works Councils often commence preliminary court proceedings to prevent action from becoming irreversible, particularly due to the statutory provisions requiring that the rights of third parties be respected.
48   WOR art. 26(4).
49   WOR art. 26(5).
50   WOR art. 27(5).
51   P.F. VAN DER HEIJDEN & A.C.B.W. DOUP, MEDEZEGGENSCHAP PER CONVENANT (Sinzheimer Cahiers No. 3, 1st ed. 1991), SDU Juridische en Fiscale Uitgeverij (The Hague).

Other examples include agreements for the desired "profile" of the supervisory board (in terms of skills and background, etc.) in "large" corporations (*see supra* Chapter 7.3.c.ii).

In the restructuring of enterprises, one common type of agreement is geared to the situation in which an international group with its top-holding company in the Netherlands intends to hive down its Dutch activities to a Dutch sub-holding company. In Dutch and international corporate practice, it is often felt that works councils of a specific country should not be in a position to be involved in matters which do not specifically relate to that country. Thus, it is almost standard practice in the Netherlands to resolve this issue by "pushing down" the Works Council to the national level only.

A variety of agreements have been concluded with Works Councils in a merger and joint venture context. By way of example, at the time of the well-known statutory merger between ABN Bank and Amro Bank, such an agreement was concluded to the effect that, in the absence of a Central Works Council at the level of the top-holding company with respect to decisions of the new top-holding company, in the interim the Central Works Council of the Amro Bank would have all of the powers that pursuant to the Works Councils Act were to accrue to any Central Works Council.

The Dutch Supreme Court ruled that the provisions of the Works Councils Act similarly apply to additional powers of the Works Council pursuant to an agreement with management[52]. The Works Councils Act states that a Works Council may be granted powers in addition to those referred to in the Works Councils Act either: (i) as provided for in a collective bargaining agreement[53]; or (ii) by means of an agreement between the enterprise and the Works Council[54]. In case the agreement provides for additional matters requiring prior consultation with, or consent by, the Works Council, the respective actions for non-compliance are similarly applicable (*see supra* Chapter 12.2.f)[55].

---

52 Judgment of March 17, 1993, HR, 1993 NJ No. 366.
53 WOR art. 32(1).
54 Amended WOR art. 32(2).
55 WOR art. 32(4). The statutory basis for agreements between the enterprise and the Works Council is similarly applicable to agreements between the enterprise and the *personeelsvertegenwoordiging* (*see supra* Chapter 12.2.e).

12.3 European Works Councils

a   **General.** The Dutch legislature has opted to implement the directive for the European Works Council (*see supra* Chapter 1.3.g) by means of a separate statute[56] (hereinafter: the "Act"), in an effort to emphasise that the Dutch Works Councils under existing legislation (*see supra* Chapter 12.2) will not be considered subordinate to European Works Councils. Instead, the powers of the Dutch Works Councils will be expanded by additional powers, *inter alia*, to appoint and remove both the Dutch members to the Special Negotiating Body (*see infra* Chapter 12.3.c) and the members of the mandatory European Works Council (*see infra* Chapter 12.3.d.i). For the interaction between the Act and the Dutch Works Councils Act, *see infra* Chapter 12.3[57].

For a good understanding of the Act, a distinction must be made between:
a   a Statutory European Works Council, formed in the absence of an Agreed Arrangement (*see infra* Chapter 12.3.d);
b   an Agreed European Works Council (*see infra* Chapter 12.3.e); and
c   any other Agreed Procedure, concluded pursuant to an Agreed Arrangement (*see infra* Chapter 12.3.e).

b   Scope

i   *General.* As a general rule, the obligations stipulated in the Act apply only to the extent no other pre-existing agreements are in place which serve a similar purpose (*see* ii below).

The substantive provisions of the Act apply to "Dutch Community-scale" enterprises and "Dutch Community-scale" groups of enterprises.

A Community-scale enterprise or Community-scale group of enterprises is considered "Dutch" for purposes of the Act if[58]:
a   the Community-scale enterprise or the "controlling" enterprise (within a Community-scale group) has its domicile or seat in the Netherlands; or

---

56   Wet op de Europese ondernemingsraden [WEOR] (Act on the European Works Councils), 1997 S.32.
57   The definitions are crucial for a good understanding of the implications of the Act. These definitions by no means correspond to the definitions in the Dutch Works Councils Act or Dutch corporate law.
58   WEOR art. 6.

b in case the Community-scale enterprise or the "controlling" enterprise has its domicile or seat outside any of the Member States, a branch or group enterprise thereof, for which the management has been appointed or is considered[59] the "central management" for purposes of the Act, has its residence or seat in the Netherlands.

The law which applies to a certain enterprise determines whether that enterprise qualifies as a "controlling" enterprise[60].

A Dutch enterprise is considered the "controlling" enterprise within a Community-scale group if it can exercise control, directly or indirectly, over another enterprise within a Community-scale group and is not itself an enterprise which is controlled by another enterprise. Control is deemed to exist if such enterprise either alone or jointly with any other enterprises controlled by it:

a appoints more than half of the members of the administrative, managing or supervisory body of the other enterprise; or

b exercises more than half of the voting rights in the shareholders' meeting (assuming all votes were cast); or

c provides more than half of the issued capital of the other enterprise[61].

An enterprise has a "Community-scale" dimension for the purposes of the Act if, for the two preceding years, it had 150 employees or more in each of two Member States, and, in the aggregate, 1,000 employees or more in all Member States[62].

A group of enterprises has a "Community-scale" dimension for the purposes of the Act if it consists of a controlling enterprise and one or more group enterprises of which two or more are established in different Member States, and, for the two preceding years, at least

---

59 As a result of the fact that the branch or group enterprise has the largest number of employees compared to the number of employees in other Member States.

60 WEOR art. 2.6. If that law is not the law of a Member State, this is determined by the law which applies to the group enterprise whose management represents the "controlling" enterprise for purposes of the Act.

61 WEOR arts. 2.1, 2.2. If more than one group enterprise meets one or more of these tests, the enterprise which meets the test under (a) is deemed to be the "controlling" enterprise, whereby the right to appoint managing directors shall prevail. If no enterprise meets the test under (a), the test under (b) shall prevail over the test under (c), without prejudice to the right to establish that yet another enterprise should be considered to be the "controlling" enterprise (WEOR art. 2.7).

62 WEOR art. 1.1.c.

one enterprise had on average at least 150 employees in one Member State and another enterprise had on average at least 150 employees in another Member State, and group enterprises had, in the aggregate, 1,000 or more employees in all Member States[63].

The law of each Member State determines whether an individual is considered an "employee". For persons working in the Netherlands, the Act defines "employees" as persons working in a Community-scale enterprise or Community-scale group on the basis of an employment agreement[64].

The Act defines a "Member State" as a country that is part of the European Union or the European Economic Area, but excluding the United Kingdom[65].

The obligations of the Act to institute a European Works Council or an Agreed Procedure rest upon the "central management" of the "Dutch Community-scale" enterprise or "Dutch Community-scale" group as defined above (hereinafter: "Dutch Community-scale Enterprise" and "Dutch Community-scale Group" respectively).

For a Dutch Community-scale Group, "central management" is defined as the central management of the controlling undertaking[66].

For a Dutch Community-scale Enterprise having its residence or seat outside the Member States, the central management for purposes of the Act is deemed to be[67]:
a a person appointed by the Community-scale enterprise, who is charged with the actual management of (one of) its enterprise(s) within the Netherlands, *or*, in the absence of such designation:
b the person or persons who are charged with the actual management of the branch in the Netherlands[68].

63 WEOR art. 1.1.d.
64 WEOR art. 3.1. Every person employed under Dutch law other than civil servants, under a contract or otherwise, is deemed to have an employment agreement, with the exception of temporary employees, contractors and independent consultants.
65 WEOR art. 1.1.a.
66 WEOR art. 1.1.e.
67 WEOR art. 1.2.
68 This branch must have the largest number of employees compared to the number of employees in other Member States in order for the Community-scale enterprise to qualify as "Dutch".

For a Dutch Community-scale Group whose controlling enterprise has its residence or seat outside the Member States, the central management for purposes of the Act is deemed to be[69]:

a the management of a group enterprise having its residence or seat in the Netherlands and designated as such by the controlling enterprise, or, in the absence of such designation:

b the management of such group enterprise in the Netherlands considered as such by the Act as a result of the fact that it employs the largest number of employees compared to the number of employees in other Member States.

The central management of a Dutch Community-scale Enterprise or Dutch Community-scale Group may decide to form a Special Negotiating Body (*see infra* Chapter 12.3.c) in order to negotiate on the formation of a European Works Council or procedure for providing information to and consulting with its employees concerning transnational matters (hereinafter collectively: Agreed Arrangements)[70]. However, central management *must* form a Special Negotiating Body upon the written request of 100 employees or more (or of their representatives)[71], provided they represent two or more enterprises or branches in two or more different Member States[72].

Central management is required to establish a European Works Council with the powers accruing to it by operation of the Act (a mandatory European Works Council formed under Dutch law hereinafter: a "Statutory European Works Council") in the event[73]:

a central management has demonstrated its unwillingness to negotiate with a Special Negotiating Body within a six-month period following a request thereto as referred to above; or

b central management and the Special Negotiating Body have not concluded an Agreed Arrangement within the three-year period[74] following such request thereto, or, if central management had indeed formed a Special Negotiating Body, within the three-year period following its formation[75].

---

69 WEOR art. 1.3.
70 WEOR art. 8.1.
71 For employees working in the Netherlands, the relevant Works Councils are considered their representatives for this purpose (WEOR art. 3.2).
72 WEOR art. 8.2.
73 WEOR art. 15.
74 The Act does not provide for a maximum period for the actual formation of a European Works Council or an Agreed Arrangement.
75 Unless that Special Negotiated Body had decided not to open or to discontinue the negotiations (WEOR arts. 15, 11.2).

The powers of the Statutory European Works Council (*see infra* Chapter 12.3.d) are thereby a benchmark for any Agreed Arrangement. Central management must ensure proper compliance with Statutory European Works Councils, Agreed Arrangements and, as the case may be, any pre-existing agreements (*see* ii below)[76].

ii   *Grandfathering Clause.* Any Dutch Community-scale Enterprise or Dutch Community-scale Group that prior to February 5, 1997 had concluded an agreement pertaining to the provision of information to and consultation with employees are exempt from the Act, provided such agreement was concluded with a party that the Dutch Community-scale Enterprise or Dutch Community-scale Group could have reasonably considered to be the representative of its employees[77]. A few large Dutch corporate groups have concluded such an agreement.

c   **Special Negotiating Body.** The Dutch members of a Special Negotiating Body are elected employees only. They shall be appointed, or their appointment shall be withdrawn, by the Dutch Works Councils of the branches or enterprises in the Netherlands[78]. The Special Negotiating Body must consist of one member of each Member State in which the Dutch Community-scale Enterprise or Dutch Community-scale Group has employees and one, two or three additional members for each Member State in which such Dutch Community-scale Enterprise or Dutch Community-scale Group has at least a quarter or more, one-half or more, or three-quarters or more of its employees respectively[79].

d   **Statutory European Works Councils**

i   *General.* The Statutory European Works Council consists of elected employees only. The Dutch members of the Statutory European

---

76   WEOR arts. 11.8, 15, 24.3.
77   WEOR art. 24.1. In order to remain exempt from the provisions of the Act, such agreements must provide, or be amended to provide within the five-year period following the effective date of the Act, that the employees or their representatives of enterprises or branches which will become part of the Dutch Community-scale Enterprise or the Dutch Community-scale Group within such five-year period will be involved in the renewal or amendment thereof or will be represented in the agreed information and consultation procedure (WEOR art. 24.2).
78   WEOR art. 10.1. In case no Dutch Works Council has been established, the Dutch members of the Special Negotiating Body shall be elected by the employees in the Netherlands (WEOR art. 10.5).
79   WEOR art. 9.1.

Works Council shall be appointed, or their appointment shall be withdrawn, by the Dutch Works Council of the branches or enterprises in the Netherlands[80]. Their appointment shall be for a term of four years[81]. If the Dutch Community-scale Enterprise or Dutch Community-scale Group has fewer than 5,000 employees, the Statutory European Works Council must consist of one member for each Member State in which such Dutch Community-scale Enterprise or Dutch Community-scale Group has employees and one, two or three additional members for each Member State in which such Dutch Community-scale Enterprise or Dutch Community-scale Group has a quarter or more, one-half or more, or three-quarters or more of its employees respectively[82]. If the Dutch Community-scale Enterprise or Dutch Community-scale Group has 5,000 employees or more, the Statutory European Works Council must consist of one member for each Member State in which such Dutch Community-scale Enterprise or Dutch Community-scale Group has employees and one, three, six or nine additional members for each Member State in which such Dutch Community-scale Enterprise or Dutch Community-scale Group has at least a tenth, a quarter, one-half or three-quarters or more of its employees respectively[83].

ii   *Powers*

    A   General Limitation
       The powers of a Statutory European Works Council are limited to information and consultation on issues which are of importance for the whole Dutch Community-scale Enterprise or Dutch Community-scale Group or for at least two branches or enterprises of the group in different Member States. These powers are moreover limited to matters concerning all branches or enterprises of the group or concerning at least two branches or enterprises in different Member States[84].

    B   Annual Consultation Meetings
       Central management is required, at least once every calendar year, to inform the Statutory European Works Council in writing and

---

80   WEOR arts. 17.1, 10.1. In case no Dutch Works Council has been established, the Dutch members of the Statutory European Works Council shall be elected by the employees in the Netherlands (WEOR arts. 17.1, 10.5).
81   WEOR art. 17.1.
82   WEOR art. 16.1.
83   WEOR art. 16.2.
84   WEOR art. 19.1.

consult it concerning the general business and anticipated pros-
pects of the Dutch Community-scale Enterprise or the Dutch
Community-scale Group. The information and consultations
with respect to such Dutch Community-scale Enterprise or
Dutch Community-scale Group must in particular address[85]:

a   its structure;
b   its financial and economic situation;
c   the anticipated developments in activities, production and
sales;
d   capital expenditure;
e   substantial changes in its organisation;
f   the introduction of new work or production methods;
g   its care for the environment;
h   any merger;
i   any relocation;
j   any reductions in the number of or closures of enterprises,
branches or important parts of the enterprise or group; and
k   the currently existing status quo of and developments in the
workforce and any mass lay-offs.

C   Special Consultation Meetings
The central management of a Dutch Community-scale Enterprise
or Dutch Community-scale Group must inform the Statutory
European Works Council of all circumstances and proposed
actions which could significantly affect the interests of the employees of two or more branches or enterprises located in different
Member States, in particular regarding relocations or closures of
branches or any mass lay-offs[86].

Upon the request of the Statutory European Works Council, central management or a more appropriate level of management having its own decision-making power, as the case may be, is required
to meet with the Statutory European Works Council for consultation regarding the circumstances or proposed management actions
under discussion on the basis of a written report prepared by management. This meeting must take place sufficiently early so that
the provision of information and consultation is still meaning-
ful[87].

---

85   WEOR art. 19.2.
86   WEOR art. 19.3.
87   WEOR art. 19.4.

The Statutory European Works Council is entitled to render non-binding recommendations with respect to the report within a reasonable time period following the special consultation meeting[88].

D   Withholding Information on the Grounds of Secrecy
Provided it can reasonably be anticipated that its disclosure would either seriously prejudice or harm the Dutch Community-scale Enterprise or Dutch Community-scale Group, central management is exempt from the obligation to provide information to the Statutory European Works Council[89]. Moreover, central management, upon reasonable grounds, is entitled to require that the information that it is to provide be treated as confidential, in which case the secrecy rules (*see infra* Chapter 12.3.f) apply[90].

e   **Minimum Requirements for Agreed Arrangements.** Subject to certain minimum requirements[91], the Act offers central management and the Special Negotiating Body ample freedom to tailor any Agreed Arrangement, resulting either in an Agreed European Works Council or an Agreed Procedure, to their respective needs.

Central management and the Special Negotiating Body may agree that for parts of the Dutch Community-scale Enterprise or Dutch Community-scale Group separate Agreed European Works Councils shall be established or separate Agreed Procedures shall apply. Alternatively, they may agree that for one or more parts of the Dutch Community-scale Enterprise or the Dutch Community-scale Group, one or more Agreed European Works Councils shall be formed and that one or more Agreed Procedures shall apply to other parts[92].

However, any Agreed Arrangement must contain provisions regarding the term of the Agreed Arrangement, the manner of negotiating a new Agreed Arrangement and the manner in which the Agreed Arrangement is to be amended to reflect any changes in the structure or size of the

---

88   WEOR art. 19.4.
89   WEOR art. 19.5.
90   WEOR art. 19.5.
91   WEOR art. 11.
92   WEOR art. 11.5.

Dutch Community-scale Enterprise or Dutch Community-scale Group or in the numbers of employees in the Member States[93].

f   Job Protection and Secrecy. Except for an "urgent cause", an employee working in the Netherlands who is a member of a Special Negotiating Body or a Statutory Works Council, or who was a member thereof during the preceding two-year period, cannot be dismissed without the approval of the Cantonal Court. The Court shall ensure that the reason for the proposed dismissal does not relate to the membership of the Special Negotiating Body or the Statutory Works Council[94].

The members of the Special Negotiating Body and the Statutory Works Council are under a strict obligation of secrecy[95]. For the effectiveness of the enforcement thereof, *see supra* Chapter 12.2.c.iv.

The same job protection and secrecy rules apply with respect to members of an Agreed European Works Council or employees involved in an Agreed Procedure[96].

g   Interaction with the Dutch Works Councils Act. Employees and their representatives have fewer powers under the Act than under the Dutch Works Councils Act. Statutory European Works Councils can deliver non-binding recommendations only (*see supra* Chapter 12.3.d.c). Central management may disregard such recommendations and is not required to suspend any actions following a negative recommendation, as is the case where a matter requires the formal advice of a Dutch Works Council (*see supra* Chapter 12.2.d.iii).

The Act does not restrict the powers of Dutch Works Councils.

---

93   WEOR art. 11.6. If the Agreed Arrangement does not provide that the employees or their representatives of enterprises or branches which are to become part of the Dutch Community-scale Enterprise or the Dutch Community-scale Group following its conclusion will be involved in the renewal or amendment of such Agreed Arrangement within a two-year period, or will be represented in the Agreed European Works Council or involved in an Agreed Procedure, central management must, upon the request of 100 or more or such employees or their representatives, form a new Special Negotiating Body (WEOR art. 11.6).
94   WEOR art. 4.8; WOR art. 21. The decision of the Cantonal Court cannot be appealed against.
95   WEOR arts. 4.4 through 4.6.
96   WEOR art. 4.1.

h   Risks of Non-Compliance. Each interested party[97] is entitled to request the Enterprise Chamber (*see supra* Chapter 9.1) to enforce of the Act, with the exception of matters relating to the job protection and secrecy rules for members of a Special Negotiating Body, a Statutory European Works Council, an Agreed European Works Council and the employees involved in an Agreed Procedure (*see supra* Chapter 12.3.f)[98].

---

97 The Minister for Social Affairs and Employment has indicated that for this purpose interested parties include the Special Negotiating Body and the Statutory European Works Council, as well as representatives of employees in other procedures for informing and consultation of employees (Memorie van Toelichting (Explanatory Memorandum) WEOR, No. 24641-3, p. 23). The relevant trade unions would therefore also qualify as "interested parties".
98 WEOR art. 5.

13   TAXATION OF COMPANIES

13.1   General

The most important taxes levied by the Netherlands from companies operating in the Netherlands are:

a   *Corporate Income Tax* (CIT)[1], which is a tax levied on profits;

b   *Dividend Withholding Tax* (WHT)[2], which is a tax levied on the distribution of profits by Dutch resident companies;

c   *Capital Contributions Tax* (CCT)[3], which is a tax levied on capital contributions into Dutch resident companies with capital divided into shares; and

d   other taxes like the *Value Added Tax* (VAT)[4], which is a tax levied on the sales of goods and services and the

e   *Real Property Transfer Tax* (RPTT)[5], which is a tax levied in respect of the transfer of Dutch real property or of shares in a real property company.

In addition, some other taxes may be due, such as certain environmental taxes, excise- and custom duties and local real property taxes.

13.2   Corporate Income Tax (CIT)

a   Introduction

i   *General.* In principle, CIT can be qualified as an ordinary profit tax based on the profits realised by companies. Nevertheless, foreign businesses generally consider the Netherlands an attractive country to establish a company. As far as the tax considerations are concerned, this is mainly due to certain specific features, such as the participation exemption (*see infra* Chapter 13.2.c), the "exemption" of foreign

---

1   Wet op de Vennootschapsbelasting [Vpb] (Corporate Income Tax Act), 1969 S. 445, *as amended.*

2   Wet op de dividendbelasting [DIV] (Dividend Withholding Tax Act), 1965 S. 621, *as amended.*

3   Wet op belastingen van rechtsverkeer [BRV] (Tax Act Legal Transaction), 1970 S. 611, *as amended.*

4   Wet op de omzetbelasting 1968 [OB] (Turnover Tax Act), 1968 S.329, *as amended.*

5   BRV, *id.*

branch income (*see infra* Chapter 13.2.i (iv)), the treatment of group financing activities (*see infra* Chapter 13.2.d) and the absence of withholding taxes on interest and royalty payments. These features, in combination with favourable tax treaties concluded by the Netherlands with other countries and the possibility to obtain advance rulings from the Dutch tax authorities, may make the Netherlands an attractive location for establishing a business operation.

ii   *Resident Companies.* Dutch resident companies are subject to CIT on their worldwide income[6]. The definition of "companies" includes *inter alia*, corporations (B.V.s and N.V.s), "open" limited partnerships (*i.e.* limited partnerships where admission and substitution of limited partners is permitted without the consent of all general and limited partners) and any other body the capital of which is wholly or partly divided into shares (including entities organised under foreign law and residing in the Netherlands)[7]. For the determination of the place of residence, the place of effective management is the decisive criterion[8]. A company incorporated under Dutch law, however, is always deemed to be resident in the Netherlands for CIT purposes[9].

iii   *Non-Resident Companies.* Non-resident companies are subject to CIT only in respect of income derived from certain specifically mentioned Dutch sources[10]. These Dutch sources *inter alia* include: (1) business profits realised through a permanent establishment in the Netherlands; (2) income derived from Dutch real property; and (3) capital gains realised on the sale of shares in and dividends and interest derived from a Dutch resident corporation in which the taxpayer has a "substantial interest"[11] which does not belong to the assets of a business enterprise.

---

6   Vpb art. 7.
7   Vpb art. 2.
8   Algemene Wet inzake Rijksbelastingen [AWR] (General Act on Taxation), 1959 S. 301, *as amended,* art. 4 and case law, *e.g.* Judgment of April 20, 1988, HR, 1988 BESLISSINGEN IN BELASTINGZAKEN NEDERLANDSE BELASTINGRECHTSPRAAK [BNB] No. 176.
9   Vpb art. 2.
10   Vpb art. 17, which refers to art. 49 of the Wet op de Inkomstenbelasting [IB] (Individual Income Tax Act), 1964 S. 519, *as amended.*
11   Generally, a "substantial interest" exists if the tax payer owns 5% or more of the share capital of a corporation; *see* IB art. 20a.

b   Tax Base and Rates

i   *General.* The CIT due is calculated on the annual taxable amount (*belastbare bedrag*), being the taxable profit less loss carry forwards[12]. The tax rate equals 35% on the taxable amount exceeding NLG 100,000. The first NLG 100,000 is taxed at a rate of 36%[13]. If the annual taxable profit constitutes a loss, this loss can be carried back to the three preceding years and any amount left can be carried forward indefinitely[14]. The tax year is generally the financial year[15].

ii   *Taxable Profit.* The taxable profit is the profit reduced by deductible gifts[16]. Profit is defined as the "total of all income derived from a business, in whatever form and under whatever name it may arise"[17]. No distinction is made between ordinary (or trading) income and capital gains. Dutch corporations are deemed to carry on their business with all their assets and liabilities[18]. Consequently, all income derived from these assets and liabilities constitutes profit.

As a general rule, the total profit derived by a corporation is equal to the difference between the equity at the moment the corporation ceases to exist and the equity at the date of its incorporation, as adjusted for (deemed) capital contributions, repayments of capital and (deemed) dividend distributions made during the existence of the corporation. As a general rule profit must be computed in Netherlands guilders. However, as from January 1, 1997 a functional currency may be applied, provided certain conditions are met[19]. For accounting purposes this was already possible before this date.

Due to specific provisions in the law, certain items of income and expenses are not taken into account when determining the taxable profits. By way of example, the benefits derived in connection with a qualifying shareholding (*see infra* Chapter 13.2.c) and the benefits derived as a result of a waiver of an uncollectible loan by a creditor[20], are generally excluded from the tax base. Moreover, expenses relating

---

12   Vpb arts. 7, 17 and 22.
13   As from 1998 the full amount will be taxed against the 35% rate.
14   Vpb art. 20.
15   Vpb art. 7.
16   Vpb art. 7.
17   Vpb art. 8, IB art. 7.
18   Vpb art. 2.
19   Vpb. art. 7.
20   Vpb art. 8, IB art. 8.

to a shareholding in a foreign subsidiary company (*see infra* Chapter 13.2.c.ii) and certain penalties are not always tax deductible[21]. Transactions with group companies should take place at "arm's length conditions". The CIT Act does not include thin capitalisation rules. However, interest expenses due on certain inter-company loans are not deductible if these loans relate to inter-company transactions which are considered tax abusive[22]. Such transactions include, *inter alia*, the creation of intercompany loans as a result of dividend payments, capital contributions, capital repayments and the transfer of shares. Under certain conditions, the interest deduction may still be recognised if the corporation can demonstrate that the transaction was based on sound business reasons.

Shipping companies may elect for a tonnage-based profit determination, provided certain conditions are met[23].

iii   *Annual Profit*

     A   Sound Business Practice
       The total profit made during the existence of the corporation must be allocated to its respective financial years in accordance with sound business practice (*goed koopmansgebruik*) and consistent accounting methods[24]. The concept of sound business practice is not defined by law. It is a dynamic concept whose meaning constantly changes on the basis of continuous case law resulting from developments in society. Important elements of the sound business concept are:
       a   the principle of matching, *i.e.* all income and expenses must be allocated to the year in which they arise;
       b   the principle of prudence, *i.e.* unrealised losses may be recognised, while unrealised profits may be ignored; the continuity of the business enterprise must be observed; and
       c   the principle of simplicity, *i.e.* the accounting method used must be manageable in view of the applicable circumstances in the situation concerned.

       The requirement of consistent accounting methods means that the accounting method used may not be changed, unless this

---

21   Vpb art. 8, IB art. 8a.
22   Vpb art. 10a.
23   Vpb art. 8, IB art. 8c.
24   Vpb art. 8, IB art. 9.

change is compatible with sound business practice and is not aimed at realising an occasional, one time tax benefit. As a general rule, profit computed in accordance with generally accepted accounting principles and adjusted for specific tax rules will be in accordance with sound business practice.

Generally, profit must be recognised when realised. The elements of sound business practice provide for some flexibility as to the moment of recognition. For example, in the situation of a hire-purchase transaction, the recognition of profits may under certain conditions be postponed until the instalments received exceed the tax book value of the assets concerned. In another example, if a fixed asset is replaced by an asset with the same economic function, the gain on the replaced asset may be rolled-over to the newly acquired asset by reducing the tax book value of this new asset. As a basic rule, the valuation of assets and liabilities for corporate income tax purposes must be made on the basis of all facts and circumstances prevailing at the end of the financial year, as known (or as should reasonably be known) at the time of the preparation of the tax return. However, facts and circumstances known at the time of preparing the tax return which occurred after the end of the financial year must be disregarded.

In brief, the following valuation rules apply. Inventory can be valued either (1) at cost, (2) at the lower of cost or market value, or (3) in accordance with the base-stock method, the FIFO, or LIFO method. Valuation based on replacement value is not allowed. In respect of receivables a provision may be made for bad debts. Fixed assets are valued against acquisition cost and can be depreciated over the useful life of the asset concerned, taking into account the expected residual value[25]. Corporations are free to choose a depreciation method, as long as it is in line with sound business practice. Generally, the straight line method is used. In case law the declining balance method has also been accepted, but only for assets whose economic use steadily declines as they become older. The amortisation of goodwill (generally over a five year period) is allowed only if it has been acquired from a third party. Goodwill included in the acquisition price of shares is generally not tax deductible. Furthermore, accelerated depreciation has been introduced for certain environmentally friendly and energy-saving fixed assets[26].

---

25 Vpb art. 8, IB art. 10.
26 Vpb art. 8, IB art. 10.

B   Special Reserves
Provided the corporation maintains up-to-date books and records a limited number of reserves may be formed under the CIT Act by making a tax deductible contribution[27]: (1) the cost equalisation or business expense reserve, (2) the self-insurance reserve and (3) the replacement reserve. On January 1, 1997 a new reserve was introduced for specific risks which arise from the activities of an internationally operated business enterprise (*see infra* Chapter 13.2.d).

The cost equalisation reserve enables recurrent expenses which do not lead to annual expenditures (for example, maintenance expenses), to be spread more equally over time. The self-insurance reserve allows a corporation which decides to assume for its own account an insurable risk, to form a reserve. In order to form this self-insurance reserve it is required that the risk concerned is insured by "most" (in practise 30% or more) other similar entrepreneurs exposed to the same risk. A replacement reserve can be formed if fixed assets (tangible or intangible) are lost, damaged or sold and the damages or consideration received exceed the book value. A condition for forming the reserve is the intention to replace or repair the asset. If within four years after the financial year in which the loss, sale or damage took place, the asset has not been not replaced or repaired, the reserve has to be released (with a corresponding increase in the taxable profits in that fourth year) unless the replacement or repair is in process, but delayed due to exceptional circumstances.

c   **Participation Exemption**

i   *General.* A Dutch resident corporation or a non-resident corporation with a permanent establishment in the Netherlands (*see infra* Chapter 13.2.g.ii) is exempt in respect of benefits derived from a qualifying participation[28]. These benefits include capital gains, actual or deemed dividends and certain currency exchange results (*see* below). On the other hand, capital losses realised in respect of a qualifying participation are not tax deductible, except, under certain conditions, for losses realised in respect of a liquidation[29], or a decrease in value during the

27   Vpb art. 8, IB arts. 13 and 14.
28   Vpb art. 13.
29   Vpb art. 13d.

first 5 years after the incorporation or acquisition of a subsidiary company[30].

Both positive and negative currency exchange results realised on loans which were obtained in order to finance the acquisition of, or the capital contribution in a foreign qualifying participation, are also exempt under the participation exemption. Upon request, the participation exemption will also apply to gains and losses on financial instruments acquired by the company in order to hedge its currency risk with respect to foreign qualifying participations[31].

ii   *Conditions.*

A   General
A qualifying participation in a Dutch resident corporation exists where:
1   the corporation owns 5% or more of the nominal paid-up capital of another corporation, with a capital which is wholly or partly divided into shares; and
2   the shares are not held as "inventory".
If shares are owned in a non-resident corporation, the following additional conditions apply:
3   the shares may not be held as a passive portfolio investment; and
4   the corporation in which the shares are held must be subject to tax on its profits levied by the central government of the country in which it is domiciled.

B   Non-Inventory Test
The purpose of the non-inventory test is to exclude from the application of the participation exemption profits derived from trading in shares in "cash companies" (*i.e.* companies which do not carry on a business, but only own cash or other liquid assets). In principle, shares held in a company which carries on an active business are not considered to be inventory.

C   Non-Passive Portfolio Investment Test
The condition that the shareholding in the foreign subsidiary company may not qualify as a passive portfolio investment is interpreted as follows. This condition is not met if the foreign sub-

---

30   Vpb art. 13ca.
31   Vpb art. 13.

sidiary itself is a passive portfolio investment company. However, this condition may still not be met even if the foreign subsidiary is an active operating subsidiary, unless the Dutch corporation performs a "real function" within the group to which it belongs[32]. This real function is considered to be performed, and accordingly the participation exemption may apply, if:

a the Dutch corporation acts as a real intermediate holding company by forming a "link" between the business activities of its (ultimate) parent company and its subsidiary; or

b the Dutch corporation is considered to be a top-holding company which is involved in management, policy making and/or financing activities.

In case of doubt, many corporations contact the Dutch tax authorities in order to try to obtain an advance ruling confirming that a foreign participation is not considered to be a passive portfolio investment.

A participation in a foreign group finance company is deemed to be held as a passive portfolio investment, unless the foreign finance company can be considered as actively involved in foreign finance activities[33].

The portfolio investment test does not apply to a shareholding of 25% or more of the nominal paid-up capital of an EC corporation domiciled in a Member State and which is not subject to special tax rules[34].

D Subject to Tax Test
The foreign tax levied from the non-resident subsidiary company should be comparable to Dutch corporate income tax, *i.e.* it should be based on the profits realised and not be an annual flat amount. It is not necessary that the foreign profits are subject to a tax rate similar to the Dutch corporate income tax rate; a low rate is sufficient. The test is also met in case no tax is actually paid due

---

32 Judgement of November 7, 1973, HR, 1974 BNB No. 2 and Resolution of October 15, 1974 No. B74/21516.
33 Vpb art. 13.
34 Vpb art. 13g. This rule is based on the EC parent-subsidiary directive (Council Directive No. 90/435 on the common system of taxation applicable in the case of parent companies and subsidiaries of different Member States, 33 O.J. Eur. Comm. (No. L 225) 6 (1990)). In certain cases, the paid-up capital requirement may be replaced with a voting power requirement.

to a tax holiday (a tax exemption which aims to stimulate the foreign economy), or due to loss carry forwards.

E   Deduction of Losses and Expenses
Although the participation exemption may be considered a favourable provision of the CIT Act, certain consequences should be considered. The acquisition costs of shares (including goodwill reflected in the purchase price of the shares) can generally not be deducted from the taxable profits. However, under certain conditions a deductible write down may be possible if the subsidiary company in which the shares are held is liquidated[35]. Moreover, as from January 1, 1997, it is possible to take into account a temporary tax deduction in respect of a decrease in value of a participation during the first five years after its acquisition[36]. The amount of this tax deduction equals the difference between the acquisition price of the participation and its reduced fair market value. For subsequent benefits (*i.e* increases in value, dividends received and capital gains realised) derived in connection with this shareholding, the participation exemption is not applicable with respect to tax deductions taken in the previous years. If after the 5 year period the fair market value of the participation remains below the acquisition price, and to the extent no benefits have been added to the taxable profits, a recapture rule will apply in the 5 subsequent years. According to this recapture rule, the tax deductions in the past will be added to the taxable profits in 5 equal instalments. In case of a sale of the participation within the 5 year recapture period, the unrecaptured amount will be added to the taxable profit at once.

Expenses incurred by a Dutch corporation in connection with a direct or indirect foreign participation that qualifies for the participation exemption, are generally not tax deductible[37]. The same applies to a direct or indirect participation in a Dutch resident corporation which realises profits through a foreign permanent establishment, if its profits are exempt due to the application of a treaty for the avoidance of double taxation or unilateral rules for double tax relief[38]. Important non-deductible expenses in this respect are interest due on, and currency exchange losses real-

---

35   Vpb art. 13d.
36   Vpb art. 13ca.
37   Vpb art. 13.
38   Judgment of November 13, 1991, HR, 1992 BNB No. 58.

ised in connection with, loans which were obtained in order to finance the acquisition of, or the capital contribution in, such a participation.

d   Group Financing Activities

i   *General.* Upon request a special reserve can be formed for the specific risks which arise from the financing of activities of an internationally operating business[39]. The rules do not form a special regime; any Dutch resident or non-resident companies which fulfil the conditions can request this treatment, regardless of whether it only carries on financing activities or has other activities as well. Nevertheless, the creation of the reserve may result in a low effective tax burden on the group financing profit realised by such company.

In order to be eligible for the special reserve, the company should truly be involved in financing activities (*see* ii below) on an international scale. The activities must be spread over at least four different countries or two different continents, thereby satisfying certain tests regarding the minimum amount of financing profits to be derived from each country or continent and the maximum amount of financing profit to be derived from Dutch resident group companies. The tax inspector is allowed to impose conditions when approving a request by a corporation to form the reserve. These conditions can be updated once every ten years. If the company does not accept these changed conditions, but still fulfils the old conditions, it is no longer possible to make new contributions to the reserve, but a taxable release of the reserve need not take place.

ii   *Financing Activities.* The international group financing activities include providing loans to group companies, the financing of participations, the financing of business assets used within the group and of business activities of the group, financial and operational leasing, licensing of intellectual property and financial administrative services. In principle, these activities should take place within the group, but they may to a limited extent have effect outside the group as well. For example, if a loan is provided to a group company which uses the proceeds to grant consumer credit to its customers, this is seen as a relevant group financing activity.

---

39   Vpb art. 15b.

iii *Special Reserve.* Each financial year in which the conditions are met, the company can contribute to the special reserve, and accordingly exclude from the taxable profits, up to 80% of its relevant group financing profit and of the proceeds derived from short-term funds available for new acquisitions (the so-called "war-chest").

The group financing profit consists of the profit from the qualifying financing activities conducted by the company itself and of Dutch taxable profits realised by other group companies to the extent these latter profits relate to a taxable release of the reserve by the company in earlier years.

iv *Release of the Reserve.* The reserve can be released, either tax-free, or subject to taxation, depending on the circumstances.

A Taxable Release
The release is taxable if it compensates a loss relating to a risk for which the reserve was formed, to the extent such loss is deducted in the Netherlands by either the company itself or a group company. For example, this may concern a write-down of a loan granted to a group company, or the liquidation of a subsidiary.

It is possible to release the reserve voluntarily in five years. The annual release to the taxable profits is then taxed at a special rate of 10%.

A mandatory release takes place if the company does not longer realise taxable profits in the Netherlands[40], if it no longer meets the test of being involved in international group financing activities, or if it no longer fulfils the conditions imposed by the tax inspector. The release is then subject to taxation at the ordinary rate of 35%.

B Tax-Free Release
Under certain conditions, the reserve can be released tax free if shares are acquired in, or a capital contribution takes place into, a subsidiary company. The tax free release of the reserve equals 50% of the investment made. The investment must lead to a real broadening of the participations within the group. The participation thus acquired should be held for at least five years, unless

---

40 For example, by transferring the place of residence abroad, or as a result of a liquidation or merger.

sound business reasons call for a different course of action. The tax free release of the reserve may even equal 100% of the investment made if (1) it relates to a subsidiary company which activities or location (political, economical, climatological factors) are, in the judgment of the Ministry of Finance, so extreme that exceptional risks are run, or (2) it relates to a capital contribution into a subsidiary company which has been held liable for an event leading to damages which the subsidiary company cannot bear itself. In calculating a possible tax deductible loss upon the liquidation of a subsidiary company, the "acquisition costs" of the shares in this subsidiary company will be reduced by the aforementioned tax free release of the reserve.

e   **Fiscal Unity**

i   *General.* Under certain conditions, Dutch corporations belonging to the same group can form a fiscal unity (*fiscale eenheid*) for CIT purposes[41]. Under the fiscal unity rules, the parent company and its subsidiary companies may opt to file a consolidated tax return. One favourable consequence of the fiscal unity rules is that losses of one fiscal unity member can be offset against the profits of another member. Another favourable consequence of the fiscal unity rules is that it is possible to carry out intra-group transactions (such as sales of goods and services, and also reorganisations) without triggering CIT liability on unrealised gains.

In order to apply for the fiscal unity treatment, the parent company must own 99% or more of the shares in the subsidiary company as from the start of the financial year. The corporations concerned must be Dutch corporations or foreign corporations domiciled in the Netherlands which have the same legal characteristics as Dutch B.V.s and N.V.s[42]. The corporations must have the same financial year. Newly incorporated subsidiaries can become members as from the date of their incorporation. Subsidiary companies owned by a fiscal unity member which meet the aforementioned requirements can also become members of the fiscal unity. If the conditions are met, an application must be made prior to the end of the financial year in which the fiscal unity should start. The fiscal unity will terminate as

41   Vpb art. 15.
42   Judgment of March 16, 1994, HR, 1994 BNB No. 191 and Resolution No. DB94/1842m (August 10, 1994).

from the start of the financial year during which one of the aforementioned requirements is no longer met. The corporate income tax due on the profits of the fiscal unity will be levied on the parent company. However, each member of the fiscal unity is jointly and severally liable for the corporate income tax due in respect of the profits of the fiscal unity[43].

ii   *Anti-Abuse Rule.* Certain complicated conditions have been imposed by the Dutch tax authorities for approving the application for fiscal unity treatment. One important condition could lead to the adverse tax result that prior to the end of the preceding financial year, as a result of the sale of shares in a fiscal unity member in a subsequent year, the assets and liabilities of that subsidiary must be revalued at fair market value. This taxable revaluation must take place if: (1) assets or liabilities were transferred between the subsidiary and another fiscal unity member such that hidden reserves were transferred between fiscal unity members, and (2) the sale of the subsidiary leads to a realisation of all or part of these hidden reserves. No revaluation is required once a period of 6 financial years[44] has lapsed between the date the assets or liabilities were transferred and the date the subsidiary's shares were sold. The purpose of this condition (generally referred to as the "16th standard condition") is to prevent abusive schemes under which assets with a tax basis below fair market value would effectively be sold without taxation. Under such schemes the assets would first be transferred to a subsidiary within the fiscal unity following which the shares in that subsidiary would be sold in a subsequent year. The first transfer within the fiscal unity would not result in taxation of the hidden reserve, while the subsequent sale of the shares would be tax-exempt under the participation exemption (*see supra* Chapter 13.2.c).

iii *Acquisition Holding.* In the past, the fiscal unity has been an important factor in structuring acquisitions of Dutch corporations. By establishing a special purpose Dutch acquisition holding company which would form a fiscal unity with the Dutch target company, the interest expenses due by the holding company on the acquisition debt could be offset against the profits of the Dutch target[45]. As a result of new measures, the interest deduction has recently been restricted to the acquisition holding company's "own profits". This restricting

---

43   Invorderingswet [Inv.] (Tax Collection Act), 1990 S.221, *as amended*, art. 39.
44   Under certain conditions a 3 year period may apply.
45   Judgment of September 27, 1995, HR, 1995 BNB No. 6.

applies for an 8 year period, if the interest is due to an affiliated company and this company did not obtain a third party loan in respect of the financing of the acquisition[46]. During this 8 year period, the non-deductible interest can be carried forward to offset future "own profits" of the acquisition holding company. After this 8 year period any amount of "interest carry forward" still available can be used to offset the future profits of the Dutch acquired company, although certain limitations still apply during the next 4 years. The same restrictions will apply if the acquisition holding company and the acquired company are merged by means of a statutory merger (*see supra* Chapter 10.3)[47].

f **Mergers and Reorganisations.** The CIT Act contains certain provisions which may exempt and/or defer the recognition of the gain realised on the transfer of a business enterprise or on the transfer of shares to another corporation.

i *Tax-Free "Business-Merger".* A corporation can transfer all or an independent part of its business enterprise tax-free to another corporation if the transfer qualifies as a "business-merger". Principally, the following conditions apply in order to qualify as a business-merger[48]:

a The transferee is, or will become subject to CIT in the Netherlands;

b The transferee will acquire all or an independent part of the business enterprise solely in exchange for new shares issued to the transferor;

c The purpose of the transaction must be to merge, on a permanent basis, financially and economically, two active business enterprises;

d The transferee must continue with the same tax basis of the assets and liabilities as the transferor; and

e The transferor must as a minimum retain the shares in the transferee for a three-year period.

The Dutch tax authorities may allow a tax-free business merger even though certain conditions may not have been met, for example the condition stated above under (c)[49].

---

46   Under certain conditions the restriction on interest deduction does not apply in the case of an acquisition where an individual is involved who is or will be employed by the acquired company.

47   Vpb art. 29a.

48   Vpb art. 14.

49   Based on EC case law (*see* the Leur-Bloem case, Court of Justice of the European Communities, July 17, 1997, C-28/95), the question arises whether this and certain other conditions may actually be imposed.

ii *Tax-Free Statutory Merger.* If assets and liabilities are transferred to another corporation through a statutory merger, the Dutch tax authorities will allow a tax-free transfer only when certain conditions are met[50]. These conditions are more or less comparable to those applicable to a "business-merger" (*see* i above), requiring the receiving corporation to continue with the same tax basis as the transferring corporation. A roll-over exemption may, under certain conditions, be obtained where there is a statutory merger between non-Dutch qualifying EC corporations (for example, between two French companies of which one has a permanent establishment in the Netherlands)[51].

iii *Tax-Free Transfer of Shares.* A transfer of shares by a corporation may be exempt for CIT purposes under the rules for the participation exemption (*see supra* Chapter 13.2.c). If the participation exemption does not apply (for example, due to a shareholding of less than 5%, or to the qualification of a foreign shareholding as a passive portfolio investment) the gain may not be recognised if the transaction qualifies as a "share-merger" under the Individual Income Tax Act[52] or if the transaction is the result of a statutory merger[53]. A share-merger exists if:

a A Dutch resident corporation, in exchange for its own newly issued shares, acquires shares in another Dutch resident corporation resulting in a voting interest of more than 50%;

b A qualifying EC corporation, in exchange for its own newly issued shares, acquires shares in another qualifying EC corporation resulting in a voting interest of more than 50%;

c A Dutch resident corporation, in exchange for its own newly issued shares, acquires shares in a corporation domiciled outside the EC, resulting in a voting interest of more than 90%.

In all three situations, the purpose of the transaction must be to merge on a permanent basis, financially and economically, two active business enterprises[54]. An amount not exceeding 10% of the nominal value of the shares issued may represent consideration other than in shares, which will be subject to tax. The tax basis of the new shares received under a qualifying share-merger is the same as the basis of the shares transferred.

---

50 Vpb art. 29a and Resolution No. DB 94/2107m (1994).
51 Act of September 10, 1992 art. IV, S. 491.
52 Vpb art. 8.
53 Vpb art. 29a and Resolution No. DB 94/2107m (1994).
54 Based on EC case law (*see* the Leur-Bloem case, *supra* p. 198 at note 917), the question arises whether this and certain other conditions may actually be imposed.

If as a result of the share-merger or the statutory merger the newly acquired shares qualify for the application of the participation exemption, a future gain on the disposal of these shares will only be exempt to the extent this gain exceeds the previous non-recognised gain[55]. Such non-recognition may, under certain conditions, also be achieved if it concerns a statutory merger between non-Dutch qualifying EC corporations[56].

g   Taxation of Non-Resident Companies

i   *General.* Under the CIT Act a non-resident company is subject to Dutch corporate income tax if it realises profits from certain specifically mentioned Dutch sources[57].

These Dutch sources include, *inter alia*: (1) business profits realised through a permanent establishment in the Netherlands; (2) income derived from Dutch real property; and (3) capital gains realised on the sale of shares in and dividends and interest derived from a Dutch resident corporation in which the taxpayer has a "substantial interest"[58] which does not belong to the assets of a business enterprise.

ii   *Dutch Permanent Establishment.* One of the most important Dutch sources of taxable income is profit derived from an enterprise which is wholly or partly conducted through a permanent establishment situated in the Netherlands or a permanent representative in the Netherlands.

The CIT Act does not contain general definitions of the terms "permanent establishment" and "permanent representative". The law only contains a fiction that a permanent establishment is deemed to be present if during an uninterrupted period of at least 30 days, activities are conducted on the Dutch part of the continental shelf[59]. Due to the absence of a definition in the law, the meaning of the terms permanent establishment and permanent representative under the application of the CIT Act must for the greater part be derived from

55   Vpb art. 13h.
56   Act of September 10, 1992, art. IV, S. 491.
57   Vpb art. 17, IB art. 49.
58   Generally, a "substantial interest" exists if the taxpayer owns 5% or more of the share capital of a corporation.
59   Vpb art. 17, IB art. 49.

case law. This case law shows that the following criteria are relevant for the interpretation of the term "permanent establishment":

a there must be a physical construction situated in the Netherlands;

b this construction must be available to the non-resident taxpayer;

c the construction must in some degree be available on a permanent basis; and

d the construction must be fitted for the business activities to be conducted.

The following criteria can be derived from case law when interpreting the term "permanent representative":

a the representative must be authorised on a permanent basis to conclude contracts on behalf of the non-resident taxpayer;

b the representative must to a certain extent be dependant on the non-resident taxpayer which he represents; and

c the proxy must be habitually exercised.

The question whether the non-resident company is a resident of a country which has concluded a tax treaty with the Netherlands could be of importance. However, the meaning of the terms "permanent establishment" and "permanent representative" under the CIT Act is not always equal to the meaning under the application of tax treaties concluded by the Netherlands. For example, a non-resident company located in a non-treaty country may be taxed with respect to its profits derived in connection with supporting activities conducted through a Dutch permanent establishment, while such an activity would not qualify as a permanent establishment under a treaty.

If it has been established that under Dutch domestic law a permanent establishment exists, and a tax treaty does not preclude the Netherlands' authorities to exercise their rights in this respect, the amount of profits to be attributed to this permanent establishment has to be determined. The direct method is generally viewed as the appropriate method to determine the taxable profits. Under this direct method, the permanent establishment is treated as if it is a separate independent enterprise which should deal on an arm's length basis with the enterprise to which it belongs. However, case law indicates that an exception to the construction of "the independent enterprise" applies in respect of certain internal payments between head-office and permanent establishment, such as interest and royalties. These payments will only be taken into account if they are due to, or received from, a third party and relate to assets and liabilities attributable to the business activities conducted through the permanent establishment[60].

h   Compensation of Losses. If the "taxable profit" is in fact a loss it can be offset against the taxable profits of the three preceding years (carry back). Any remaining amount not carried back can be carried forward indefinitely[61]. Losses are offset in the order in which they were incurred. If a company ceases its operations entirely, or almost entirely, any losses incurred in the period prior thereto can only be compensated with future profits if at least 70% of its shares are still held, directly or indirectly, by the same shareholders. The same rule applies to a carry back of losses realised through a newly started business activity if the losses are carried back to profitable years prior to the year in which the company (almost) entirely ceased its former business activities. These rules try to combat the trading in loss companies.

i   Foreign Source Income

i   *General.* Dutch resident corporations receiving income from foreign sources may under certain conditions be entitled to relief in order to avoid a tax claim in both the Netherlands and the foreign source country on the same income. This double tax relief is based on tax treaties for the avoidance of double taxation or on Dutch unilateral rules for double tax relief. If no tax treaties or unilateral rules can be applied, the amount of foreign tax paid can generally be recognised as a deductible expense[62]. In case a tax credit would normally be applied the corporation may also opt for non-recognition of the tax credit and deduct the amount of foreign tax paid as expense.

ii   *Unilateral Rules for Double Tax Relief.* The Decree for the avoidance of double taxation ("BVDB")[63] includes the most important unilateral rules for double tax relief. Under the BVDB, Dutch resident taxpayers can claim an exemption or a credit in respect of certain items of foreign source income. These unilateral rules can only be used if no tax treaty for the avoidance of double taxation (*see* iii below) is applicable[64]. An "exemption" (*see* iv below) can, *inter alia*,

60   Judgments of 7 May 1997, HR, 1997 BNB no. 263 and no. 264.
61   Vpb. art. 20.
62   Vpb art. 10.
63   Besluit voorkoming dubbele belasting [BVDB] (Decree for the avoidance of double taxation), 1989 S. 594, *as amended.*
64   BVDB art. 1.

be claimed in respect of profits realised through a permanent establishment present in another country, provided the profits are subject to tax levied by that other country[65]. Foreign income taxes paid by a Dutch resident taxpayer in respect of interest, dividends and royalties received from certain developing countries may, under certain conditions, be credited against the Dutch taxation due on these items of income[66]. The so-called "participation exemption" (*see supra* Chapter 13.2.c) is also considered a unilateral rule for the avoidance of double taxation. This participation exemption excludes dividends received by the Dutch corporation, including foreign dividends, from corporate income tax. If the participation exemption applies, no credit or deduction of foreign withholding tax levied will be given[67].

iii *Tax Treaties for the Avoidance of Double Taxation.* The Netherlands has concluded many tax treaties for the avoidance of double taxation. Generally, these tax treaties require the Netherlands, *inter alia*, (1) to "exempt" (*see* iv below) profits realised by a Dutch resident person through a permanent establishment in the other treaty country, and (2) to credit the Dutch tax liability for the amount of withholding tax levied by the other treaty country on interest, dividends and royalties paid to the Dutch resident recipient. In addition, these tax treaties provide for a reduction of withholding taxes which may be levied by the source country on dividends, interest and royalties.

iv *Exemption for Foreign Branch Income.* Under the unilateral rules and tax treaties for the avoidance of double taxation, the Netherlands "exempt" the income attributable to a foreign branch (permanent establishment; *see* ii and iii above). This "exemption" does not imply that the foreign branch income is actually excluded from the Dutch taxable base. The foreign branch income is included in the worldwide taxable income, while the relief for double taxation is calculated by means of a reduction of the Dutch tax due on that worldwide income. This reduction equals the average rate of Dutch tax due on the foreign branch income (so-called exemption with progression)[68]. For corporations, this method of double tax relief is generally equal

---

65 BVDB art. 2.
66 BVDB art. 4.
67 *See infra* Chapter 13.2. for the possibility to credit the amount of foreign dividend withholding tax paid against the amount of Dutch dividend withholding tax.
68 As from January 1, 1999 the "exemption" as applicable under the unilateral rules will be replaced by a credit method if the foreign branch is mainly engaged in passive financing activities (BVDB art. 10).

to an exemption. It should be noted that this method of double tax relief allows for the deduction of foreign branch losses from other Dutch source taxable income. A recapture rule applies if the branch becomes profitable in subsequent years[69].

j   Administrative Aspects

i   *Filing Tax Returns.* CIT is levied from a corporation through an assessment raised by the competent tax inspector[70]. This assessment is based on the tax return which should be filed every year[71]. This tax return shows the taxable amount realised during the tax year concerned. The tax inspector sends a tax return to the corporation if he believes that it may be subject to CIT[72]. If the corporation is subject to CIT, but has not received a tax return, it must request the tax inspector for a tax return within six months and two weeks after the end of the tax year[73]. The tax return must be completed and filed by the corporation within the period indicated by the tax inspector, which is generally within 6 months after the tax year. If requested by the corporation, the tax inspector may grant an extension of filing of the tax return[74].

ii   *Assessments.* During and after the tax year concerned, the tax inspector may already impose one or more provisional assessments based on information to be provided by the corporation[75]. These provisional assessments will be offset with the final assessment[76].

The tax inspector must impose the final assessment within three years after the tax year concerned[77]. This three-year period is extended by the period for which the tax inspector granted the corporation an extension of filing of the tax return.

---

69   BVDB art. 3. This article provides for the "per country method".
70   Vpb art. 24.
71   AWR art. 6.
72   AWR art. 6.
73   Uitvoeringsregeling Algemene Wet inzake rijksbelastingen 1994, [UAWR] (Implementing Decree on General Act on Taxation) art. 2, 1994 S. 114, *as amended.*
74   AWR art. 9.
75   AWR art. 13.
76   AWR art. 15.
77   AWR art. 11.

Under certain conditions the tax inspector may impose an additional assessment if he believes that the final assessment was too low[78]. Generally, this additional assessment can only be imposed if this takes place within five years after the tax year concerned and the additional assessment is based on facts and circumstances not known to the tax inspector at the time of the final assessment. The five year period may be extended to a twelve year period if the additional assessment relates to foreign source income[79].

iii *Appeal.* The final and additional assessments can be challenged by the corporation in a pre-proceeding by sending a notice of objection (*bezwaarschrift*) to the tax inspector within six weeks after the date of the assessment[80]. The tax inspector must decide on the objection within 1 year[81]. The decision of the tax inspector can be appealed against before the Tax Court[82], with a further right of appeal to the Supreme Court on questions of law only[83].

13.3   Dividend Withholding Tax (DWT)

Profit distributions made by Dutch resident companies of which the capital is divided into shares are subject to DWT at a rate of 25%[84]. The tax must be withheld by the distributing company[85]. If the dividend is received by a Dutch resident taxpayer, the DWT can be credited against the Individual Income Tax or CIT due[86]. If the dividend is paid to a non-resident taxpayer, the withholding tax is generally a final levy. However, the DWT can under certain circumstances be reduced, for example, due to the application of tax treaties or domestic provisions implementing the EC parent-subsidiary directive[87]. Under these last mentioned domes-

---

78   AWR art. 16.
79   AWR art. 16.
80   AWR art. 22j and art. 23, Algemene Wet Bestuursrecht [AWB], (General Administrative Law Act) art. 6:7, 1994 S. 1, *as amended.*
81   AWR art. 25, the 1 year period may be extended by 1 additional year.
82   AWR art. 26.
83   Wet Administratieve Rechtspraak Belastingzaken [WARB] (Act on Administrative Jurisdiction in Tax issues) art. 19, 1956 S.323, *as amended.*
84   DIV arts. 1, 5.
85   DIV art. 7.
86   AWR art. 15; IB art. 63 and Vpb art. 25.
87   Council Directive No. 90/435 on the common system of taxation applicable in the case of parent companies and subsidiaries of different Member States, 33 O.J. Eur. Comm. (No. L 225) 6 (1990); DIV arts. 4a, 4b.

tic provisions, generally, no Dutch withholding tax is due if the dividend receiving EC Corporation owns 25% or more of the share capital in the Dutch corporation. If the shares are held by a corporation and qualify for the application of the participation exemption (*see supra* Chapter 13.2c), no DHT needs to be withheld on distributions to the recipient[88].

Profit distributions subject to DWT include disguised dividends and liquidation proceeds paid to the shareholders to the extent these payments exceed the paid-up capital recognised for tax purposes[89].

A repayment of capital is generally not subject to DWT. In the case of a share-for-share exchange the new paid-up capital, which equals the fair market value of the contributed shares, may not be fully recognised for Dutch tax purposes[90]. Only the recognised amount of capital paid on the contributed shares will be recognised as capital payment to the newly issued shares. The excess amount (the "tainted" part) will be subject to DWT. This rule counters potential tax avoidance. By way of example, in the absence of this provision, a shareholder in a corporation with a substantial amount of retained earnings could transfer his shares under a tax-free share-for-share exchange to another corporation and have the retained earnings distributed tax-free to that other corporation. Thereafter, the latter corporation could repay the capital created under the share-for-share exchange without DWT. However, the aforementioned rule subjects the tainted part of the capital to DWT.

In respect of foreign dividends received by a Dutch corporation, which are exempt under the application of the participation exemption (*see supra* Chapter 13.2.c), it may be possible to obtain relief in the Netherlands from foreign withholding tax levied on these dividends. This relief can be effectuated by means of a reduction of the Dutch dividend withholding tax, provided the foreign dividends received are redistributed by the Dutch corporation within two years and certain other conditions are met[91].

---

88   DIV art. 4.
89   DIV art. 3.
90   DIV art. 3. An exception applies to the contribution of shares in a non-resident corporation (Resolution No. DB 89/4235 (1989)).
91   DIV art. 11.

13.4   Capital Contributions Tax (CCT)

a   General. Capital contributions to Dutch resident companies with capital divided into shares are subject to a 1% CCT[92]. These contributions not only include the amount equal to the paid-up nominal value of the shares, but also share premium (*agio*) paid in excess of the nominal value, and deemed capital contributions. If the capital contribution is paid in kind, the CCT is calculated on the fair market value of the contributed property[93]. The CCT is due by the capital receiving company and deductible for CIT purposes[94].

An exemption can be claimed in the case of a merger or an internal reorganisation, qualified for CCT purposes[95].

b   Exemptions

i   *Merger.* A merger for CCT purposes exists if:

a   A Dutch resident corporation acquires 75% or more of the shares (or increases its interest to 75% or more) in another corporation residing within the EC, in exchange for newly issued shares in the Dutch acquiror ("share-merger"), or

b   A Dutch resident corporation acquires all of the assets and liabilities or the entire business enterprise or an independent part thereof of another EC resident corporation in exchange for newly issued shares in the Dutch acquiror ("business-merger").

If an exemption is claimed under a share-merger, the shares acquired may not be transferred and the interest may not be reduced below the 75% within a five-year period following the exempt transaction; otherwise, the tax saved under the exemption will still be due (a so-called recapture claim). The recapture claim does not apply if the new transfer qualifies under the merger or under the internal reorganisation exemption, or if the acquiror is to be liquidated[96].

---

92   BRV arts. 32, 36.
93   BRV art. 35.
94   BRV art. 38.
95   BRV art. 37.
96   Uitvoeringsbesluit belastingen van rechtsverkeer [UBBRV] (Implementing Decree on Tax Act Legal Transaction) art. 14, 1971 S. 393, *as amended*

A 100% shareholding may qualify as an independent part of a business enterprise under the business merger exemption[97]. Claiming this exemption could be an alternative to the share-merger if it concerns a shareholding in a non-EC resident corporation (not qualifying for the share-merger) or if the intention is to avoid the recapture claim under the share-merger.

The Dutch Supreme Court considers the restriction, that the contributing corporations should be residents within the EC, to be a violation of the non-discrimination article as included in certain treaties for the avoidance of double taxation[98].

With regard to a statutory merger, an exemption can be claimed based on published tax policies[99].

ii *Internal Reorganisation.* For CCT purposes, an internal reorganisation is deemed to exist if a Dutch resident corporation acquires all of the assets of the same kind from other group companies residing in the EC in exchange for newly issued shares in the Dutch acquiror.

Under both the merger exemption and the internal reorganisation exemption the Dutch resident corporation is allowed to make a payment other than in shares to the extent not exceeding 10% of the nominal value of the shares issued in connection with the transaction.

13.5 Other Taxes

a   **Real Property Transfer Tax (RPTT).** The acquisition of Dutch real property is generally subject to a 6% RPTT on the fair market value of the transferred property[100]. The RPTT is due by the acquiror[101]. A taxable transfer includes not only the transfer of the legal title to the real property, but also the transfer of the economic interest in the real property. Dutch real property includes shares in real property corporations (*i.e.* corporations mainly engaged in investing in Dutch real property)[102]. The

---

97   Judgment of April 27, 1994, HR, 1994 BNB No. 207.
98   Judgments of April 27, 1994, HR, 1994 BNB Nos. 207, 209 and 210.
99   Resolution No. 285-13707 (1995) and Explanatory Notes to draft statute No. 21031.
100 BRV arts. 2, 14.
101 BRV art. 16.
102 BRV art. 4.

transfer of shares in such a corporation will be subject to RPTT if the purchaser acquires or increases a substantial shareholding (in general an interest of one-third or more).

Under certain conditions, an acquisition of real property is exempt from RPTT if the transfer is connected with a qualifying merger or internal reorganisation[103].

b   Value Added Tax (VAT). VAT is levied in respect of the delivery of goods and the rendering of services by "entrepreneurs"[104]. The tax is based on the consideration charged[105] and to a large extent based on EC Directives. In principle, VAT is born by the final consumers of the goods and services. The various entrepreneurs performing taxable transactions practically act as collectors on behalf of the Dutch tax authorities. The amount of VAT to be paid by an entrepreneur is generally the VAT due on its own turnover reduced by the VAT paid to other entrepreneurs. As a consequence, VAT is not a cumulative levy. The general VAT rate is 17.5%. Necessity goods and services (for example, food and medicines) may be subject to the lower rate of 6%, while exports are generally subject to a zero rate.

103 BRV art. 15 and UBBRV arts. 5a, 5b.
104 OB art. 1.
105 OB arts. 8, 9.

AMSTERDAM
Apollolaan 15
1077 AB Amsterdam
P.O. Box 75088
1070 AB Amsterdam
The Netherlands
Tel: (31-20) 574 1200
Fax: (31-20) 671 8775
Telex: 14291 (lex nl)

ROTTERDAM
Weena 70
3012 CM Rotterdam
P.O. Box 74
3000 AB Rotterdam
The Netherlands
Tel: (31-10) 403 4777
Fax: (31-10) 414 9388
Telex: 23395 (lex nl)

BRUSSELS
Avenue de Tervueren 268A
B-1150 Brussels
Belgium
Tel: (32-2) 778 2211
Fax: (32-2) 763 2185

ANTWERP
Mechelsesteenweg 267
2018 Antwerp
Belgium
Tel: (32-3) 285 3434
Fax: (32-3) 285 3444
Telex: 72748 (eurlaw b)

BARCELONA
Avenida Diagonal 550, 4º 1a
08021 Barcelona
Spain
Tel: (34-3) 200 7177
Fax: (34-3) 202 3098

KORTRIJK
Pres. Kennedypark 37
B-8500 Kortrijk
Belgium
Tel: (32-56) 235 111
Fax: (32-56) 235 110

LUIK
Rue Simonon 13
(Place de Bronckart)
4000 Luik
Belgium
Tel: (32-41) 544 310
Fax: (32-41) 527 511

LUXEMBOURG
Rue Ermesinde 67
P.O. Box 5017
L-1050 Luxembourg
Luxembourg
Tel: (352) 468 946
Fax: (352) 468 957
Telex: 60736 (zflaw lu)

MADRID
Antonio Maura 7
28014 Madrid
Spain
Tel: (34-1) 531 2501
Fax: (34-1) 531 3530

NEW YORK
Swiss Bank Tower, 23rd floor
10 East 50th Street
New York, N.Y. 10022
U.S.A.
Tel: (1-212) 759 9000
Fax: (1-212) 759 9018

PARIS
Avenue Franklin D. Roosevelt 1
75008 Paris
France
Tel: (33-1) 4953 9125
Fax: (33-1) 4289 1460

SINGAPORE
24 Raffles Place
22-01-01 Clifford Centre
Singapore 048621
Singapore
Tel: (65) 533 5332
Fax: (65) 533 0313

JAKARTA (associated office)
Ali Budiardo, Nugroho,
Reksodiputro
Niaga Tower, 24th floor
Jalan Jenderal Sudirman Kav. 58
Jakarta 12920
Indonesia
Tel: (62-21) 250 5125
Fax: (62-21) 250 5121